Presented To:

_____

From:

_____

Date:

_____

Prayer,
Quantum Physics,
and Hotel Mattresses

Prayer,
Quantum Physics,
and Hotel Mattresses

DISSOLVING THE BARRIER BETWEEN
THE SEEN AND THE UNSEEN

JIM BERGE

DESTINY IMAGE® PUBLISHERS, INC.

P.O. Box 310, Shippensburg, PA 17257-0310

"Promoting Inspired Lives."

This book and all other Destiny Image, Revival Press, MercyPlace, Fresh Bread, Destiny Image Fiction, and Treasure House books are available at Christian bookstores and distributors worldwide.

For a U.S. bookstore nearest you, call **1-800-722-6774.**

For more information on foreign distributors, call **717-532-3040.**

Reach us on the Internet: **www.destinyimage.com.**

ISBN 13 TP: 978-0-7684-4101-7

ISBN 13 Ebook: 978-0-7684-8865-4

For Worldwide Distribution, Printed in the U.S.A.

1 2 3 4 5 6 7 8 / 16 15 14 13 12

Contents

Introduction

While traveling through Minnesota a while back, I stopped to see my good friend Lee. As usual, we ended up in deep conversation about the life of Christ, which we often struggle to fully understand. The summer night was warm, but surprisingly there were no mosquitoes on the front porch. "Do you think there's a relationship between prayer and quantum physics?" Lee asked. "Do you think prayer can affect reality on a subatomic level?"

Hmmm.

I call myself an armchair physicist. In other words, I love reading about big bang theory and quantum physics, but I don't know how to solve differential equations, even though I had to prove I did before I could get my B.S. in Engineering more than 25 years ago. So the question intrigued me.

Yes, I knew there was an intimate connection between physical reality and the spiritual realm, but I had never before attempted to think through what that would look like or how it would work. It had to have something to do with quantum physics, though. And brain waves. And anger and emotion and pain. And love. The interface at which the physical meets the immaterial—whatever it looks like and however it functions—affects every aspect of our lives. When I propose to move my finger in such a way as to type the letter "K" on my keyboard, an immaterial thought must precede the action, which turns into electrical brain waves, which stimulates the proper nerves, which instructs the proper muscles, which turns the immaterial thought into a physical reality—words on a screen. The naturalist would argue that it is nothing more than brain waves and chemicals. I believe, however, that every action, word, thought, and motive actually originates in a place much deeper and unseen.

"Well," began my four-year-long answer to Lee, "I've experienced for myself how prayer and thought can literally change physical circumstances. There must be some connection between the worlds of prayer, thought, and emotion and that of physical reality." This question sparked an interest in exploring what it might look like at the interface between the physical world we are so familiar with and the spiritual dimension of our universe.

Certainly, if there is a place from which immaterial thoughts and desires ascend, then there has to be an intersection at which the immaterial thing meets its material consequence. Thoughts have results. They cause things to happen. There is power in spoken words. Psychosomatic illnesses are real. Thoughts and ideas have created both havoc and Heaven on this Earth for millennia. I think about moving my fingers in a particular way, and beautiful music comes from my guitar. But these same fingers also have the potential for great harm. Whether good or evil, my actions originate in the unseen realm, and if there is any possibility of uncovering the association between these immaterial catalysts and their physical manifestations, it could very well be at or near the level of reality that is touched upon by quantum physics and quantum mechanics.

So there is a place where the unseen world of thoughts, desires, and emotions meets the physical world of flesh and bones, dark chocolate, and sandy beaches. This interface between the seen and the unseen is the authority behind every action large and small. Its rock-solid, yet completely unpredictable rules govern every war that has been fought, every personal argument that has been won, every love that has been lost, every movement, every breath, every vibration of every molecule of matter that has ever existed in the entire universe.

Have you not felt it? Have you not stood at the edge of the sea and felt that your heart is bigger and deeper than you had realized? Do you not know deep down that the physical beauty and incomprehensibly complex world that surrounds you has roots that go much deeper than the colors of the spectrum, sound waves, the periodic table of elements, and mathematical formulas? In this interface between the seen and the unseen lies the secret to a life that makes sense and provides a compelling reason to live and love and laugh. That beautiful sunset has something in common with your very spirit within you.

This place of interface harbors an incomprehensible intensity of energy, yet peace is there. Love and justice are as meaningful here as the rules of quantum physics. For no one can honestly deny that every physical action, every word breathed, every synapse fired, every move of a finger was born out of this immaterial substance. And because the movements of many fingers over time have produced the Bible, the writings of Mahatma Gandhi, documents of world governance, and the compassion of Mother Teresa, we can know beyond doubt that tremendous power and authority await us there. Whether the fruit is good or bad depends on whether we accept that this place is real and what we determine to do with that knowledge. In an age of relative values, not everyone accepts that good and evil are as distinct as they really are. Consequently, they do not experience the amazing life that is awaiting them.

What do these things have to do with quantum physics? When the molecules, atoms, and quarks that constitute all matter are broken down to their most basic level of existence, science is still left with questions. And it is near this place where we will find information pointing to some of the truths describing another realm of existence. It is in this other realm where immaterial thoughts turn into actions with physical consequences. Could it be it is at or near this level of existence that God enters into our sphere and encourages us to make physical changes to the world surrounding us for the betterment of all human beings on Earth? It is at this point that modern science admits it can't quite explain what happens, but I believe that God can. The science behind what we will be discussing here is profoundly complex, but our discussion will be very simple. It is founded in fundamentals and is something I believe every human being can participate in. I trust you will find that it reveals an amazingly diverse and intimate portrait of a Creator God who is very personally interested in the details of your everyday life.

As we face a challenging world in which religious thought may seem irrelevant to some, it is possible to gain the understanding that all things are sacred, all things can be made holy, all things have been made and exist for God, all things are infused with the beauty of God, and this is made manifest in innumerable ways. Life, work, play, music, art, science, spirituality, tools, invention, ingenuity, and humor can all be used for God's purposes because that is the very reason all these things were originally created.

Soon after my conversation with Lee, I began typing some stream-of-consciousness thoughts, not necessarily in any meaningful order. I was in the middle of a business trip, staying in a generic hotel. So I sat on the hotel mattress and put my computer on my lap and began typing. Out came an 11-page paper entitled "On Quantum Physics, Prayer, and Hotel Mattresses." That paper evolved into this book, the title representing the triune state of reality that surrounds us: prayer, representing the spiritual realm; quantum physics, representing science and the created universe; and hotel mattresses, representing the everyday stuff of life that we must deal with moment by moment.

I know I may be pushing some limits here. My primary goal is to get us all thinking about such things, so please be patient with me, and don't judge my science because, although I am a robotics engineer (or "enginerd" per my wife), I am not a scientist. Nor am I a theologian, so I also appreciate some grace at that point. These are ideas, but I don't want this book to be about my ideas and me. It's about a God who not only had the intelligence to create such an unfathomable universe, but also gave us the foresight and brain-power to study it, learn about it, and come to some conclusions about the amazing person who thought it all up. This book is about reveal-ing a particular part of God that perhaps you have not spent much time thinking about, but could have a dramatic impact on your view of just how real, personal, and loving He really is. I am hoping that it will be the cause and fodder for many a conversation and will pro-vide many "Aha!" moments for readers.

To this end, I have not created a hard and fast outline of chapters with each chapter focusing on a particular aspect of the discussion. We'll roam from here to there, to various parts of the universe and its ultimate realities, then back to Earth for some relatively grounded talk before taking off again. This book has become more a journal of my thoughts about these things rather than a textbook-style excur-sion into scientific topics that could potentially be as exciting as watching paint dry. In fact, much of the material is based on excerpts from my journal, so think of it more as a conversation. I have come to realize that every good thing we choose to think about ultimately comes from God, through His mind and Spirit at work within us, and it is intended to be directed back toward God as an act of honor and worship.

In short, this book is:

A conversation. I invite readers to join me in my favorite activ-ity—sitting around the campfire together, each with his and her own stick to poke the fire and play with the coals, talking about deep things and why they matter.

A challenge. A thorough knowledge of this unseen realm and a proper response to its workings by each and every individual could catalyze our connectedness as a single human race.

A dose of reality. Many books, seminars, and "experts" today are teaching a form of "scientific" spirituality that is not based in reality. Quantum physics has some seemingly mystical qualities about it, but it is still science. There is a realm of existence where the immaterial meets the material, but this does not necessarily require that all of reality is based on mystical un-reality. We will try to take a fair and levelheaded approach to the link between the spiritual and physical worlds. What we find may surprise you, but it should also make a lot of sense.

A mind-stretching experience. The concepts discussed in this book are accessible to everyone, but the ideas may be new to many. Some of your long-held beliefs may be bent or challenged, but the goal is pure: to discover together how we can use our knowledge of science and spirituality to create a life that is worth living.

Stretching far beyond either prayer or quantum physics, the topics we'll be discussing together apply to every imaginable aspect of life. Crucial to surviving and thriving in this evolving age of knowledge and technology is an understanding of how knowledge, wisdom, and technology will affect our lives for either better or worse. However, equally as important, but overlooked by many modern pundits, is the discussion on the limitations of knowledge to solve our global crises. As ultimate reality comes closer and closer to revealing itself, we see as a far more beautiful creature than we had first imagined— compelling, maybe even frightful at times as it challenges some of our cherished assumptions. But always alluring, offering an overwhelming sense of peace as we finally come to understand.

As we enter this realm, we necessarily approach the world of spirituality, which brings us to the heart and soul—or should I say Spirit?—of this book. Let us approach this Spirit together as we ascend onto the plateau where the air is a bit fresher, the sky a bit bluer, and we can freely breathe truth and awareness—perhaps for the very first time.

Thanks for joining me by the campfire.

CHAPTER I

Iconoclast

Don't mistake the religion called "Christianity" for relationship with God. The very thing Jesus condemned while He walked this earth is the same thing popular atheist authors like Christopher Hitchens gripe and moan about: religion. When God enters your world, He does it not with religious tradition and a list of rules to follow, but with a promise of life that transcends what you see with your eyes. Blind religious tradition kills that process. I hate that kind of religion. Jesus hated it. It's just more of the same old lies that have forever plagued humanity.

Christians are called to something new—to literally be new creatures. This is what appeals to many who decide to follow the precepts and example of Jesus Christ. Many of us, at some point in our lives, realize that doing things our own way just isn't working, so our decision to follow Jesus is an adventure into a new, fresh, and amazing way of living, full of promise and change for the better. Those who follow Jesus make a decision to *be* different, not just to experience new things and get their lives together, but to change the very way they perceive life and reality. We who have made this life-changing decision ought to be actively struggling to break out of our old patterns of thought. In other words, God wants us to be a family of iconoclasts.

An iconoclast is one who attacks established dogmas and conventions of thought. And while those who oppose Christian principles often call Christians "dogmatic" in a demeaning way, the truth is most Christians—at least true Christ-like Christians who actually love their neighbors—are free from dogma and religious thinking. At least we should be. This comment may come as a surprise to many non-Christians, especially those who are outspoken critics of Christians, but the truth is many who call themselves "Christian" are only acting out a surface rendition that is void of truth and power. Some of the strongest critics of Christianity don't seem to understand that their biggest complaints about Christians are identical to Jesus' biggest complaints about the religious leaders of His day.

Those who would choose to follow the example and principles of Jesus Christ in this world are called to think differently than those who do not know Him. Jesus is neither limited by nor confined to the parameters imposed on Him by the physical creation, and as His followers, we also have freedom to live in and experience that same freedom from natural constraints. Just think about the possibilities of living a life that is not constrained by the physical world, the things we see with our eyes, the mundane circumstances of everyday life, and the inane system of media, money, and mayhem so prevalent in today's society! Many non-Christians remain limited because they see Christianity as a lifestyle that severely limits their freedom, but the truth is precisely the opposite. Modern churches may emphasize long lists of "don'ts" but Jesus is concerned with the "dos." Life with Christ is all about incredible freedom to become everything that the God of the universe designed you to be, a role that is exponentially more enormous and fulfilling than anything the natural world can dream up.

Renewed Minds

God instructs us "...be transformed by the renewing of your mind..." (Rom. 12:2). The word transformed in the original Greek is metamorpho'o, making this transformation as thorough and life-changing as the metamorphosis of a caterpillar into a butterfly. Our caterpillar stage is the one in which we are born and raised, and by nature, we perceive all of life from the viewpoint of physical constraints and natural boundaries. Dirt and grass is the only world a worm can know. But Jesus promised us that we will do greater works than He did (see John 14:12). When we begin our metamorphosis into the butterfly, we will indeed be transformed in our minds so that we are actually able to see and interpret things from God's eternal perspective—on the wing, looking down from above, unlimited by our physical five senses.

In his excellent book *Iconoclast: A Neuroscientist Reveals How to Think Differently,*[1] Gregory Berns discusses how the brain of a person who has stepped outside his or her historical boundaries of thought and achieved something truly new and fresh—an iconoclast—literally sees things differently than others. An iconoclast perceives reality from a different angle than everyone else and in so doing opens up realms of possibility previously unknown to humankind. We are embarking on just that kind of journey in this book. According to Berns, one of the crucial prerequisites for breaking out of conventional thinking is to regularly expose one's own mind to new thoughts, ideas, and experiences. This breaks old synaptic connections in our brains and forces new connections to be made, which stimulates new thoughts, new ideas, and breakthroughs in all aspects of life.[2] We will be discussing some things that perhaps you haven't thought about before. And that's good for you.

God expects us to change. He tells us so in Second Corinthians 3:18, where He describes us as *"being transformed into His image with ever-increasing glory."* He instructs us to *"work out your salvation"* (Phil. 2:12) because relationship with God is a process, not a static state of being. We are constantly changing, we are constantly learning more about God and His character, and we are constantly growing and maturing in Christ. Change is not only encouraged, but it is absolutely crucial in relation to our walk with God. This change is wrought by the renewing of our minds and hearts, which is a result of our exposure to the truth and power of a Living God who is personable and knowable. And change is accomplished in our minds and our belief systems by exposing ourselves to ever-increasing revelation of God's character and His plans and purposes.

The apostle Paul was taught to think differently when God knocked him off his horse. He was on his way to kill some Christians, but God got a hold of him and taught him to think in a completely new way. He thus became one of the greatest teachers of all time.

Peter had a huge change in his thought processes, being embarrassed to even walk with Gentiles due to his deeply ingrained sense of racism toward anyone who was not Jewish. God healed that through a vision, convincing Peter that no human being was ever again to be considered unholy, but all are invited into the abundant life that Christ offers (see Acts 10). This was a tremendous cultural change in his thinking.

Change can be good. We ought to be changing daily, if for no other reason than we know and serve an infinite God and there is a lot to learn from Him and about Him. What I want to emphasize is that growth often occurs when our assumptions about reality are challenged. When we hear things that are new or unclear to us, we don't need to run away screaming with our ears covered for fear that our minds will be infected with something that isn't biblical. Jesus ate in the pubs and taverns with the "sinners." He was criticized for it by the religious leaders of the day because such behavior was considered unorthodox and evil. He ate supper with Zacchaeus, one of the most despised thieves in town (see Luke 19). Jesus was not afraid to have discussions with people about the real stuff of life, about their struggles and their downfalls. He wasn't afraid of exposing Himself to the language and stories flying about inside the pub. He was confident of what He believed and did not feel threatened by anyone or anything. Truth be told, He probably had a lot more fun hanging out with the guys in the tavern than he would have in the temple.

Modern Iconoclastic Debates

Divisions in the Church can become absurd and damaging in nature when people refuse to consider change. "Open theism" and the age of the Earth are two examples of hot topics that cause deep divisions in the Body of Christ, and I think this is ridiculous and tragic. We don't have the time or space here to unpack those ideas, but a very brief explanation will help.

Open theism states very generally that God can indeed be changed. He has given over certain levels of authority to humans and has subjected Himself in certain ways to human will. He is not completely sovereign, and God's will does not always automatically happen. The simple fact that some choose not to follow Him demonstrates this. His will is that all should know Him, yet many choose not to. Therefore, God is not utterly sovereign in human affairs, having subjected Himself in certain ways to the free will decisions of human beings. This debate is a matter of great division and mudslinging among Christians.

The debate over the age of the universe is also in this same category. Some believe that the universe was created in a creation event that took literally six, twenty-four-hour days. Others believe that God unfolded the universe over billions of years, perhaps consistent with the big bang theory. This is an issue that is peripheral to the basic tenets of Christian faith and belief, yet it causes great division in the Church, to the extent that one Christian will call another a heretic or at least a false teacher. Truth is, if someone chooses to believe in open theism or an ancient universe, these beliefs really have nothing to do with the eternal state of our souls. As Christian brothers and sisters, we ought to be exhibiting a lot more grace than we do during debates about issues that are actually peripheral to our faith.

Homosexuality is another hot topic among Christians today. Regardless of one's opinion on the morality of homosexuality and the condition of the souls of homosexuals, the truth remains that traditional Christian knee-jerk reactions against the gay community effectively nullify any effort that some Christians would make in reaching them. Consider the woman caught in adultery who was brought before Jesus. In those days, the religious leaders reacted to such people the same way many act toward the homosexual community today. They wanted to stone her to death, and they wanted Jesus to sanction it. He didn't. In fact, He did not have a single word of condemnation for her. He actually ended up taking to task those who wanted to condemn the woman (see John 8:1-11).

The same thing happened with the woman at the well who was living with someone she wasn't married to (see John 4:4-42). The reactions of the faithful Jewish folks, especially the religious leaders, toward these women are a perfect parallel to the reactions the gay community receives from many parts of society. If we follow through to the conclusion of the matter, we will have to conclude that Jesus' response to gays today would very likely be similar to His response to these women: "Neither do I condemn you. Let's go have lunch and talk about life."

Why all this talk about our reactions to controversy? Because we close off our minds, by our canned and uninformed responses, to the possibility of uncovering any new truth, not to mention we often offend lots of people in the process, or at least convince them that Christians are closed-minded bigots who are interested in neither truth nor love. There was a time when the Earth was the center of the universe. This was a spiritual principle that the Church insisted upon. It was the Church, not his scientific peers, that convicted Galileo Galilei of heresy when he published materials stating the Earth actually revolved around the sun. Sometimes, unfortunately, there is a price to pay for being iconoclastic.

Open-mindedness is good. This does not mean we have to blindly accept anything thrown at us. As Steve Taylor wrote in one of his songs, "You're so open-minded that your brain leaked out."[3] No, to be properly open-minded begins by being absolutely sure of where you stand. Be convinced of the truth and the basic principles of that truth. We add much to the teachings of Jesus that is not there. It's all about fundamentals. If you believe homosexuality is morally wrong, that's your choice and that's fine. We simply need the discipline to shut our mouths before we scream and yell condemnation every time we're confronted with it. I believe that sex outside of marriage is wrong, but I have friends who don't agree, and they're still my friends.

I also have gay friends. I have Christian friends with whom I disagree about hell and the rapture and the interpretation of the Book of Revelation, but I still love them. Once I am convinced of where I stand on an issue, and that it is consistent with the truth found in the Bible, then I am free to be open-minded about discussing things I may disagree with, because simply giving light to those issues will not change my convictions about what I know is true. In fact, I might just learn something new. At the very least, it's an opportunity to discuss issues at length, confirm why I believe the way I do, and have some quality time with the person or people I'm conversing with.

Learning to think differently is crucial, both when becoming a new believer in Jesus and while working out our relationship with Him. One thing is true about God—He is totally unpredictable. Once we think we have Him and His ways figured out, He might just blindside us with a curve ball. This is so He can establish Himself in our lives as the Source, the Provider, the Truth, and the Way. We learn to think in ways that may sometimes contradict traditional common sense, in ways that may contradict the things we see with our eyes and pick up with our five senses, and we learn to live a Proverbs 3:5 kind of life: *"Trust in the Lord with all your heart. And **do not lean** on your own understanding"* (NASB).

Now, *that's* thinking differently! And that's what we'll be doing together during the course of this book. I want to invite you to open your mind to what God wants to reveal to you, trusting that He is strong and wise enough to preserve His truth as we explore what may be to you some new limits of thinking. You might read a few new ideas. Open your mind. Dare to be an iconoclast. Dare to let God's Spirit lead your mind and spirit into something new.

Endnotes

1. Gregory Berns, *Iconoclast: A Neuroscientist Reveals How To Think Differently* (Boston: Harvard Business Press, 2010).

2. Ibid.

3. Steve Taylor, "Whatcha Gonna Do When Your Number's Up?" *I Want To Be A Clone* (Sparrow Records, 1990).

CHAPTER 2

Quantum Physics Primer

So just what is quantum physics all about? I will try to quickly describe some of the basic features, but I want to keep it within the context of our subject, that is, that interface where the material world meets the invisible world. Quantum physics describes the way things happen in the subatomic world with the tiniest of particles. But the word *particles* may be a bit misleading, since we have discovered that those little balls of matter called *electrons, protons,* and *neutrons* we learned about in high school are not really balls of matter at all, but are more like little concentrations of energy. The electron, often viewed as a ball rotating around the atom's nucleus, is actually a cloud of probabilistic existence[1] surrounding the center of the atom. They say it has zero mass, but it still possesses an electrical charge. Let that spin around in your brain for a while.

An electron really can't be directly observed. There is a proven stipulation of quantum physics called the Heisenberg Uncertainty Principle that states if we look at or measure the position of an electron, then other crucial information about it is lost. Also, at the moment we observe the electron, it basically gives that electron a position and an identity in the realm of the natural. In other words, our observation or measurement can cause that electron to become real. I suppose that must be very frustrating for scientists, who then must realize not only that their observations affect the experiment, but they must also determine how the experiment was changed and accommodate these changes as they interpret the results. Weird stuff, I know, but scientifically real nevertheless.

Quantum physics and quantum mechanics try to explain the activities in this subatomic world and seek to harness whatever usefulness or utility can be gleaned from this knowledge. This utility is then used not only to facilitate further study of both the very small and the very large (the important laws of quantum physics have as much to do with the origins of the universe as with the subatomic world), but also to improve our lives on a macroscopic level, for instance in the study of microbiology and medicine.

Quantum Physics is often presented as a whole different animal than classic Newtonian physics, which deals with the stuff we're all familiar with such as billiard balls bouncing off each other and cars with crash test dummies slamming into brick walls. Newtonian physics has to do with gravity, mass, acceleration, force, and inertia. This is the stuff typically studied in high school physics classes, and it deals with phenomena that are very familiar to all of us who live in a primarily "physical" environment.

Quantum physics is just as scientifically provable, but makes less sense to our intuitive rational minds. For example, quantum physics says a particular electron can suddenly appear over there instead of here where I think it should be. This has to do with an uncertainty principle that says there is a statistical probability that this could actually happen. In fact, it actually does happen. It can be proven mathematically, but intuitively it makes no sense.

This is one reason why it gets increasingly difficult to pack more power into a computer chip: in order to get a chip that can do more calculations, more microscopic electronic pathways must be etched into the material the chip is made of. But as these pathways get more numerous within a fixed space, they also get tinier and tinier (to the tune of millions per computer chip) and the distance between them gets smaller and smaller to fit them all onto the computer chip. Eventually, there would be only a few molecules of matter separating one of these electrical pathways from the next. This makes it easier for an electron to suddenly appear on the far side (the wrong side) of an allegedly solid boundary of material, not because it physically pokes its way through, but because quantum physics mathematically says it can and might appear where it shouldn't be (this is called quantum tunneling).

Quantum physics indeed represents a very strange world, one in which chance and uncertainty play a big part, and it is precisely this strangeness that lends a spiritual quality to the study and explanation of quantum physics. Just stand in front of the physics section of any major bookstore and notice the spiritual content of many book titles. They use words like God and Tao. These physicist authors are onto something.

The thing about quantum physics is that it helps explain a lot of science that remained a mystery to humankind for millennia. In spite of its strange behavior and weird consequences, which caused Albert Einstein to at first reject its premises, this science has incredibly expanded our knowledge of how the universe works. After considering the sometimes (seemingly) random behavior of matter on a quantum level, and stating that, "God does not play dice," eventually Mr. Einstein changed his tune, forced to accept the validity of quantum physics because it helped explain the rest of his universe.

Science and the Bible

While I will be mentioning a lot about quantum physics, I want to emphasize the role that science in general plays in this discussion. God created the universe, a fact made evident from the incomprehensible amount and quality of information and design that is ubiquitous in all of creation. The whole of science comprises the language God chose to express these physical truths that in turn are all designed to point us toward Him (see Rom. 1:20). I believe that if humankind would approach scientific study with the foundational premise that the universe is created by God, and it is our responsibility and honor to figure out how and why He did it, then the strides we could make in scientific progress would far surpass our imagination. God made an incredible, unfathomable universe, and we continue to learn more and more about it—and about Him—*through science.*

I greatly appreciate organizations like Hugh Ross's Reasons To Believe (www.reasons.org), because they have made a career of studying the universe and reporting what it tells us about God. Science is real, testable, and trustworthy to a large extent. The primary goal of these scientists is to expose truth, and it displays exciting, wonderful, incredible images to us of a God who cares, a God who loves us, and a God who really went overboard making a beautiful place for us to live and love and interact with Him and with one another.

I will be taking at face value much of what modern science has discovered. Some believe we ought to be much more skeptical about scientific discovery and the "agenda" lurking behind the work of many scientists today. The truth is that most scientists are in it for the love of discovery and will simply report the facts once it is established that they are actually "facts." There are many conservative Christian scientists who largely agree with the general conclusions wrought by the scientific community at large, and for these people I am grateful.

We must keep in mind that the science that is telling us the approximate age of the universe is the same science that allows us to safely fly passenger planes six miles above the ground, upload to Facebook from our iPhones, and cure diseases. Either we trust science or we don't, and I believe strongly that God gave us the language and methods of science so we could learn more about who He is and the wonders He has in store for us. To reject science is to reject a primary language and means of communicating that God has gifted to us.

You may be getting the idea by now that I think quantum physics can help explain some of God's modus operandi here on earth. *"God is Spirit"* (John 4:24), so many of the truths He expects us to learn are discerned in a purely spiritual way apart from science, physics, or even common sense. But God also chooses to communicate in the language of physical realities, more commonly known as science, depending on the message He is trying to get across. For example, no matter how much I try, I just can't find any information about the speed of light in the Scriptures. Nor can I find anything about the resonance of a carbon atom or cosmic background radiation or how water gets from the roots of a tree all the way to the top of its upper-most branches.

In other words, the Bible simply is not a science textbook. It is not meant to be. There are innumerable scientific facts that do not appear in the Bible, so we do God and the world a great disservice by demanding that everything to be gleaned about the universe and about reality can be found in the Bible. We often believe that the Bible must always take precedence in all things, but sometimes this may not be the best approach. If my leg is broken, I don't want my doctor searching for the cure in the Bible! Perhaps he can pray for me, but I really hope he has some medical experience in treating a broken leg. The Bible is God's best revelation to humankind about the fall and redemption of human beings and the way in which God works in and through individual lives, people groups, and societies to bring about that time when all things are put under the rule of Jesus Christ (see Eph. 1:10). Until then, we have the exhilarating experience of discovering all that God has prepared for those who love Him, and much of that discovery is through scientific endeavors.

But even science is not our primary focus. Our attention is on Jesus Christ and the life that He is envisioning for us. When Jesus worked miracles and gave the crowds miraculous signs of God's power, He was specifically and overtly using the power of science and quantum physics to make changes to the physical realities that the people experienced. He did it out of love; He accomplished it through the power of God the Father; and very importantly, He told us that we will do *"greater works than these"* (John 14:12 NASB). We, as believers and followers of Jesus, ought to be wielding the same power and authority that He did while He walked this earth.

But how? Are we supposed to just snap our fingers and see miraculous healings, water turned to wine, and storms calmed? Well, yes, that's what the Bible says. But there are some prerequisites. We must be sure we are working these miracles out of love for God and love for others, not for our own advancement or pride. We ought to be able to recognize the spiritual realm upon which all of reality is actually built. We must actually believe that God not only can (faith), but that He *will* (belief) do these things through us. Yes, there is a difference between faith and belief.

This is all easier said than done, I know. But that's why God is inviting us on this journey with Him, a journey on which we will learn that the process—not the destination—is in fact the big thing. He wants us to learn that the things we come to believe—and most importantly the people we become—are what make the difference between a life of mediocrity and a life of abundance. He wants us to realize how His will and His presence are literally woven throughout all of His physical creation, including your mind and body. And He wants us to discover Him—a God of such grandeur, such love and beauty, such incredible intelligence, such gentleness and compassion, that we can't help but fall in love with Him all over again.

Endnote

1. This "probabilistic existence" means that a law of quantum physics called the Heisenberg Uncertainty Principle is at work here. This law states that an electron (or any fundamental unit of matter) can only be defined by stating a statistical chance of what that particle might be doing at any given moment. Chance, in other words. It is uncertain what and where an electron actually is until it's observed, and at that moment it "chooses" a state of being—a position, for example. But at that same moment, the observer loses other information about that electron. Weird but true.

CHAPTER 3

The Spirituality of Quantum Physics

Quantum physics can help explain lots of interesting phenomena we have observed, and it can be tested and verified with mathematics and experimentation. At the end of the spectrum where particles of energy become exceedingly small (at the subatomic level, tinier even than the fundamental particles like neutrons, protons, and electrons), it has been proven an important method of describing reality, albeit a strange and unfamiliar reality. But at that most elementary level, at that point where matter and energy become almost infinitely tiny, at that point where our math and understanding begin to fail, could this be where these strange quantum realities begin to express spiritual truths?

It's no coincidence, as you stand in front of the physics section in the book stores, that you see many titles that include spiritual overtones, many even including the word "God," "Tao," and "Spirit." When we come to the end of our science (either heading toward the infinitely small at the center of elementary subatomic "particles" or heading toward the very large and the study of the origins of the universe), we come face-to-face with the need to explain what caused all this in the first place or what conditions existed before it all began. And many experts and laypeople alike turn, at this point, toward some higher power as an explanation, as the first cause, or the prime mover.

It is not uncommon to call on some kind of deity to explain unknown or unfamiliar phenomena. From the days of old, events like eclipses and earthquakes caused many to fall on their faces and plead with the gods to spare their lives. It's no different today. Physicists with a bent for writing and pontificating—those who are more in touch with their spiritual or mystical side I suppose—understand that there is a missing piece to their puzzle, a piece that in the minds of some can only be explained by a being higher, smarter, bigger, and better than us. The language these mathematicians are trying to speak requires using words and phrases that point toward the infinite and the divine.

When our mathematical formulas finally break down—which they do when we try to calculate everything that happened during the first trillionth of a second before or after the big bang—then a new language is required. And if, from a Christian viewpoint, this divine is the Creator God we know from the Bible, then this language must be able to describe the very spiritual character of all things material, from quarks to quasars. But if our language is only able to describe something, then it isn't as useful as it might be. If it had power—literally—to change reality, then we would be onto something big. We might actually discover something about why the universe exists. Stephen Hawking—Director of Research at the Centre for Theoretical Cosmologoy at the University of Cambridge and author of many books on physics and the origins of the universe, including the classic laymen's physics book *A Brief History of Time*—says,

> The usual approach of science of constructing a mathematical model cannot answer the questions of why there should be a universe for the model to describe. Why does the universe go to all the bother of existing?[1]

How the Spirit Realm Interacts
With the Physical Realm

If we pray and God somehow tells us to do something (however that looks to each of us individually), then that spiritual advice turns into a thought, which turns into electrical brain waves, which can then become a physical reality. For instance, we read in the Bible that we ought to feed the poor. You read the printed words with your eyes, the message is interpreted by electromagnetic signals in your brain, somehow your will is affected, and a decision is made. You take some cash, give it to the local Salvation Army, and they host a turkey feast on Thanksgiving Day for the homeless in your town. Thankful people praise God as a result.

A spiritual principle (with no physical form or reality whatsoever) has just resulted in a physical action that not only has physical ramifications, but also fulfills a commandment made by an immaterial God and spiritually blesses the recipient. It goes full circle: spiritual-physical-spiritual. I think this is one of the most amazing things in the world. At some point along that path of cause and effect, the spiritual met the physical (and vice versa). But how does that work?

Spiritual worship,
resulting in a philanthropic desire.

Physical action which meets a physical need,
bringing an attitude of worship.

I believe that there is biblical evidence that confirms God has spiritually woven quantum realities throughout the universe as we know it. The idea is that if quantum reality—or at least our modern understanding of it—indeed underlies all of the physical and visible matter with which we are so familiar, then it must be at or near that level of reality where this spiritual and physical interface takes place. And if it's true that at the most basic level of existence things actually exist in or near to a spiritual condition, then perhaps there really is no "interface" to speak of. Perhaps all of reality, traditionally conceived of as a juxtaposition of physical against spiritual, is indeed just purely spiritual after all.

Although he probably wasn't thinking it at the time, this may be the underlying foundation of what William Tyndale was thinking when he wrote,

> Now if thou compare deed to deed, there is a difference betwixt the washing of dishes and the preaching of the word of God; but as touching to please God, none at all.[2]

If we are in God's will, then singing hymns can be altogether as holy as playing ball with a child because God Himself and His truth permeate all of matter, existence, and reality. This is why we are encouraged to *"fix our eyes not on what is seen but on what is unseen. For what is seen is temporary but what is unseen is eternal"* (2 Cor. 4:18). The unseen is the eternal reality that we must be focused upon.

But what about this juxtaposition of spiritual reality against physical reality? Can quantum physics have anything to say about how that interface operates?

Einstein concluded that mass equals energy, and science continues to support his discoveries. If matter is indeed energy at its core, and all of matter and energy was created "from that which cannot be seen" by nothing more than God's thoughts, then there must be some kind of intimate spiritual reality underlying all of the physical matter that fills the universe, including the chairs we sit on, the food we eat, and the molecules that comprise our own bodies.

If there was nothing first except God, and then God created something using only His will for raw material, then the simple law of cause and effect implies that if God (who is spiritual and non-material) was the only possible cause, then the effect (the physical universe) came wholly from the stuff of our immaterial God and must at least have some immaterial aspect or character to it. What if, because everything we see and touch and feel and smell is immaterial at its core, we have had to derive this distinction between physical and spiritual as a crutch to help us study and understand the universe?

Had Adam and Eve never fallen, we may have intuitively known all this without the need for the crutch of a "physical dimension." After all, God walked and talked with them! What must that have looked like? Perhaps, as Jacob witnessed angels going up and down the ladder (see Gen. 28:12-13) and Elisha saw the angel troops on the hillsides (see 2 Kings 6:16-17), we too would have been able to clearly see this spiritual realm. The fall of humanity may well have blinded us to this spiritual universe surrounding us, leaving only echoes that we must now spend millenia trying to decipher.

I have stated that perhaps God is woven in and through everything, but I want to be careful not to drift too far toward pantheism here, which claims that all things in the universe comprise God. I can easily see where such a belief system gets its fuel, but I want to make it clear that, while I believe all things are completely and thoroughly permeated by God's presence, all things taken together do not comprise God. At one time long ago, all of creation was perfect and flawless until sin crept in. I believe the first humans to have fellowship with God originally had no concept of a division between what was spiritual and what was secular. Since God permeated all of creation and it was created in perfection, everything was considered holy and consecrated for Him, from the dirt Adam tilled to grow food to the words and concepts shared in the cool of the garden between the humans and their loving Father. God did, after all, call it *"very good"* (Gen. 1:31).

Sin changed all that, but it did not obliterate our understanding of reality. Sunsets are still beautiful. Roses still smell lovely and sweet. Really good dark chocolate or big, bitter, hoppy India pale ale still taste heavenly. Love and relationship and good discussion and great wine and delicious food still feed our souls and cause us to give glory to God. We can still bring Heaven to earth—*"...Your will be done, on earth as it is in Heaven"* (Matt. 6:10). We can still study the universe and experience it through all of our senses, but it takes more work now. It's not as easy to understand.

Our knowledge continues to evolve and our understanding gets a little clearer as time passes, but as Paul says in First Corinthians 13, we see things dimly now, but some day we shall see clearly. Until then, quantum physics might just be our best glimpse into how the interface between physical and spiritual realities works. Then we must draw some conclusions about what we will do in light of that information.

Examples of Quantum Physics

Let me describe a couple things scientists are talking about that I think emphasize the spiritual aspect of quantum physics. Fascinating experiments have been done to prove that time can travel backward (see Chapter 32, "Prayer Changes the Past"). Sounds too farfetched? It's being confirmed in laboratory tests.[3] By performing some very innovative and fascinating experiments, scientists have observed the effect happening before the cause. Our understanding of the direction of time has remained consistent for millennia, and we have only dared to explore that idea in science fiction writing, but now we are developing scientific proof that perhaps there can be a dimension (God's) that defies the supposedly relentless arrow of time.

Consider gravity. Have you thought much about gravity? Gravity holds the earth in its orbit around a sun that is 93 million miles away. In my mind, that is itself an amazing miracle. Here's a force that we have been intuitively aware of for the entire history of humanity. It affects us intimately with every single physical action we do; yet, no one can explain how it works. Electromagnetic energy can be transferred in little packets called photons, but not gravity. Some speculate that a similar particle called the graviton must exist, and this must be the particle or entity by which gravity is transmitted, but they haven't proved yet that it exists.

Gravity acts through almost infinite distances. It's what caused galaxies and stars to coalesce in the first place; it maintains our atmosphere down here on the surface of the Earth, where it can protect us from outer space; and it just so happens that the strength of the gravity on Earth is precisely what it should be to sustain life and cause it to thrive. What is this miraculous force? Where does it come from? How does it act through hundreds of millions of miles of empty space? How does the mass of the moon pull on the water in our oceans to cause tides? Is it an essence that perhaps God can "see"? Is it simply His power, His will, His word that keeps things together? *"...All things were created by Him and for Him. He is before all things, and in Him all things hold together"* (Col. 1:16-17).

I realize that most of us modern westerners are going to have trouble relating the unseen spiritual realm to the visible physical world in which we seemingly live our lives, and tougher yet is the understanding of how the realities of quantum mechanics might be involved. A lot of this stems from the natural tendencies that were culturally formed in us during the industrial revolution. The phenomenal success of technology during the past two centuries has created in us a very strong propensity toward scientific and naturalistic thinking, resulting in a body of God followers who are wholly dependent on logic and cause/effect thinking in all aspects of their lives. Any interpretation of life that includes or requires thinking bordering on the mystical or mysterious seems unnatural and un-Christian from the outset.

God is Bigger than the Bible

We have become accustomed to interpreting biblical truths from a strictly pragmatic viewpoint, dissecting every chapter, verse, and word into absolute, strict, literal constructions of language, verbs, and verb tenses—while losing sight of the mystery, beauty, and breadth of applications to which we can apply these eternal spiritual principles. We should not live as if the only activities that are allowed in the Church and in spiritual life are those specifically found in the Bible. This is simply inconsistent with the truth of the Bible and the actions of our own biblical heroes.

Consider, for example, God whittling Gideon's army down to 300 so he could go out and surround the enemy who had 160,000 troops (see Judg. 7). Or God sending Moses, an old man with a stick and a speech impediment, to rescue more than a million Israelites from bondage to a despotic ruler (see Exod. 3). Capture a city by walking around it for a week and expecting the walls to fall down? C'mon. (See Joshua 6.) And Naaman being told to go wash in the river seven times to be healed of leprosy (see 2 Kings 5). None of these stories should be interpreted as a manual on how to capture cities, lead slaves to freedom, or cure leprosy. The whole point of these stories is to show the consistent *unpredictability* of God's methods.

The Bible itself is a miraculous document, but the truths that it conveys are so broad, permeating, and far-reaching that we really must be open and willing to embrace a broader, bolder, more spiritualistic, and dare I say mystical interpretation of it. *Why* did God whittle Gideon's army down to 300? *Why* did God instruct Moses to go to Egypt alone to stand up against the planet's most powerful ruler? There are deeper issues here than the methodology. The *principles* are what we are to discover and apply to our lives.

If the Bible says not to commit murder, then I should obviously take that most literal meaning to heart. However, the *principle* of killing a body made of flesh and bones is not the most fundamental issue that God is talking about here. He's showing us the innate value in human life. It's a sacred thing, and there is a reason why every society to ever exist on this planet understands the value of the human life and the tragedy that lies in senseless abuses of it. Feed the hungry, do not murder, care for the downtrodden—these are all common themes in the Bible, and they all point to the inherent goodness and value in human life.

Christian Mysticism

Let's be clear about what I mean by "mystical," so my fundamentalist friends will understand where I'm coming from. The dictionary has a couple different definitions; so let's look at what the *New Oxford American Dictionary* says:

mystical | ˈmistikəl |

adjective

1 • of or relating to mystics or religious mysticism: *the mystical experience.*

• spiritually allegorical or symbolic; transcending human understanding: *the mystical body of Christ.*

• of or relating to ancient religious mysteries or other occult or esoteric rites: *the mystical practices of the Pythagoreans.*

• of hidden or esoteric meaning: *a geometric figure of mystical significance.*

2 • inspiring a sense of spiritual mystery, awe, and fascination: *the mystical forces of nature.*

• concerned with the soul or the spirit, rather than with material things: *the beliefs of a more mystical age.*

The second definition is the one I'm more interested in right now. Christian mysticism to me is simply recognizing the side of reality that we don't see with our eyeballs; in other words, the life of the spirit. Westerners are consumed with what we can see and touch, but Eastern societies (including the paradigm from which all the biblical writers lived and wrote) have a characteristically more spiritual or mystical approach to all of life.

In the same way, every biblical principle one can point to has this unseen or mystical value in it. There may be some extremely practical advice in the Bible about finances, relationships, health, and spiritual life, but every one of those principles is built upon the foundation of the unseen, a principle that is actually more important than the illustration. This is why Paul prayed that his readers might have the eyes of their hearts enlightened (see Eph. 1:18). The eyes of our hearts can see things that the eyes in our heads can't.

We are dealing with words like *mystical* and *unpredictable*, but also with quantum physics and science, and we are searching the deeply hidden meanings of these and similar concepts. Therefore, this journey is not just about science. It's not just about Christianity, about God, or about your personal concept of who or what God is. It's about stepping back a few huge steps (maybe a few light-years!) and looking at all of these things from a new perspective. It's about seeing things in a completely different way than you are accustomed to seeing. It's about calling on the resources deep in your spirit to see things that are true about the depths of physical reality, and seeing how that affects your understanding of life, material reality, and spirituality. Then comes the most important part: once you learn what life really is, what are you willing to do about it?

Endnotes

1. Stephen Hawking, *A Brief History of Time* (New York: Bantam Books, 1998), 198.

2. William Tyndale, quoted in "A Theologian For Today," *The Tyndale Society*; http://www.tyndale.org/TSJ/2/werrell.html; accessed on August 18, 2011.

3. Paul Davies, *About Time: Einstein's Unfinished Revolution* (New York: Simon & Schuster, 1995).

CHAPTER 4

Biblical Proof of Quantum Physics?

My friends Henry and Hugh will be joining us occasionally during our discussions in this book. Imagine Henry as an older man with an English accent and Hugh as a middle-aged family man trying to make sense of life.

Henry: My good friend, I must admit that the stars never fail to fascinate me!

Hugh: How so, Henry?

Henry: Huge, glowing masses of hydrogen, I know, but beautiful nevertheless. Always churning, always wriggling, twinkling...as if they're unhappy with their fate and are trying to throw off that shell of fire and burst free.

Hugh: You know, I've read that it can take a million years for a photon created in the heart of a star to reach the outside and escape.

Henry: Extraordinary!

Hugh: Just think of the tremendous gravity in a star like the sun. Its mass is a few nonillion pounds.

Henry: *Nonillion?* Are you making that up?

Hugh: No, it's just one of those things that sticks in my hyperactive brain. A nonillion is a number to the 30th power, so it's like a million, million, million, million, millions. Or consider that it's a trillion times a trillion times a trillion...plus another billion. Or you could say...

Henry: Please, Hugh! My brain is already spinning!

Hugh: Hehe...sorry, Henry. I like numbers.

Henry: Let's agree that the sun is quite heavy.

Hugh: Agreed. Therefore, the gravity on the surface of the sun is proportionately higher than that on earth.

Henry: The sun's gravity must be quite impressive in order to keep the earth in its orbit at this great distance.

Hugh: 93 million miles.

Henry chuckles at his friend's obsession with numbers.

Hugh: The sun could explode, and we wouldn't even know it for eight minutes since the light from the explosion would take that long to get here.

Henry: Is God not the most amazing engineer in existence?

Hugh smiles and leans back in his chair, noticing that the branches from the crepe myrtle in his back yard perfectly frame Orion's Belt.

* * * * * * * * * * *

Is there biblical *proof* of quantum physics? OK, so maybe *proof* is too strong a word, but now is a good time to look at a couple examples of what the Bible might reveal about such things. Paul wrote, *"By Him [Jesus] all things were created: things in Heaven and on earth, visible and invisible…and in Him all things hold together"* (Col. 1:16-17).

This reminds me of a quandary modern scientists find themselves in. What happens when you force the positive poles of two strong magnets together? It's impossible! The closer you push similar magnetic forces together, the stronger they repel each other. So why does the nucleus of an atom hold together? You have a bunch of positively charged particles in extremely close proximity that ought to repel each other with violent force. When we are actually able to break those tremendous binding forces, the energy is so intense that we have explosive results. It's called a nuclear bomb. Those particles ought to reject one another violently, yet they hold together.

GUT

Scientists couldn't explain that, so they just gave it a name and called it the "strong nuclear force." This is one of the four fundamental forces in the universe that scientists have identified, the other three being the weak nuclear force, electromagnetism, and gravity. The all-consuming exercise (for some physicists) for the past several decades has been the search for a common unifying force underlying all four of these. It's the holy grail of physics, and they call it the Grand Unifying Theory (GUT).[1] I think they might be barking up the wrong tree. The Bible verse above explains it clearly to me. In Christ *"all things hold together."*

One of the challenges to finding the GUT is gravity. Electromagnetism can be defined as being transmitted through particles and/or waves, but not gravity. Scientists speculate that a particle called the graviton actually exists, and it is the mechanism by which gravity is transmitted through space (much like the photon is the particle by which light or other electromagnetic waves are transmitted). The existence of the graviton is so important to some in their quest for the GUT that they write books about it like *The God Particle* by Leon Lederman. But no one has yet seen a graviton or proved that it exists.

What if they never find a graviton? I would just refer them to Isaiah, who said that God spread out the Heavens (see Isa. 48:13). I think gravity might be God's power keeping things in place. Once again, in Christ *all things are held together*. Does it negate science to glibly claim that it's God and not gravity, or does it dumb down God's power by equating His power with a physical force? Can we say that because God uses gravity that it's ultimately God holding the universe together, just like when I swing a hammer, it was me who built the house, not the hammer? Where do we draw the line between God's abilities and the tools He uses to get His work done? What's the difference?

Does God not have the right to use whatever forces He deems necessary to accomplish His purposes? If He chooses to use scientific processes, that's OK with me. If He chooses to change people's minds by challenging their assumptions, that's OK too. If He wants to speak directly to someone's heart and bypass his or her skeptical brain, then He's just being God. I think it's completely logical and permissible to say that the power of God's intention is holding the universe together, and so is gravity. Which is which? Are they the same? Does it really matter?

God established a bunch of physical laws by which the universe operates and we do best when we abide by them. If I decide to jump out of a plane without a parachute just for fun, trusting God to temporarily put the law of gravity on hold until I can gently touch down, I will probably not have such a gentle landing. This is not because He doesn't love me or doesn't want to care for me. This same force of gravity that could threaten my life was put in place for my benefit.

For example, it's gravity that keeps the air on Earth close to the surface so we can breathe, and allows the airplane I'm jumping out of to fly. When we disobey God's laws—be they moral laws or physical laws—there can be real consequences.

But what role do science and theology have in explaining gravity? Perhaps we will discover a graviton. Then we will know the mechanism that God uses to hold all things together. The discovery of the graviton should not worry Christians, but cause us to rejoice that we have taken one step closer to figuring out just how God created the universe. Is God any less omnipotent if He chooses to use gravitons to hold the universe together rather than simply his "miraculous power"? Either way, the previously mentioned Scripture attributes the ongoing stability of "all things" to Jesus, the original Designer and Creator. And we know that one of the tools He uses is science and the natural laws He has put in place.

Quantum Physics at Work in the Bible

Do you need more biblical proof? How about Shadrach, Meshach, and Abednego surviving the fiery furnace? (See Daniel 3.) There are some cool quantum physics going on there! Fire is a bunch of carbon and oxygen atoms going berserk, and their violent collisions, releases of energy, and outbursts are what cause fire to burn our flesh. Those photons are flying around so fast and hard that they disrupt the actual atomic structure of the stuff they run into. In this example, the bodies of the soldiers that threw our three friends into the furnace were burned. But the three were not harmed.

It's interesting that the Bible states there was not even a smell of smoke on their clothes after they came out of the furnace. Some sub-atomic protection was there to prevent those violent photons from melting them and to prevent their clothes from acquiring the particles of smoke and particulate from the fire. Sure, God simply protected them supernaturally, but how? Is it a crime to wonder about the mechanism God used? Does it betray a lack of faith to surmise that God used a miracle of quantum physics to protect them? Or does using scientific principles make God much more amazing because He is able to command the behavior of matter on a subatomic level?

Creation

The most obvious example of quantum physics in the Bible is the creation of the universe. What was created did not come from nothing, as our popular "creation ex nihilo" theology teaches. The Bible says the universe was created from "what cannot be seen" (see Heb. 11:3). Whether we choose to subscribe to the big bang creation scenario or not, it still remains that creation ex nihilo sounds an awful lot like re-arranging energy (which cannot be seen) into matter (which can be seen). This process, discovered by Albert Einstein just a few decades ago and summarized in his famous equation E=MC2, is 100 percent, pure quantum physics. What this equation means is energy (E) is equal to mass (M) multiplied by a constant (C2), which has to do with the speed of light. Mass is energy. The solid stuff we call matter is just a bunch of little concentrations of vibrating energy. It's the electrical forces between the subatomic particles that cause things to feel solid beneath our feet or fingers. And all the material in the known universe was and is fashioned from this energy soup, clinging to itself in every imaginable configuration.

$$C\left(T_{\mu\nu} - \frac{1}{2}g_{\mu\nu}T\right) \simeq C\left(T_{\mu\nu} - \frac{1}{2}g_{\mu\nu}T\right)$$

$$\simeq C\left[\begin{pmatrix} \rho_0 & 0 & 0 & 0 \\ 0 & 0 & 0 & 0 \\ 0 & 0 & 0 & 0 \\ 0 & 0 & 0 & 0 \end{pmatrix} - \frac{1}{2}\begin{pmatrix} \rho_0 & 0 & 0 & 0 \\ 0 & -\rho_0 & 0 & 0 \\ 0 & 0 & -\rho_0 & 0 \\ 0 & 0 & 0 & -\rho_0 \end{pmatrix}\right]$$

$$\simeq \frac{C\rho_0}{2}\delta_{\mu\nu}$$

$$H = -\frac{\hbar^2}{2m}\int d^3r\,\phi^\dagger(\mathbf{r})\nabla^2\phi(\mathbf{r}) + \int d^3r\int d^3r'\,\phi^\dagger(\mathbf{r})\phi^\dagger(\mathbf{r'})U(|\mathbf{r}-\mathbf{r'}|)\phi(\mathbf{r'})\phi(\mathbf{r}) = GOD$$

When Genesis says, *"...and there was light"* (Gen. 1:3) this is not just some mundane event that we ought to accept blindly on faith. This describes the behavior modification of electrons and photons being arranged into their familiar particle/wave format we know as the electromagnetic spectrum. God was commanding that energy/matter to begin acting a certain way from that moment on. Whatever one's view on the age of the universe, most of us—Christians and scientists included—agree that there was a moment in the history of the universe when energy/matter began acting in ways that it previously had not. Quantum physics in action!

When Isaiah says that God spread out the Heavens, this is not merely our Creator putting together a Lego-style universe, placing one star here and a galaxy there according to whimsy. It describes an infinitely complex interplay between massive stars, galaxies containing billions of stars, nebulae, and other deep space features, the gravity that acts throughout the universe to control the positions and motions of all things, the unfathomable characteristics and consequences of bizarre creations like black holes, the very mysterious existence of dark matter (which according to some physicists may comprise the majority of mass in the universe, even though it is undetectable), and in the middle of it all a tiny planet populated with beings that God loves enough to die for.

When Genesis says that people were made *"from the dust of the ground"* (Gen. 2:7), this is not merely some miraculous event at some specific point in time. Yes, it was miraculous, but it specifically describes the rearrangement of myriad molecular elements into a specific configuration such that the subatomic nuclear and electrical bonds were held together in such a way as to form a complete, functioning human body. When God breathed the ghost into the machine, that mass of atomic particles—those trillions of little balls of energy being held together by the will and Word of God—became a portal bridging the visible realm of the universe with the invisible spiritual realm of God's Spirit. From that moment until now, God has had as intimate a relationship as can be imagined with these created beings, since His life force, creativity, and the authority of His thoughts and words permeate our very bodies and spirits. What an incredibly intimate relationship! No other piece of God's universe (to our knowledge, unless there are beings on other planets) enjoys such a thoroughly personal relationship with its Creator, since we are permeated both physically and spiritually with His energy and character.

I could go on and on discussing the myriad miracles in the Old and New Testaments, all of which depend chiefly on the performance of matter and energy playing according to the rules of quantum physics. Yes, the Bible contains plenty of proof for the existence of quantum physics. Or might it be more accurate to say that quantum physics provides proof of the authenticity of the Bible?

For thousands of years, humankind has read stories in the Bible that defy physical explanation. God has blessed you and me by placing us at a specific time in human history such that we can now begin to understand the mechanisms behind those miracles. We may not be able to perfectly re-create any of these miraculous events (yet), but we certainly are beginning to understand more thoroughly how they may have happened. And every step closer we come to discovering the scientific methodology that God used to create, and continues to use in His ongoing creation of the cosmos and of His Kingdom on Earth, the closer we come to the heart of the Living God, who loves us with an undying love. This entire, unbelievable universe was created specifically for you and me; all its wonder and magnificence, all its unknowable glory, all its indescribable beauty, are for you and me. Now, *that's* a love worth finding!

Endnote

1.   Timothy Ferris, *The Whole Shebang: A State of the Universe(s) Report* (New York: Simon & Schuster, 1997), 217.

CHAPTER 5

Seeing in the Spirit

Ever thought much about Elijah? He's a very interesting character from the Old Testament. Here was a man who had a great grasp on that unseen realm that we often struggle to see. I would like to start by sharing a few stories about him:

> Elijah said to her, "Don't be afraid. Go home and do as you have said. But first make a small cake of bread for me from what you have and bring it to me, and then make something for yourself and your son. For this is what the Lord, the God of Israel, says: 'The jar of flour will not be used up and the jug of oil will not run dry until the day the Lord gives rain on the land.'" She went away and did as Elijah had told her. So there was food every day for Elijah and for the woman and her family. For the jar of flour was not used up and the jug of oil did not run dry, in keeping with the word of the Lord spoken by Elijah (1 Kings 17:13-16).

This is very similar to the miracle Jesus performed when feeding the 5,000. He created bread out of nothing, expanding five loaves into a huge surplus of food that fed thousands of people. Quantum physics galore was happening in front of the disciples' eyes as energy was rearranged into bread and fish in the hands of Jesus. Here, Elijah also called upon God to perform some serious science—creating oil in the jar so that it never ran dry. This is the same miracle of creating substance from the invisible realm that happened at the creation of the universe. Either God created more oil where there was none, or He duplicated the molecules of oil that were in the jar. Either way, science was performed in a very impressive way.

> *Some time later the son of the woman who owned the house became ill. He grew worse and worse, and finally stopped breathing. She said to Elijah, "What do you have against me, man of God? Did you come to remind me of my sin and kill my son?"*
>
> *"Give me your son," Elijah replied. He took him from her arms, carried him to the upper room where he was staying, and laid him on his bed. Then he cried out to the Lord, "O Lord my God, have You brought tragedy also upon this widow I am staying with, by causing her son to die?" Then he stretched himself out on the boy three times and cried to the Lord, "O Lord my God, let this boy's life return to him!"*
>
> *The Lord heard Elijah's cry, and the boy's life returned to him, and he lived. Elijah picked up the child and carried him down from the room into the house. He gave him to his mother and said, "Look, your son is alive!"*
>
> *Then the woman said to Elijah, "Now I know that you are a man of God and that the word of the Lord from your mouth is the truth"* (1 Kings 17:17-24).

The context of the story shows us that Elijah's cries for the boy's life are what moved God to bring him back to life. God did not instruct Elijah to pray that way, but Elijah—through his relationship with God and his boldness before the throne—asked God to do the miraculous on behalf of the boy and his mother, and God "heard Elijah's cry" and obliged.

One more story, but this one is about Elisha:

And Elisha prayed, "O Lord, open his eyes so he may see."
Then the Lord opened the servant's eyes, and he looked and
saw the hills full of horses and chariots of fire all around
Elisha (2 Kings 6:17).

This is a classic representation of that unseen realm that surrounds us, the realm of "Heaven," or the "eternal hereafter," or however we envision it. I believe this is the realm of existence where we go after our physical bodies die and where those loved ones who have gone before are residing now. They can see the angel warriors surrounding us. They can see the spiritual warfare being waged for our time, energy, and souls. Maybe they're cheering us on!

These angel warriors are of the same army that surrounds you and me, and their powers and abilities are there for us every day. And I believe that the extent to which we can take advantage of their power and work in our lives is governed by our awareness of that realm of existence and our belief that God really means what He says:

For He will command His angels concerning you to guard
you in all your ways; they will lift you up in their hands,
so that you will not strike your foot against a stone (Psalm
91:11-12).

If we remain ignorant of the angels protecting us, I'm pretty sure they'll continue their duties anyway. However, if we learn to cooperate with God's desires, the protections He has put in place for us, and the beings He has appointed to watch over us, then how much more might we benefit from their presence? If I'm in the trenches during armed conflict, how much better off will I be if I'm cognizant of the forces in the trench with me and aware of their abilities, the orders they have received from their Commander, and their modes of doing battle?

Eternal Eyes

What all of these stories above illustrate is that Elijah and Elisha had eternal eyes. They could readily cross over between the seen and unseen which, in practical terms, eliminates the difference between the two. If Elijah could see the eternal perspective of angels on the hillsides, then there really was no difference to him between what was temporal and what was eternal. I believe that this is a goal we all ought to be striving for as we learn and grow and mature in Christ. We *have* the Spirit of Christ, right now. Within our spirits *are* all the provisions, wisdom, eternal perspective, and knowledge we will ever receive.

The key is learning to manifest all of this in our everyday lives, our everyday circumstances, and in our everyday relationships. We need to "Elijah" ourselves by the inner workings of God's Holy Spirit in our hearts and minds. And as the characteristics of His Spirit are made manifest in our lives, we too will gain a perspective that will dim the horizon between the two realms and allow us to participate in the truly supernatural realm where God lives and breathes.

CHAPTER 6

The Kingdom of Heaven Is Here

An important consequence of this quantum spiritual reality existing right here under our noses is that it should help us more consistently live as if the Kingdom of God is present, now, right here where we live. We know the Kingdom of God is here (see Matt. 11:12) and that we ought to be striving to see things happening here on Earth as in Heaven (see Matt. 6:10). The Kingdom of God is unseen and immaterial in nature, but these events that take place in order to bring God's Kingdom to Earth have physical manifestations.

You have probably heard the saying, "That person is so heavenly minded he's of no earthly good." The implication is that it is not appropriate to only dream of a future in Heaven, because God's purpose for us includes our impacting the lives of our neighbors and friends here and now, in our neighborhoods, churches, and places of employment. How? By helping financially, by providing food to those who are hungry, by taking an elderly house-bound neighbor some supper, by encouraging each other and praying for each other. If we accept all things physical, mental, spiritual, and emotional as spiritual realities, then I believe it will become more natural for us to treat other humans, animals, resources, our planet earth, and all things with much more respect and care.

For example, Christians have sometimes been accused of not caring for the environment, especially with the strong association of Christians with the political right in America. But the fact is that, of all people, followers of Jesus ought to be the most concerned about protecting our environment because it is a holy creation, a precious gift given to us by a holy God who wanted to create the very best home in which we can live and experience life. Being of some "earthly good" is a biblical mandate for all believers because it is primarily through physical acts of kindness that God's love is effectively shown. As James wrote:

> What good is it, my brothers, if a man claims to have faith but has no deeds? Can such faith save him? Suppose a brother or sister is without clothes and daily food. If one of you says to him, "Go, I wish you well; keep warm and well fed," but does nothing about his physical needs, what good is it? In the same way, faith by itself, if it is not accompanied by action, is dead (James 2:14-17).

Let us continue with the idea that Jesus meant it literally when He said, "The Kingdom of Heaven is at hand" (Matt. 3:2 NASB). Perhaps we can gain some insight into this spiritual reality that underlies everything we see and experience. Remember the angel armies that Elisha saw surrounding him and his servant? This story beautifully portrays one of my visions of Heaven and the "other side." Perhaps the life awaiting us after our physical bodies die may be surrounding us where we are now. But *surrounds* is such an inadequate Newtonian word, since it seems to limit our thinking to three-dimensional space. Maybe *permeates* would be a better term. What if all of reality, including the eternal reality where God exists with those who have gone on before, is the same reality we live in, but is simply not normally visible to us nor accessible by our three-dimensional limitations and our five senses? If those chariots of fire were surrounding Elisha and his servant all that time, but were not visible until their eyes were enlightened and enabled to see that dimension of existence, then perhaps it's safe to assume that this is indeed that actual reality that surrounds us at all times.

Is this the same as Heaven? It's impossible to say for sure. We simply have no way of knowing what it's really like until we experience it, but for sure there are significant spiritual realities surrounding us right now, and that dimension of existence permeates the time-space universe where we live. This is why I believe that our physical actions have immediate and penetrating spiritual consequences. It is not as if the consequences of the harsh words we speak or the refusal to help someone in need are limited to some distant reaction or deny us of some future spiritual blessing. While this may surely be part of the truth, I see it more like the consequences of our selfishness and soulish behavior are real and immediate and have significant effect on the fabric of the spiritual/physical interface that controls the existence of all things, the fabric of life itself.

The story above suggests this, as does Hebrews 12:1, which talks about us being *"surrounded by...a great cloud of witnesses...,"* and Numbers 22:31, which reports, *"Then the Lord opened Balaam's eyes, and he saw the angel of the Lord standing in the road with his sword drawn...."* Should we take *surrounded* literally? We realize that the Bible is full of figurative language, poetry, apocalyptic language, metaphors, and similes, and we have to be careful about insisting on pure literal interpretation at all times in all cases. But to choose the word *surrounded* is peculiar to me, unless it actually means what it says. The author could have chosen *preceded by* or *presented with* instead. If this cloud of witnesses surrounds us, as did Elisha's invisible army, and if God's angels guard us and even protect us from harm as the Psalmist claims (see Ps. 91), and if God is everywhere at all times, then perhaps this eternal world we look forward to is right here under our noses, and the passage into eternity may not be as unfamiliar and spooky a thing as we have been thinking.

What Does Heaven on Earth Look Like?

We know that when we begin our authentic walk with God, He places a life force within us that will go on forever. In the words of Scripture, we gain *eternal life*. This eternal life begins now, here on Earth, not after we physically die. Because we lose our physical bodies when we die, this immaterial and immortal part of us lives on in an unseen dimension. This unseen dimension is just as much a part of me now as it will be after I shed this temporary dwelling place. If this unseen and eternal part of me is just as real and eternal now as it will be in eternity, then should I not be taking advantage *right now* of all that this unseen realm has to offer me?

What if you could see with perfect eyes? What if the colors, fragrances, and all the physical manifestations of all creation could be experienced and understood perfectly with no limitations of your five senses? What if you could see like an eagle, able to spot a mouse in the grass a mile away? What if you could literally *see* the pain in the hearts of the people around you? What if you could see the sinful intent of a person who is about to cause pain to another? What if you could see trouble coming, know when and where it's going to hit, know how to avoid it, and know how to defeat your enemy before he even starts the fight?

Big-screen, big-budget movies are made of this stuff, and this is the kind of insight that is offered to us if we simply choose to live in that realm of the Spirit where God offers us wisdom, knowledge, shrewdness, and discernment (see Prov. 2:1-11). While it's true that First Corinthians 2:9 says, *"No eye has seen, no ear has heard, no mind has conceived what God has prepared for those who love Him,"* most people leave it at that and don't continue to the best, most important part of the sentence. Paul goes on to say, *"but God **has** revealed it to us by His Spirit…"* (1 Cor. 2:10). We can get a glimpse of this awesome reality (the real reality, not the physical reality) if we just open our spiritual eyes.

It really is possible to live there, in that place where insight and spiritual discernment trump our five senses and our logic. In fact, God invites you to live there because that's where He hangs out. He loves you and wants to share His Kingdom and His perspective with you. That's what *"on earth as it is in Heaven"* means (Matt. 6:10). The Kingdom of Heaven is here now. It surrounds us, permeates us, helps us, heals us, and it provides for us—all because we have been placed *in Christ* and the Father has already given us—past tense—all things through His Son.

Let's look a little closer at this statement *"on earth as it is in Heaven"*:

- Is there any doubt in Heaven?
- Any disease?
- Any sin?
- Any pain?
- Any arguments?
- Any depression?
- Any weakness of the will that allows our emotions or mental condition to roam out of control?
- Any accusation, regret, or sorrow?
- Any hatred between parents and children?
- Any mistrust between husband and wife?

Now, are you ready to really dig in deep?

- In Heaven will there be any boundaries or restrictions between what you see and what you believe?
- Will there be any anomalies between what you

believe and what you do?

- Between what you do and who you are?

- In Heaven, will the actualization of your true character—including the manifestation of who you truly are at the level of your deepest dreams and desires—be lacking in any way?

- Will the absolute expression of your deepest personality—precisely the way God created you and intended you to be and act and do—be missing any component or virtue?

- Will the tasks you are expected to accomplish overcome your resources, your abilities, your commitment to see them through, or your ability to complete them with excellence?

- Will there ever be any doubt or hesitation about what God is expecting you to do, to be, to accomplish?

After answering all these questions, are you ready to begin experiencing Heaven on earth?

I believe we must take the declaration of Jesus that the Kingdom of Heaven is here, and His prayer that we ought to ask for and expect things to be on Earth as they are in Heaven, as literally and as simply as we possibly can. In the past (fundamental literalist that I was), I had taken these concepts to simply mean happiness, lack of sin, and whatever other ethereal characteristics I thought Heaven must have. Now I realize it goes far deeper than that. God created you the way you are for a reason. You are to become the Bride of Christ, and He does not want to spend the rest of eternity with a nasty, ignorant, or lethargic woman. He made you specifically the way you are because your deepest dreams, desires, and personality are exactly what He wants for His eternal companion.

If you can achieve that expression of your true eternal self while still walking this Earth in flesh and blood, what a tremendous expression of Christ that would be to the world around you! And as each one of us accomplishes this milestone as a part of the Body, the Building, the Nation that is the whole of God's children, then the world cannot help but be turned upside down! Now, *that's* what I call the Kingdom of Heaven. *That's* what I call Heaven on Earth. The Kingdom of Heaven is here, and God wants to share it all with us, here and now, in our flesh and bones, in our hearts, minds, bodies, and spirits.

CHAPTER 7

The Spirit Web

I'm not especially literate in the language of dreams and visions. When I say things like, "I had a vision," what I typically mean is that I had an image in my mind of a certain reality, and this vision was a bit more real than just a thought, but not quite as real as seeing something with my eyes. I hope that makes sense, because I want to describe what I feel was a vision I had at a conference I attended in 2008.

We had just finished some incredible praise and worship, and the whole crowd was standing in front of the platform listening to the leader of the conference. It was near the end of the three-day event, and this was the day we would all be going home after an awesome experience. Graham Cooke was standing on the platform praying, and I envisioned that each of us in that building was very literally a concentration of God's energy in space-time.[1] Each person was made up of a mass of brilliant white jiggling particles in the physical realm, connected behind the scenes by a source of energy in the spirit realm that caused each one to appear as a glowing mass.

We have discussed that the atoms and molecules of which matter is constructed consist of vibrating points of energy, so each person is a mass of these little entities. This is not new age mumbo-jumbo; this is literally what science tells us. Keeping in mind that we physically exist as concentrations of energy, remember that we are also God's conduits from His unseen world toward the visible world around us.

So we are these vibrating sources of physical energy, infused with the spiritual energy of God's Spirit. Scriptures tell us that it is the mighty power of God that works through us and that it's His divine power that supplies everything we need for our life (our physical needs) and godliness (our spiritual needs) (see 2 Pet. 1:3).

Each Christian's physical presence on this planet is a literal portal into eternity, a glimpse into the "other side," a connection for the people around them to the blessings, love, and gifts that God wants to spread throughout the earth. Most of the time, when God chooses to touch the lives of humans, He chooses to do it through the words, actions, or prayers of another human. No matter how we describe it, each of us individually represents—very literally—concentrations of God's character and life force in space-time toward the people we encounter. His love ought to flow through us, and also His grace, His mercy, and His encouragement—His energy! Non-believers do not have this characteristic (see Rom. 8:7-8), so it is a tangible presence that surrounds us God-followers wherever we go and sets us apart from the rest of the world. I suppose there are a hundred ways to describe this, but it will all be metaphorical language because we are trying to express a spiritual reality in the language of physical phenomena.

An important part of life in the Spirit is that we are also connected to each other because we are all one in the Holy Spirit: *"Make every effort to keep the unity of the Spirit through the bond of peace"* (Eph. 4:3). The Bible metaphorically describes our unity in the Spirit in many similar ways: as a Body (see 1 Cor. 12) held together by ligaments and sinews (see Col. 2:19), as a building (see Eph. 2:20-22), as a nation (see 1 Pet. 2:9), and so on. As one body, we cannot be separated. This, of course, is spiritual language because of course we are physically separated. But, as a single spiritual body connected by muscles and sinews, which I believe the apostle Paul uses as a metaphor for our love for God and for one another, we are literally connected to one another.

Back to my vision: I pictured each individual as a mass of energy particles, each one a conduit into the supernatural realm. As each person left the conference, after having been charged up by God's Spirit, a web or a net stretched out between us so that each person was connected by a glowing cord to all the others. Our spiritual connection enabled us to cover the whole country—actually the whole world—with this net of God's energy, so that none should be unaffected by God's web of love and influence.

We are connected to each other in a very real sense, and there is an energy that engages us with each other and stretches across infinite distances. These webs connecting us are love, compassion, and the gifts of the Spirit, and they literally connect heart with heart.

Recognizing the Spirit-to-Spirit Connection

Haven't you felt it? Haven't you met someone with whom you almost immediately developed a spiritual connection? This is not necessarily based on similar likes or dislikes, certain qualities of personality, or any other type of similarity, except that you both resonate with a particular expression of God's character, and this creates a bond that cannot be broken for the rest of your lives. This bond is like a string that attaches your heart across distances to the hearts of those who are also in Christ, and these interconnected strings form the web I envisioned, covering all of creation. It not only connects spirit with spirit, but those who do not know Christ get tangled up in the influence you possess as a conduit of God's love and Spirit. They get a shot of God's energy, and therefore, they get a taste of what Christ is like even though they may not understand what they are experiencing.

This Spirit web is a very real way in which I personally experience the crossover between the seen and unseen realms and what makes me hungry for more of the latter. If we can truly understand and visualize that unseen network of Spirit connections, then distance and separation become meaningless regarding the building of relationships and the spiritual encouragement of one another. We ought to be able to "do Church" over great distances. I admit that there's no substitute for face-to-face contact, but long-distance Church can become a reality if we can truly understand things from the perspective of the unseen realm that undergirds everything we see and touch.

A wormhole is a hypothetical feature of space-time that could connect distant parts of the universe. A trip that may require traveling at the speed of light for millions of years might be done instantaneously. Pundits surmise that such a feature might arise from the near-infinite gravity near a black hole that could warp space-time to such an extent that it folds inward and opens a rift to another part of the universe. As we have discussed, gravity is an unknown and unseen force, but it is bent by large concentrations of matter, and it gets bent completely out of shape near a wormhole. Weird stuff, I know, but I'm working toward an illustration here.

Wormholes and Spiritual Connections

My best friends live far away from me, thousands of miles away. I see some of them only of couple times a year if I'm lucky. But I love them no less. They inspire me, and I gain energy from them. I feel closer to them than to many of my local friends. They are part of my inner web, and I feel their presence even when I am alone. I am connected to them by a heartstring, and it gives me a glimpse of that realm that surrounds me, but cannot be seen. In that unseen place, distances are meaningless. Physical distance is reduced to nothing, the limitations of time and space and my physical body are null and void, and I can have Spirit fellowship across any distance because there is a wormhole surrounding me that allows instantaneous time-travel in the Spirit realm. That infinite gravity that opens up the rift in space-time is God's character working in and through me, and it transcends physical time and space.

Imagine that you had a room in your house with a hundred doors, each of which would take you instantaneously to the home of a different friend or loved one. Imagine further that instead of taking you to that person's house, it took you directly to an expression of his or her spirit and you could sense what they are feeling or experiencing. Perhaps you could even see these things without their knowledge, not in a sordid, Peeping-Tom way, but in a Spirit-led revelation of the difficulties and emotions that others are experiencing. Armed with this information, you could then pray for them, think and brainstorm about their circumstances, and discuss with God what you will say to them, or what you will do for them when you see them face-to-face or talk to them on the phone.

This is precisely the kind of life we can and ought to be living. These heartstrings, these doors of access, these methods of seeing into the invisible realm where time and distance are meaningless, are God's ways of inviting us into His eternal perspective so we can effectively pray, prophesy, and do battle on behalf of the people in our lives. By touching them in this way—by instantaneous time travel via the Spirit web—we can build each other up and encourage each other immediately over great distances.

This concept could be further illustrated by thinking about telephones. What an incredible technology! When I answer my cell phone, there is an amazing sequence of events behind the scenes that conspire to allow me to talk to my Honey, even when she's a thousand miles away. Her cell phone is connected to a network via electromagnetic signals that are beamed through physical space to her phone. These invisible electromagnetic waves follow all the wacky rules of quantum physics that have to do with electromagnetism. This is Einstein stuff we're talking about here. Even if she's traveling down the highway at 70 miles per hour, the cell phone signal remains connected to her phone.

As her line connects to the network, the signal enters physical-relay stations located in physical cell-phone towers close to her. Pieces of our conversation are then transmitted through physical wires or fiber optic cables to various places, through switching mechanisms, through a computer that can bill my wife for the air time she's using, then on toward the tower that's closest to me (how it knows which tower I'm near is a miracle to me!). Then it's up the tower to the transmitter and across miles of air space into my cell phone. As I travel down the highway the signal is smoothly handed off from one tower to the next, so I can have a continuous conversation over a distance of dozens of miles.

If I am in a big city, then all the while there are a thousand other cell-phone conversations passing right through my body, but I don't hear them, because my personal cell phone is not translating them. All the electromagnetic waves for all the local radio stations, television stations, cell phone communications, satellite transmissions, and all sorts of other stuff are passing through my body continuously, yet I am only able to understand and translate those for which I have the proper device (a television or radio tuned to a particular channel, for instance).

Now let's think of all this electromagnetic mumbo-jumbo in terms of the Spirit Web. When I dial my cell phone—that is, when I need to interface with a friend or loved one—it's a plea for intervention. It could be tears, it could be some good news I want to share, and it could be a request for prayer for healing or a number of other needs. This spiritual, unseen need is transmitted wirelessly into the network that is the Body of Christ—the friends and family that make up my inner circle. I can ask specifically and verbally for intervention, or someone close to me may get a message directly from God through the Spirit wire that I need some kind of attention. The message may be transmitted to a central station where it is logged in—the church or my local fellowship of like-minded believers and loved ones.

Many people may be informed of my need and many will pray and begin interceding with God on my behalf. God hears, of course, and may choose any number of ways to answer and meet my need. That answer is then transmitted back through the network, sometimes via a prophetic word of encouragement or advice, sometimes directly from God to my cell phone (my inner spirit). The answer always begins as an immaterial desire or command from Heaven, issued on my behalf. The manifestation of that answer may be a physical miracle or something immaterial like encouragement or a word of knowledge or word of wisdom. This Spirit web surrounds me and penetrates my physical being at all times. The more attuned I am to its function and the messages that are flying about, the more I can receive, interpret, and take advantage of the messages that pertain to me and my condition. It all depends on the hardware in my hand.

To translate these invisible messages, I need a few tools, just like I need a cell phone in my hand to translate that one specific electromagnetic transmission among thousands that is meant for me. I need knowledge of the Bible and God's *modus operandi*. I need sensitivity to His Spirit speaking in a still, small voice. I need love and forgiveness because hate and unforgiveness block Spirit communication and cause so much background noise that I can't hear the conversation. I need a desire to hear God's voice. I need an understanding of my place in His Body so I can properly interpret the messages I receive and turn them into love and blessings toward others. I need some humility so I can apply the advice and principles I learn in a way that will build others up rather than tear them down.

The Spirit web is a phenomenon that I want to understand more and more as I live my life. I believe there is an amazing power lying there in wait for us. We have learned to harness the power of electromagnetic transmission for millions of beneficial uses, and it's time we learned to harness and use the power of the Spirit web to encourage and love one another, to do battle against the enemy, and—most importantly—to remain intimately connected to our Creator. I encourage you to pray about it. Ask God to plug you into a depth you have never experienced before so that you can have supernatural insight about your own life, the lives of those you love, and even the lives of those you run into in your day-to-day life who may need a word from God. Once you start operating in the Spirit web, you'll never want to go back!

Endnote

1. The term *space-time* refers to the four-dimensional universe that most scientists base their studies and beliefs on. The three physical dimensions have been shown to be intimately integrated with time, the fourth dimension in our universe, by Albert Einstein's theories of relativity. Time and space can in some ways be the same according to quantum physics.

CHAPTER 8

Rules By Which
We Live

God has planned a relationship with you that has its roots in a different realm. It has its roots in a different dimension of thought, action, and experience. And we're always wanting God to invade this realm, but you know the real purpose of God is to pull you into His. That's why He put you "into Christ." Because Christ is living in a different realm than we are living in. And we are getting pulled into the realm of Jesus, so we think as He thinks. Therefore we are not subject to the natural world, nor are we limited to an earthly experience. —Graham Cooke[1]

What might it really mean for us to *not* be subject to the natural world or limited to only earthly experiences? Do you believe that it's possible to live above and beyond the natural world? Does this kind of talk amount to a bunch of flighty, religious mumbo-jumbo in your mind? Would you rather have a faith that is grounded in what you can see, touch, and feel? Let's read Romans 12:1-2:

Therefore, I urge you, brothers, in view of God's mercy, to offer your bodies as living sacrifices, holy and pleasing to God—this is your spiritual act of worship. Do not conform any longer to the pattern of this world, but be transformed by the renewing of your mind. Then you will be able to test and approve what God's will is—His good, pleasing and perfect will (Romans 12:1-2).

I would like to pay special attention to verse 2 where it says, *"Do not conform any longer to the pattern of this world...."* This alone shows us in black and white that the standard we are to strive for is *not* of this world. Since we are clearly instructed to *not* confirm to this world; we *must* strive for something above and beyond what we can see and touch and sense with our purely physical senses. This alone should be enough to kick us out of our lethargy and get us dreaming and striving for a supernatural perspective on things.

Do Not Conform to This World...

I have historically understood Romans 12:1-2 in light of sin and the struggle with the flesh. To me, *"Do not be conformed to this world,"* meant, "Do not sin like the world does" or "Do not succumb to the temptations of the world." I was a good evangelical boy, always concerned first and foremost with sin. As usual, my interpretation was tragically limited in its scope. I finally got it while listening to a CD of Graham Cooke's teaching on this passage while driving through the snow and misery of a Chicago winter. Taking Graham Cooke's quote above into consideration, I came to understand that *"do not be conformed to this world"* refers to any and all of the world's assumptions and strictly naturalistic interpretations of all things.

Those who do not know Jesus are restricted to a world consisting only of what they can see and touch. Christ followers, by understanding that we are not subject to the natural world, nor are we limited to an earthly experience, understand that Romans 12:2 leads us to a worldview that does not follow the same cause and effect rules that the world follows. Jesus is not subject to the natural world, and He is not limited to earthly experiences, nor are we since we are in Christ. This is why we must learn to follow our hearts, *not* our minds (see Prov. 3:5-6). The *world* trusts their understanding; we *don't*. We trust in God and His usually unorthodox methodology; the world *doesn't*. The *world*—at least us western societies with our naturalistic mind-set—trusts its own capacity to reason, being strong believers in cause and effect.

The world would have us believe that our employers are the ones who provide us with money; therefore, we must work for food and provision. But Jesus tells us that we must start with the all-consuming goal of putting the Kingdom of God and His righteousness first in everything we do and think, and then all our provisions will be given to us (see Matt. 6:33).

The world would have us believe that when medical science has done everything they possibly can for a terminally ill patient, then there's no other choice but to go home and die. While I would never discourage someone from seeking medical help, I nevertheless know that miraculous healings and other supernatural wonders are not uncommon in the world of those who are in tune with Christ.

The world would have us believe that happiness can only come from things that make us feel good, either physically or emotionally. But Christ wants us to learn through experience that we can have peace and happiness no matter what our circumstances.

Rules of the Kingdom

The rules that govern the Christian's existence are nothing like those by which the world abides. But it's not just that we follow a different set of rules, but a far *superior* set. The rules of the Kingdom are unlimited in their scope because they are supernatural and *not* limited by anything physical, natural, or human. We are not subject to the limitations that natural laws define, nor are we limited to experiences that can only be explained or quantified by earthly or natural parameters. Our lives ought to be lived on a plane above and beyond simple natural explanations, and the supernatural ought to become normal to us.

What exactly does the word *supernatural* mean to you? To me, it means anything that cannot be caused or explained by strictly natural phenomena. It's *beyond* natural. *Above* natural. *Higher than* natural. I find it interesting that most of the supernatural miracles of Jesus required some serious science to pull them off. As we will explore elsewhere, turning water to wine, healing diseased body parts, feeding 5,000 with a few loaves of bread, immediately calming a storm—all these miracles required some awesome authority over the world of science and quantum physics. So when Jesus spoke and something miraculous happened—something that we consider supernatural and something that requires an awesome display of scientific prowess—what does this say about the relationship between the miraculous, other-worldly, supernatural powers of Jesus and the qualities of quantum physics?

I want to live in that realm of existence. I want to live a life that is focused on the supernatural and is never limited by gravity, Newtonian physics, and common sense. I want to live in the dimension where Jesus operates, where the Holy Spirit is able to make physical changes by breathing supernatural power across the boundary between the seen and the unseen. I want to have my own personal access to the power that transcends my own brain's ability to comprehend. Why? Because, to tell the truth, I'm not all that impressed with what the world has to offer.

So, how do we make this all come to pass in our lives?

Spiritual Vision

I'm coming to understand that the formula is exceedingly simple. We must simply believe. That's the whole formula in its simplest form. Just believe. Believe that these things are true. Believe Matthew 6. Believe Proverbs 3:5-6. Just believe it and live as if it's all literally true. It's easier said than done, of course, but a crucial prerequisite to the abundant life of the Spirit. We must pull ourselves (or let God pull us) out of our evangelical tunnel vision and set our eyes on God's supernatural, unpredictable, unexplainable, and sometimes totally whacked-out ways, because this is the only way true miracles, abundance, provision, and spiritual advancement can happen in our lives on a regular basis. Laws of finance, government, societal norms, cultural momentum, and common sense limit the world. But in order to experience miracles, we must operate on a plane that is not subject to such limitations. This place of unlimited existence, of extreme possibilities, of miraculous provisions, surrounds us all even now. Problem is, most of us just can't see it. Therefore, we can't have it.

You see millions of images with your eyes every day, but you only retain a very small number of them as concrete memories. Why? You see thousands of things, but you don't retain them because you weren't looking for them. There are many tricks and tests whereby we can prove how little of the superfluous information in an image, conversation, or piece of text is actually retained versus the information that we are actually interested in. Let's say I'm telling you how much I enjoyed the clowns at the circus. Then I show you a photograph of the busy circus performance and ask you to count how many clowns are in the picture. When I take the picture away from you and then ask how many *lions* were in the photograph, there is a very small chance that you'll know the correct answer, because you weren't looking for lions.

When we go about our lives without an intentional desire to see God at work in this "other" realm about which we are learning, we will miss most of what He has prepared for us. On the other hand, if we *"fix our eyes not on what is seen but on what is unseen..."* then our spiritual vision is adjusted to pick up the wavelengths that God uses to communicate with us (2 Cor. 4:18). This realm of existence surrounds us at all times, but because of our naturalistic mindset, we rarely see that dimension of life.

It's all about what we believe, and we so often limit what God can do in our lives simply because of our naturalistic viewpoint of life. If we can't rely on God to reveal to us His own realm—unlimited by any earthly or natural constraints—then we will not experience the extent of what He has planned for us. This lack of "God assignments" and our sentence to a strictly earthbound existence are what it means to be *"conformed to this world."* But transformation, as Romans 12:2 goes on to explain, comes from the renewing of our minds. Minds that can see into the spiritual realm, that can be led by our spirit-level communications with the Holy Spirit, that can believe in and unwaveringly trust in the realm of existence where real change is made, are the minds that God will use to instigate some incredible and long-overdue change in this world.

Let's look at Romans 12:2 one more time: *"Do not be conformed to the pattern of this world...."* The Greek word *pattern* here is *metamorpho'o*, the same root word that gives us the concept of metamorphosis.[2] When a caterpillar experiences metamorphosis and turns into a butterfly, absolutely everything about its existence changes completely. Before, it crawled, but now it can fly. Before, it was a worm, but now it's a beautiful butterfly. Before, it was earthbound and could only see an inch in front of its face, but now it can fly high and see great distances. Before, it ate leaves, but now it drinks sweet nectar. Nothing of its former shape or habits remains.

About that information that we don't retain—the first step is to actually see it, to notice it. We obviously cannot retain what we have not experienced. So we *"fix our eyes not on what is seen but on what is* unseen." To fix one's eyes is an exercise of discipline and intentionality. We can't accidentally focus on something. And tapping into that unseen realm cannot help but metamorphose us into creatures that are no longer bound to this earthly, strictly physical existence. We will gain a higher elevation. We will be able to look down into our lives from a high position of power and clarity and, therefore, will not be blinded by the circumstances that conspire to block the light from our lives. We will drink of the sweet nectar of the Spirit rather than eat the sticks and twigs of earthbound existence. We will soar effortlessly rather than crawl slowly about on our bellies. We will be living in *freedom*!

This unseen realm of existence transcends the vibrating of atoms and the organization of molecules. In this realm, molecules and subatomic particles are rearranged into new limbs, healed retinas, vanquished cancers, and clean arteries. Chemical imbalances are righted and the unfathomably complex interactions of hormones and enzymes within a human body are corrected on an atomic level. These physical changes are brought about by nothing more than the intentionality of God Almighty, the very same power that created the entire universe by His mere words! If God's words and desire can create this amazing universe in all its immense glory, then certainly He can heal bodies and minds, cleanse emotions, release captives, and bring joy. And here's the cool part: He wants to use *you* as the vehicle to accomplish all this!

Co-laboring With God

While God will sometimes break in unannounced, He normally prefers to work through a human agent to accomplish His work. I suppose there are many reasons for this, but chief among them must be His desire to knit us together into body life. He makes clear that all of us believers here on Earth make up one body (see 1 Cor. 12:12-27), and it seems one of His primary intentions is to teach us to recognize one another and the importance we each hold in the lives of people around us. This, in turn, is motivated by God's desire to simply love. It's His love that compels us to pray for one another and lay hands on one another for healing. It's His love that should be the motivation for all prayer and miraculous healings and provisions. This love is what binds us together as His Body and gives us the ability to truly love, even to love those who seem on the surface to be unlovable.

To transcend the natural world that surrounds us; to live our lives in such a way that we do not base our decisions on our physical circumstances; to sense and understand the unseen realm in which God's unseen forces change our visible reality; and to actually appropriate that authority and power to bring change to the people and circumstances around us is to live the life that Jesus originally intended for us. These are the rules by which we ought to live.

Endnotes

1. This quotation by Graham Cooke is taken from a recording of his conference entitled "Permission Granted," held at The Mission in Vacaville, CA. The focus of the conference was the incredible permissions we have because God has placed us "in Christ."

2. Strong's Numbers Online; http://strongsnumbers.com/greek/3339.htm; accessed August 18, 2011.

CHAPTER 9

Thoughts Make Things Happen

houghts and words make things happen. They can ruin nations or build up the emotions of someone who's feeling down. A solitary thought can change the world. The process of doing anything begins with an immaterial thought, and the consequences of that immaterial thought can create incredibly far-reaching physical effects.

One of my favorite lines in literature is from Charles Dickens' *Great Expectations*: "This was no nominal meal we were going to make, but a vigorous reality." What does it take to turn the dream of an awesome experience—something that exists at first only in someone's mind, in this case a meal to be remembered—into a vigorous reality?

Scientists have a relatively good theory about what happened when the universe was created. They do the math backward in time until a few millionths of a second after the big bang went bang! But even modern science admits that we cannot discern what happened just as the bang began and everyone agrees that we certainly cannot logically or mathematically understand, prove, or accurately speculate about how or what existed prior to the bang. We simply have no method, no math, no language, and no framework to prove or even express it.

Well, God had a thought. A really big thought:

I'm going to create a universe, and these people that I put there will be awestruck by it. I have to make it big enough so they will never be able to understand it fully, but not so overly complex that they can never learn about it. It has to be complex enough that it will continually amaze them and vast enough that they will appreciate the one who made it.

God is not satisfied with doing anything average. He has to make things incredible. He didn't just make a universe with stars and quasars and billions of galaxies, but He made wine; and tens of millions of insect species; and an animal that looks like a beaver, but has a duck's bill; and plants that we can eat that taste really good. He created people in such a way that when they laugh really hard, they sometimes squirt food out their noses.

Thoughts make things happen.

A thought culminated in the 9/11 World Trade Center tragedy.

A thought led to Mother Teresa's orphanages and hospice centers.

A thought led to the attempted extermination of Jewish people under Hitler's regime.

A thought led to the development of machines that can fly 300 people from Los Angeles to Tokyo in a matter of hours.

A thought led God to extend Himself throughout a physical space that ultimately became our universe. At some point long before creation, He was all that existed. Therefore, something of God must have been used to create the universe. The artist/painting analogy is useful, but only to a point. Like an artist, God is not the same thing as His creation. He created the universe like an artist creates a painting.

The subject matter, the vision, the aesthetic all come from within the artist who is creating something apart from Himself.

But unlike an artist, God did not have raw materials that existed apart from Himself. There is nothing that exists that is eternal other than God Himself, so the stuff of which the universe is made had to have its origin in God unlike the painter whose raw materials (brushes, paint, canvas) were pre-existing apart from him or her.

There was nothing first except God, and God created the universe using only His will for raw material. So mere cause and effect implies that if God (who is spiritual and non-material) was the only possible cause, then the effect (the physical universe), having come wholly from the stuff of our immaterial God, must at the very least have some immaterial aspect or character to it. When God used the big bang to create the universe, He was saturating all things with Himself—His creativity, His scientific knowledge, His purposefulness, His humor—and He concluded when it was all done that it was very good. Of course it was good! It was God manifesting His own character through one of His best and most complex revelations about Himself—the physical universe!

Am I reducing God to less than omnipotent by suggesting that perhaps a scientific explanation underlies miracles like the creation of the universe? Well, I don't believe that a God who could design and create the universe as we see it in all its unfathomable glory and immeasurable immensity, by using methods consistent with quantum mechanics, is any less worthy than a God who mysteriously makes matter out of nothing with no scientific explanation. The former also requires a fantastic, infinite God, and in my opinion makes more sense because God then gave us the ability and the mission to do science and discover how He accomplished it all. He gave us the ability to do science by making it possible to discover the intricacies of the natural laws He put in place. I believe that with every fascinating new scientific discovery we get a new glimpse of the incredible genius of the God who created it all.

The Spiritual and Physical Realms Coexist

Had Adam and Eve never introduced sin into the equation, we may never have had the need to distinguish between the spiritual and physical realms of existence. Perhaps, as Jacob witnessed angels going up and down the ladder, we too would have been able to clearly see this spiritual realm. After all, the Bible tells us that Adam and God walked and talked together. The fall of humanity may well have simply closed our eyes to this spiritual universe surrounding us, leaving only echoes that we must now spend millennia trying to decipher. Or perhaps the physical world and the spiritual world were one and the same in Adam's day. After all, Romans 8 tells us that the creation was also wrecked by sin and it groans as in the pains of childbirth (see Rom. 8:22).

This wall between the seen and unseen may have been created at the same time, and in the same manner, as the wall that sin created between humanity and the God who loves us. This wall of sin created severe limitations in Adam and Eve's ability to function as they were designed to function. The Bible says their eyes were opened and they could see that they were naked, but if we think about it a little deeper, we must conclude that this became a form of bondage. Before, they had complete freedom in the garden, and they were not ashamed. Now they felt they had to cover up their bodies.

This is bondage, not freedom. This is limitation not openness. In the same way, sin caused a limitation—a wall—between the spiritual and physical realms because humankind could no longer relate to God in the way it had. No longer did they have the unbridled freedom they once had. God separated Himself from humanity because of their sin, but His creation was still made of the same stuff.

Although the wall had gone up, the matter of the universe and the physical laws that define it mostly stayed the same. God's character, beauty, and scientific brilliance still permeate all of existence.

If everything is permeated by God's presence (He is omnipresent after all; see Ps. 139), then one of the necessary conclusions is that every human being on this planet is also permeated by God's presence. Therefore, we are all—those who know God personally as well as those who don't—connected somehow to one another. That's why war and hatred are so destructive. Not only is harm done to one person or a group of people, but the unity that is inherent in all of humanity is severed, also causing a rift in the created order. You cannot murder your neighbor and remain unaffected by it at a quantum level.

If it is true that God permeates everything, then the language of quantum physics ought to—at the very least—shed some light on His creation and His methodology. We may see things dimly now, but we are not totally blind. Whether we are living our lives according to a God-centric worldview or not, we are still subject to the rules and laws of existence that God has defined. And I'm not only talking about physical laws here. In fact, I'm not so sure there's much difference between the physical laws God has put in place and His spiritual laws like "love one another" and "pray for one another."

Where there is harmony of thought and intention, the atmosphere tends toward peace, even if that harmony is not of an overtly "spiritual" nature. The guys getting together to smoke cigars and play cards are displaying a kind of unifying spirit that displays the quantum effects of unity of thought. When Bubba has one too many and insults his brother's wife, then, despite their friendship, emotions rise and faces turn red—physical manifestations of a non-physical disunity in spirit. Adrenaline pumps and a host of microbiological consequences ensue, some of which can be described only in terms of quantum, mechanical processes even though their origin was in the immaterial realm—in thoughts.

God, in all and through all, is a matter of profound spiritual debate, which we do not have room for here. For the purposes of our conversation, we should keep the assumptions as simple, but as true as possible, namely, that the presence of God permeates all of matter and, since matter is energy, and the atoms and subatomic stuff of which our bodies and brains are made are matter, then He permeates us at an exceedingly intimate level. Does this end at that interface between the physical and spiritual? What if someone is not living a spiritual life? Is an atheist permeated by God to the same extent as a worshipper of God?

Today's popular atheist writers won't like to hear this, but the answer is yes. The very moment one of them decides to change his or her opinions about God and begin following Him, God is right there to immediately answer the prayer. He is actively pursuing a right relationship with all of His creation,[2] and that pursuit takes on a whole new level of meaning and depth when applied to His pursuit of human beings. This pursuit takes place at three varying and increasingly intimate levels and intensities. But of course we would expect a trinity, wouldn't we?

A New Creation

The first level is that of the spirit. The spirit is the deepest level of existence for a human being. When we begin a relationship with the Living God, our spirit comes alive and a new creature is created that did not previously exist: *"Therefore if anyone is in Christ, he is a new creature; the old things passed away; behold, new things have come"* (2 Cor. 5:17 NASB). This spirit being is actually one with God's Spirit. This is a concept that is supposed to be understood by

Christians, but I think many of us really don't appreciate the power inherent in the concept.

When we fully grasp what it means to be literally one with God's Spirit, the power in that truth will change a person radically and eternally. All of the promises of God, all the power of Christ, all the character and perfection of the Spirit and of Jesus Christ Himself, are ours here and now. It's in our spirit, because it literally is Jesus living within us. Problem is, we don't always experience all this provision and power because we need to learn how to appropriate it and bring it into physical manifestation. That's the entire purpose of life in the Spirit—to bring God glory by learning how to come into all the fullness of God's plans for us.

As we learn these disciplines, the process changes our souls, the second level of existence of the human creature. The soul is the interface between our spirit—or in a broader sense, the immaterial world we have been discussing—and the physical body that carries us around. The soul can be defined in many ways, but includes our emotions, our will, and our mind. As the Holy Spirit manifests inside us, the soul changes more and more into the character of Jesus. As our spirit, which is one with God's Spirit, rises up, and the strength and discipline of our will increases, we are better able to love, to control our moods and emotions, to give sacrificially, and to put others first. All of these actions have some sort of physical manifestation. That's where level three, the body, comes in.

The body itself is self-explanatory, but it is by no means easy to describe. In all its glory, the human body is an unbelievably complex system of chemical and mechanical processes, all of which rely heavily on quantum mechanics and subatomic activities. But one of the more fascinating things about the human body is its vulnerability to influences from the unseen realm. Emotions, tragedies, joyous events, as well as mental and emotional strain, all leave their mark on our mental and emotional state, the quintessential example of the link between the visible and invisible realms in which we simultaneously operate. Thoughts and words have a huge impact on the physical body and, therefore, on all of physical reality.

That words and thoughts have power to affect physical reality is a concept that is strongly supported in Scripture:

> *Reckless words pierce like a sword, but the tongue of the wise brings healing* (Proverbs 12:18).

> *Pleasant words are a honeycomb, sweet to the soul and healing to the bones* (Proverbs 16:24).

> *The tongue also is a fire, a world of evil among the parts of the body. It corrupts the whole person, sets the whole course of his life on fire, and is itself set on fire by hell. All kinds of animals, birds, reptiles and creatures of the sea are being tamed and have been tamed by man, but no man can tame the tongue. It is a restless evil, full of deadly poison* (James 3:6-8).

Given that we have such clear descriptions and straightforward instructions about the power and authority of our words and thoughts, how much more cognizant must we be about their eternal consequences? And by this I don't mean to emphasize the negative consequences of our thoughts and words, because that's a tired and all too predictable evangelical response (often more concerned about what we're doing wrong than breaking free). No, I want to emphasize a lifestyle that takes advantage of the incredible, latent power that arises from the unseen realm that permeates us and launches us into a style of existence that really takes advantage of and experiences *"all the fullness of God"* that Paul talks about in Ephesians 3:19. The power of our thoughts and words to change physical reality is tremendous, and we ought to focus at all times on strengthening and building up each other by the words we speak.

The unseen realm is where God makes His authority freely available to us so that we can change our lives and touch the lives of the people around us. Let's learn to use that power and authority to bring God's Kingdom down—on Earth as it is in Heaven!

Endnotes

1. Charles Dickens, *Great Expectations* (London, England: Penguin Books, 1996).

2. Romans 8:19-22 discusses the groaning of the physical creation as it waits for its delivery from decay. I interpret this eventual redemption of the creation as part of the universal redemption that God has been seeking ever since the fall of humanity.

CHAPTER 10

Viva La Sparks!

Henry is walking on the sidewalk toward Hugh's house. Afar off, he sees Hugh on the front porch looking quite sullen and glum. Since Hugh is rarely without a smile, Henry is concerned for his friend. Henry walks up the stairs and sits unannounced in the chair near Hugh, who sits with his chin in his hand looking down at the floor.

Henry: Hugh, my boy, you seem a bit glum today. May I enquire as to the reason?

Hugh: Hi, Henry. I dunno, just kind of melancholy today I guess.

Henry: I see...this gorgeous weather's got you down?

Henry smiles because it's 75 degrees and sunny, with a mild breeze, but Hugh doesn't respond.

Henry: These insufferable songbirds making too much noise for you?

Hugh almost cracks a smile.

Henry: Surely it must be that your promotion last week is simply putting too much money in your pockets, and you are cracking under the strain.

Hugh: Well, Henry...I guess I never thought I would

be subject to a mid-life crisis. I always figured I was the type that could handle pretty much anything. Nothing really bothered me; nothing really caused me to be down in the mouth...

Henry: Are you thinking about something specific here, Hugh?

Hugh: Well...you know, here I am in my 40s. Life sometimes seems like it's passing me by. I can't really look back and point to any great impact I've had on anyone. I see pain in the world everywhere I look, but I honestly haven't done much about it. Certain events in my life a few years ago set me back, and as you know, I had to start all over. I ought to be farther along! I ought to be...I dunno...more financially stable, more spiritually mature, more in control of my emotions. I don't know; guess I'm just babbling.

Henry: Hmmm...I see....

A moment passes.

Henry: Do you love God, dear friend?

Hugh: Of course! With all my heart. In fact, my relationship with Him these past few years has been the best in my life. I guess...well...I guess I'm learning some hard lessons, but I've put enough life behind me to realize that the tough things I've been through are actually good for me. That's really the only time I ever learn anything important. The only time I really get close to God is when times are tough. Ya know?

Henry: Well, that's one little bit of silver lining to fix your gaze upon.

Hugh: Yeah, but things just don't feel like they gel for me. I'm not where I want to be. I know the things I want to be doing, but I just don't do them.

Henry: The old Romans 7 syndrome, eh?

Hugh: Yeah, yeah, exactly. And I feel like I'm only accomplishing a fraction of what I could for God's Kingdom, so He must feel at least some disappointment about that.

Henry: Hmmm...I see. Tell you what. Allow me a rather direct question please.

Hugh: Sure.

Henry: Have you been busy hating God?

Hugh: What?

Henry: Have you been busy hating....

Hugh: I heard you! It just kind of took me by surprise!

Henry: Well?

Hugh: Well, no; of course I haven't!

Henry: Have you been purposefully trying to ignore or disobey Him?

Hugh: No, not purposefully. Perhaps negligently at times, but not on purpose.

Henry: So it would be safe for us to conclude that your heart is actually on God's side?

Hugh: Sure it is; no question about that.

Henry: So maybe your perspective just needs a little adjustment.

Hugh: My perspective on what?

Henry: I believe it was William Tyndale who said, "There is no work better than to please God; to pour water, to wash dishes, to be a cobbler, or an apostle, all is one…to wash dishes and to preach is all one, as touching the deed, to please God."[1]

Hugh and Henry both sit in silence for a moment.

Hugh: Wow.

Henry: I concur.

Another pause.

Hugh: Henry, that's one of the best things I've heard in a long time.

Henry: Hugh, my friend, if we were to somehow gain God's perspective on things, I am convinced that it would change us immediately, dramatically, and forever. The years of your life may not seem impactful to you from your present perspective, battling the doldrums as you seem to be, but in God's eyes I am sure the list of good things you've accomplished for His Kingdom and for your fellow humanity—including your family, friends, business associates, and the thousands of people you have indirectly touched through your professional life—is quite impressive.

Hugh: Huh! Washing dishes and preaching the Word…same thing in God's eyes…His perspective… God's perspective…an eternal perspective. Henry, this is why I call you a friend, in the deepest sense of the word.

Henry: So, I believe you were about to offer me some iced tea…

* * * * * * * * * * *

Hebrew tradition attempts to make all things sacred and remove the line between what we typically see as sacred and secular. In their excellent book, *The Shaping of Things To Come*, authors Michael Frost and Alan Hirsch discuss and juxtapose the Hebraic and Hellenistic interpretations of life and consciousness. Of special interest is their discussion of the Hebraic understanding of the shekina glory of God.

Quoting Hebrew scholars, the authors offer one metaphor of the *shekina* as holy sparks that are present in all things, waiting to be released by those who use their tools, skills, and resources for God's glory. As the hammer strikes the nail, holy sparks fly, releasing God's glory for the world to behold. As the guitarist strums her instrument, holy sparks ignite passion within the hearts and minds of those listening and draw them upward to greater heights of awareness. As the artist wields his brush, holy sparks illuminate the eyes of the beholders, and they are blessed and inspired by the beauty. A child learning her math and the janitor keeping the hallways squeaky clean provide the holy sparks in their important spheres of influence.[2]

Francis Schaeffer also touched on this truth when he stated that in the eyes of God, it is no more holy to sing songs of worship on Sunday morning than to play ball with your child, as long as it is done with love and the proper appreciation of God. The point is that the reasoning and motivation behind our every action should be the unveiling of God's glory, and that unveiling should be manifested in every mundane, physical action we partake in every moment of every day. Whether the sparks get released—or perhaps more accurately, whether we notice the sparks ourselves—depends on our own perspective. The limited perspective of the natural or soul-obsessed mind will not notice the good that God does through us every day. The enlightened perspective of the Spirit will recognize

God at work in even the mundane things of our existence and will give God glory.

How are the holy sparks manifested in the mundane and ordinary of everyday life? If God's presence is interwoven throughout all matter and space, then the artist creating, the worker laboring, the poet writing, and the mother nurturing are using matter and energy for redeeming purposes and thereby justifying and authenticating it. The proper use of matter and thought and energy can redeem people and build them up psychologically, emotionally, mentally, and spiritually. But don't we already know intuitively that this is so?

All things can be sanctified and made holy for God's work depending only on the attitude with which we approach them. In this context, I'm using the word *sanctified* to mean used for building people up and fostering peace and rest and love as commanded by our Lord. And it looks as if God has made this particularly easy by weaving His truth and love and grace throughout all the matter in the universe. Did Mahatma Gandhi do good work? Did his kindness and gentleness cause the shekina sparks to fly? How about Mother Theresa? How about the kindly lady who makes a casserole for her elderly neighbor who has a difficult time getting up and about? *Viva la sparks!*

Paul wrote that there is *"one God and Father of all, who is over all and through all and in all"* (Eph. 4:6). As human beings caught in a physical existence, we tend to categorize and classify everything, as if the delineation between physical and spiritual really exists. I don't think such a line exists. It's like sleeping—no one can tell the moment they fall asleep; we just fade from one form of consciousness into another. What if this other realm of the Spirit is really just another form of consciousness or just another perspective of the viewpoint(s) we already have? What if the apostle Paul's encouragement to allow the eyes of our hearts to be enlightened (see Eph. 1:18) will actually lead us to the point where we can see these other dimensions of reality in our own spirits? What if, whenever we did an act of either purposeful kindness or some rote responsibility like paying the bills, we could literally see the shekina glory of God send sparks flying in all directions? If we could actually see these events in the Spirit realm, might it make a difference how we see ourselves and the crucial role we each play on this planet?

If God is through all and in all, then perhaps this entire physical universe is just another continuing real-time expression—just another revelation—of God Himself. God speaks many languages—science, revelation, Scriptures, beauty, music, art, written words, and spoken words. God really loves a good conversation with people who love Him. He wants to talk with you about the perspective you hold on the realities that surround you. He wants to hear you talk to Him about your strengths and weaknesses, and He wants to encourage you to give it all to Him so He can arrange some spark-worthy events in your life. He'll hold you up in your weak points and send people into your life to build you up in those areas. He will identify to you how to further build on your strengths.

Don't worry about the weaknesses—focus on knowing Jesus Christ and His will and seeking first His kingdom and His righteousness (see Matt. 6:33). Focus on the strengths and gifts He's given you, and work to make them even stronger. The specific gifts God has given you are His reason for placing you on this earth. We all have a reason for being here, no matter what your life experiences or history tell you. You are deeply loved by God, and He has big plans to prosper you, not to harm you (see Jer. 29:11). You have your share of sparks stored up just waiting to be released by your acts of love, kindness, and forgiveness and by you exercising your specific gifts.

When the shekina glory sends sparks flying, then you'll be able to *"test and approve"* God's will (Rom. 12:2) and will begin to see things more clearly from His Heavenly perspective.

Endnotes

1. William Tyndale, quoted in "Quote Library," *Beliefnet.com;* http://www.beliefnet.com/Quotes/Christian/W/William-Tyndale/There-Is-No-Work-Better-Than-To-Please-God-To-Pou.aspx; accessed August 18, 2011.

2. Michael Frost and Alan Hirsch, *The Shaping of Things To Come* (Peabody, MA: Hendrickson Publishers, 2003).

CHAPTER 11

Unity

There is a concept in quantum physics that seems to defy reality, but has been proven scientifically in laboratories. The concept of entanglement shows us that two particles of matter can be created as a "matched pair."

The entanglement manifests itself in this way: whatever we do to one of the particles, the other particle is also immediately affected in like manner—at the exact same time, regardless of the distance between the particles. Imagine that the effect is seen in both particles at the same moment in time regardless of their distance from one another. Then imagine that we greatly increase this distance. Let's say we separate these paired particles by 1,000 miles. Separate sensors monitor the effect of our input on each particle, and we see that the particles responded at exactly the same time in exactly the same way. Now we separate the particles by ten million miles, or maybe even by ten million light-years. The laws of science state that nothing can travel faster than the speed of light, including information flow. If the particles are separated by ten million light-years, it ought to take ten million light-years for the information to get there. But regardless of the distance between the two particles, we get the same results.[1] Even though instantaneous reactions at these distances defy the fundamental rule of science that prohibits anything from traveling faster than the speed of light, that's exactly what we see as a result of these experiments. The effect on the separated, paired particles happens instantaneously. Quantum entanglement is strange, but true.

Now let's apply this newly gained knowledge to our discussion on obliterating the boundary between the seen and unseen. If these two worlds are simply different manifestations, or different interpretations, of a single reality, then our spiritual entanglement with the Holy Spirit, and with one another as believers in Christ, is the same.

The Spiritual Realities of Christian Unity

Scripture is clear on the concept of unity. Unity with Christ, unity as the Body of Christ, and unity with the Holy Spirit are all solid biblical principles. What God says can happen immediately regardless of where we are located in this universe. What happens to you may very likely be felt or "experienced" by another, especially someone who is emotionally very close to you. But even if we don't share common experiences, the concept of unity and spiritual entanglement is still very valid and biblical.

We are to weep with those who weep and rejoice with those who rejoice (see Rom. 12:15). We are to carry one another's burdens (see Gal. 6:2). We are to pray for one another (see James 5:16). All these activities are examples of being spiritually entangled with one another in love and mutual support. This is one of the areas in which westernized Christianity seems to be faltering terribly lately. We are a very independent people when we ought to be learning interdependence. The word *entangled* may sound like it has a negative connotation, but in reality this kind of unity feeds and supports individuals and helps us to grow stronger than we could in isolation.

What happens when we pray for someone who is physically far removed from us? Prayer causes things to happen, very often from a significant distance. A huge amount of prayer is offered up for people who are far separated from us, but this does not affect the power of prayer in the least. Yes, it is God who is answering these prayers and actually affecting change in that person's life, no matter where they are physically. And when God decides to step into the physical reality of a person you are praying for from 2,000 miles away, and He intervenes with physical healing, creating new flesh and bone, or healing an injury or illness, or correcting a mental or emotional problem, it is precisely through spiritual entanglement that change happens.

When the centurion approached Jesus about healing his servant (see Matt. 8:5-13), the healing took place that very moment, even though the sick servant was a long distance from Jesus. The centurion began walking home, and it took him some time according to the Scriptures. When he returned home, he learned that his servant had been healed on the previous day at the very moment the centurion was conversing with Jesus. Distance was meaningless. The power of prayer traveled through space and healed instantly, because in the spirit realm there is no limitation imposed by physical constraints.

Wormholes Echo God's Ability to Connect People Supernaturally

Remember the theoretical phenomenon in the universe called a wormhole? It could possibly be caused by a gravitational field so strong that it warps space-time in upon itself, opening one point in the universe to another extremely distant point. It could theoretically connect two vastly separate places in the universe as if they were adjacent to one another.

In the same way, the Kingdom of God connects people, resources, faith, healing, wisdom, and knowledge. When we pray for one another, instantaneous change can happen, regardless of distance. But this is only the beginning. Imagine what can happen when people begin to think alike. Imagine what could happen if all the

Christ-followers in the entire world began to follow the specific leadings of God that have to do with the direction He's taking the human race at that moment in history. Imagine if God could simultaneously train up an army of warriors all around the world, using various methods and teachers, but with the same message and tactics. This is, in fact, what is happening right now, and it's exciting!

As He has throughout all of history, God has specific plans for His Body on Earth today. He transcends time and space to bring a unity of thought and intention to His people across the globe so that they are all on board with what's happening. This kind of unity is not just about similar goals and directives, but it gets down into the hearts of individuals and changes them from the inside out, creating a Body of believers who are all on the same wavelength when it comes to love, unity, forgiveness, grace, and supernatural ministries. This is one of the reasons why the Bible teaches so often and so forcefully about unity. If we want to be in on the upgrades that God is dishing out, then we need to be plugged into His Spirit and remain familiar with what He's trying to accomplish in the world.

I saw a science fiction show once where a spaceship was located near a wormhole. The crew had learned how to safely travel in and out of the wormhole to transport their ship to various places in the universe. This is a perfect parallel to the access we have to God's activities and ideas in other parts of the world. We should not be restricted by physical space. We should become skilled in "time travel," the ability to know what's going on somewhere without having to take the time to go. Albert Einstien showed us that time and space are actually identical. We can't physically get somewhere in space without investing a given amount of time. But in the Spirit, it's a different story.

In the Spirit, we transcend the limitations imposed on us by a physical universe, even the limitations of quantum physics. We are not subject to distances or any other physical limitation. We are commanded to trust in the Lord for absolutely everything and reject what our own logical understanding tells us (see Prov. 3:5-6). And we are instructed to do it as a team!

All of this insight, wisdom, understanding, knowledge, power, and love are meant to be communal in nature. Distances cannot touch the unity of true Christ-followers. Physical circumstances cannot stop the purposes of God. He is in the process of not only growing and maturing each of us individually, but also knitting us together as a Body, placing each of us in the position where we can do the most effective work for His Kingdom. Each of us is an important part of the Body with a specific purpose:

> Now the body is not made up of one part but of many. If the foot should say, "Because I am not a hand, I do not belong to the body," it would not for that reason cease to be part of the body. And if the ear should say, "Because I am not an eye, I do not belong to the body," it would not for that reason cease to be part of the body. If the whole body were an eye, where would the sense of hearing be? If the whole body were an ear, where would the sense of smell be? But in fact God has arranged the parts in the body, every one of them, just as he wanted them to be. If they were all one part, where would the body be? As it is, there are many parts, but one body.

> The eye cannot say to the hand, "I don't need you!" And the head cannot say to the feet, "I don't need you!" On the contrary, those parts of the body that seem to be weaker are indispensable, and the parts that we think are less honorable we treat with special honor. And the parts that are unpresentable are treated with special modesty, while our presentable parts need no special treatment. But God has combined the members of the body and has given greater honor to the parts that lacked it, so that there should be no division in the body, but that its parts should have equal

concern for each other. If one part suffers, every part suffers with it; if one part is honored, every part rejoices with it. Now you are the body of Christ, and each one of you is a part of it (1 Corinthians 12:14-27).

Just as our paired electrons can experience the same effect even when separated by vast distances, so we can experience both the encouragement and miracles that result from other brothers and sisters in Christ praying and interceding for us and the very real and powerful effects of God's Spirit working directly in our lives to heal, encourage, guide, and instruct.

Endnote

1. Scientists don't actually need to separate particles by millions of miles or millions of light years. Our instruments now are accurate enough to measure these minute time references at distances more reasonable for the laboratory, say a few miles or several thousand feet. For more on these time-based experiments, see Paul Davies, *About Time: Einstein's Unfinished Revolution* (New York: Simon & Schuster, 1995), 168-173.

CHAPTER 12

Science,
Simplicity, Style

Science is of great value in describing the way the universe operates. It is inextricably linked to the quality of life on this planet. Like any other idea, power, resource, machine, skill, or strength, science itself is merely a tool and is therefore amoral. It can cause great harm in the wrong hands or great benefit in the hands of the good and trustworthy. But science can only go so far in describing ultimate reality.

Some scientists have tried to boil down matters of the heart to just a complex set of chemical reactions, but most of the general public (and a very large contingent of scientists) know that there is more to reality than what we can touch and measure.

In *The Spiritual Brain: A Neuroscientists's Case for the Existence of the Soul*, authors Mario Beauregard (neurobiology specialist from the University of Montreal) and Denyse O'Leary argue that certain spiritual experiences must originate from outside the physical body and brain. Beauregard studied Carmelite nuns during their ecstatic spiritual experiences and concluded the source must be something (I would argue Someone) outside the body. "Within each neuron, the molecules are replaced approximately 10,000 times in an average life span. Yet, humans have a continuous sense of self that is stable over time."[1] If consciousness and self are only physical results of chemical reactions in the brain as naturalists claim, then where does this continuous self-awareness come from? How is it preserved?

Christianity and Science Are Not in Conflict

Is this other realm a separate reality that operates independently of our minds, brains, and the physical world? Most of us live our lives like it is, or we just seldom bother to think about it, or we don't want to mess up our neat theology by blending it with the mess inherent in scientific discovery.

What if...

...science and spirituality are two different languages expressing the same truths?

...the discovered universe and the spiritual revelations of the Bible are ultimately completely compatible and it's only *our interpretations* of both that seem to sometimes contradict?

...scientific discovery could eventually lead to a deeper understanding of the link between the realm of emotions and thoughts and that of wars, strife, peace, and unity?

...the language of quantum physics is a valid attempt to describe activities at or near that boundary between the material and immaterial worlds?

...science is one of the primary languages that God uses when He speaks to us?

...modern scientific discoveries can actually teach us about God?

It is clear from Scriptures that God is omnipresent (see Ps. 139). As the Prime Mover,[2] His presence is necessarily woven throughout all of creation. He is as much present in a beautiful sunset as in the sanctuary, in the physics lab as in the seminary. God is the Ruler of all things (see 1 Chron. 29:12) and the Creator of all things (see

John 1:1-3). The loftiest goal of science, then, ought to be the discovery of how the Creator created, what mechanisms He used, what laws are in effect to make such a creation possible, and how we can harness that knowledge and intellectual power for the good of all humankind. Like making really good dark chocolate. Or a guitar that sounds like an angel is playing it even though it's just me.

A brilliant designer named Ross Lovegrove uses precisely this paradigm of studying God's inventions and adapting them to his designs. He calls himself "Captain Organic" based on his love for and study of organic designs. What he's actually doing is adapting God's designs into his work, although I have not heard him describe his work in this way. I have no idea what his spiritual leanings are, but regardless of his ideology, his methods are rooted in the handiwork of the original great Designer.

One of the more fascinating aspects of this design methodology is that it yields designs that are the strongest, most elegant, simplest, and often the most aesthetically appealing. The caption in one of his designs says it all: half the weight of its nearest competitor. Clean and simple. Elegant. Perhaps it's a bit of irony that he named it the "Supernatural."

FURNITURE
My new SUPERNATURAL gas injected polymer chair for Moroso weights 2.5 kilos. it's fat free: half the weight of its nearest competitor.

As we pursue science, design, knowledge, spirituality, and life in general, it ought to become clear that simplicity and elegance are attributes worth striving for. Don't most of us complain that our lives have become too complex? Almost everyone I hear, from friends and family to productivity pundits, tell me how busy and complex and inorganic life in western civilization has become. How many people do you hear complaining that their lives are too simple and elegant? I don't believe I've ever heard such a complaint, although I wish this, instead of the former, was the problem we were dealing with.

The Simplicity of Creation

In the realms of spirituality, quantum physics, and creativity, elegance and simplicity seem to be key. If and when a Grand Unifying Theory (GUT) is ever discovered, we can be sure it will be a simple, elegant solution that will cause a lot of physicists to do the "Wow, I should've had a V8" head slap. Why? Because that's the way life is. Complexity breeds unrest and messiness. It betrays a lack of skill in a chosen art or craft. Long ago, I noticed a pattern in life that required a descriptor, so I coined Berge's Theorem of Irreducible Complexity. It states that for any problem, there is one solution that is the most elegant, most simple, and most beautiful. And the important corollary is that *this one solution may be exponentially difficult to find*. It takes lots of work and determination to reduce a design to its bare minimum.

Yves Chouinard, founder of Black Diamond climbing gear and the Patagonia outdoor clothing company, describes the process of design simplification in his excellent book *Let My People Go Surfing*. In his early days, when he was designing hardware for mountain climbers, his goal was to make the most simple, clean, and elegant pieces of hardware available. While his competitors strengthened their products by adding gussets and extra material for strength, Chouinard focused on removing anything that was not absolutely necessary. The result was hardware that was simultaneously the simplest and most elegant, yet the strongest and most functional. There is wisdom in subtraction, but it is not necessarily easy.[3]

The beautiful, smooth, and organic design of a belay/rappel device from Black Diamond.[4]

If design and functionality have their origin in the greatest of designers, then this leads me to a couple of necessary conclusions. First, these designs from the ultimate Designer are bound to be the most elegant and functional, or in other words, the best. Second, the concept of simplicity of form and function must extend throughout creation because it represents a fundamental principle. Physicists admit this when they dream about the GUT. Chouinard dreams about it in his designs of climbing hardware. Lovegrove strives for it in his organic designs of furniture, cars, and airplanes. We all long for it—although perhaps not consciously. And since this fundamental principle of simplicity extends throughout all of existence, then it also applies to the fundamental laws that govern time and space, including quantum physics, sciences of all sorts, spirituality, and everything in between.

Quantum physics is the search for these most fundamental of truths. The search for the GUT, string theory, big bang theory—it all is in essence the search for simplicity. Everything known to human-kind can be simplified to its most basics constituents:

- All the physical matter in the universe is nothing but little balls of energy clinging together.

- The GUT is nothing but one single force that acts upon all known matter.

- All of life in the Spirit boils down to love (see 1 Cor. 13).

- Even the most complex construction known to humanity, the human brain, really boils down to a bunch of brain cells connecting to one another through synapses (yes, I'm oversimplifying here, but not too much).

In my personal experience, the most precious moments are the simplest. The best chocolate is a high quality piece of pure bitter-sweet. The best times are sitting around talking with my sweetheart or with family or friends. The best wine is a simple, classic caber-net sauvignon made from one variety of grapes. The best dessert is crème brulee, which contains only five ingredients. The most beau-tiful music is the sound of my guitar on the back porch. The most beautiful sunset moments are simple reflections of evening sun off the ripples on a lake.

The best pleasures in life are the simplest, yet they are by no means easy to achieve. A really great wine is just fermented grape juice, but imagine the work that goes into it! It took nature millen-nia to create just the right soil. It takes decades to grow just the right vines and a cumulative knowledge that stretches back centuries to create the perfect cabernet. Then the wine spends several years in an oak barrel, aging to a perfect bouquet and flavor, before it is bottled. This process is simple, yes, but it is not easy. Remember the corollary to Berge's Theorem of Irreducible Complexity: that most elegant and simple of solutions may be very difficult to find.

If it were easy to make incredible wine, everyone would be doing it. If it were easy to combine cocoa and sugar into a world-class chocolate, everyone would be famous. If it were easy to understand the ultimate mysteries in the universe, then it would demean the value of our incredible and loving God. That's why we must work diligently at this discipline of science, design, style, and complexity, as it relates to the discovery of the universe and learning how God created it all. Everything that God created has an elegant, stylish, simplistic side, whether we're considering the chromatic musical scale and its scant 13 notes or Albert Einstein's famous, incredibly profound, yet simple, equation: $E=MC^2$.

Christianity Is a Simple Solution

Isn't a life spent following Jesus also the most simple, elegant solution? People tend to make things so complex! Hindus worship millions of gods. How can anyone possibly keep up with that? Some belief systems are so complex; it's amazing anyone can even understand them! But walking with Jesus is very simple. Just believe what He says. That's it! We believe, and that leads to trust. When we trust God for everything, life becomes so much clearer and easier. Not pain free by any means, but easier. In the middle of the pain, there is a Comforter. In the middle of the confusion, there is a Counselor. In the middle of the disease, there is a Healer. In the middle of the battle, there is a Warrior King who would lay down His own life for you.

The universe is mind-bendingly complex, yet it is all fashioned from tiny vibrating blobs of energy. God is unfathomably complex, yet He became a simple craftsman and walked, ate, worked, and slept among us. With a classic and timeless style that every human being on Earth ought to be mimicking, and with a simplicity and purity that astonishes, Jesus performed amazing miracles, used the laws of Quantum Physics to prove to others the power of His Father God, and loved like no one else has ever loved.

Endnotes

1. Mario Beauregard and Denyse O'Leary, *The Spiritual Brain: A Neuroscientists's Case for the Existence of the Soul* (New York: Harper One, 2007), 114.

2. *Webster's Dictionary* defines *Prime Mover* as "a self-caused agent that is the cause of all things." This term is often used to describe God as existing from the eternal past and causing, or creating, all things in the universe.

3. Yves Chouinard, *Let My People Go Surfing* (New York: Penguin Press, 2005).

4. See www.blackdiamondequipment.com

CHAPTER 13

The Power of Faith

Hugh is in the front yard, gazing up into a tree.

Hugh: Jump, Honey! I'll catch you!

Henry: My, oh my, old chap. What seems to be the difficulty today?

Hugh: Oh...morning, Henry! My daughter somehow found herself up this tree, and she's afraid to jump into my arms.

Henry: Hmmm, yes, I see. Clara, dear, you can trust your Daddy! I happen to know that his arms are quite strong enough to save you!

Clara does not want to budge and her 6-year-old lips begin to pout.

Hugh: Clara, honey, it's just like when you jumped off the jungle gym at the playground. I caught you then!

No response except for a few more tears of fear.

Hugh (quietly so Clara can't hear): I think she just doesn't have enough faith in her Dad's strength.

Henry: I wouldn't be so sure, dear friend. I think she has plenty of faith. She just doesn't believe that you'll catch her.

Hugh: What? What's the difference? Faith and belief are the same thing.

Henry: Are you quite sure of that?

Hugh: Well, knowing you, there is a very good reason for your question!

Henry: Remember, when we prayed for your wife, Margie, to be healed of her pneumonia?

Hugh: I do, far too vividly, I'm afraid.

Henry: And she wasn't healed.

Hugh: Right. Always wondered about that. Hang on, honey! I'm going to go get a ladder in a minute!

Henry: Did you have the faith that God had the power to heal her?

Hugh: Of course! There was never any question there.

Henry: So, why wasn't she healed?

Hugh: Well, I guess it just wasn't His will at that time. I guess...Well, maybe He had some greater good in mind by keeping her bedridden. Or maybe...maybe I didn't have enough faith. Or...well, I have to admit I just don't know!

Henry: Were these the kind of thoughts you were thinking that night we prayed for her?

Hugh: Well, of course. I mean, isn't that normal? We don't see God heal every time, so it must not have been His will that time.

Henry: So, is it safe to say that you had *faith* that God *could* do it, but you didn't *believe* that He actually *would*?

Hugh notices Clara finally making her way down the tree, the same way she went up.

Hugh: Way to go, honey! Great job! I'm so proud of you!

Henry: Well?

Hugh: Yeah, I heard you. I'm just not so excited about answering you.

Henry has a good chuckle.

Henry: That's the difference, my dear friend, between faith and belief.

Hugh: Honey! You did it! Hooray!

Hugh gives his little girl a hug.

Hugh: What made you change your mind about coming down?

Clara: I didn't believe you were going to help me any time soon!

* * * * * * * * * * *

I find it interesting that the New International Version (1984) and the New American Standard translations of the Bible treat the subject of faith differently in Hebrews 11:1. The NIV (1984) defines faith as an action, as if it is a verb: *"Now faith is **being sure** of what we hope for and certain of what we do not see."* Faith is the activity of *being sure* or *certain*. On the other hand, the NASB (and KJV) define faith with a noun: *"Now faith is the **assurance** of things hoped for, the conviction of things not seen."*

I believe that faith is a substance, because Jesus made statements like *"Your faith has healed you"* (Matt. 9:22; Mark 10:52). The Bible says faith *is* this, and faith *is* that. I am more inclined toward the NASB and KJV renditions of faith as a noun. The original Greek uses nouns for the words translated *assurance (hupostasis)* and *conviction (elenchos)*.[1] They are clearly nouns, and I believe God prefers that we understand them that way.

Faith is a thing that God can see in us and a thing that we possess. We should not be looking at faith as an event, but as a lifestyle. This too is more in line with the idea of faith as a noun. Think of the lifestyle of physical fitness. This is something that people can see in us. It's a state of being, and good health is understood as a noun. It's something we can possess if we take the proper steps to secure it. People may say to someone who's fit, "You have good aerobic conditioning," or "You have good muscle tone." It's something to possess.

We tend to equate faith and belief, but I think faith is the noun part of the equation, and the presence of faith helps us to do the verb part—to believe. To make faith a part of our lifestyle, we need to acquire it as we would acquire knowledge. If we wrongly tried to express knowledge (a noun) as a verb, it might sound like this: knowledge is the acquisition of facts and learning. No, *learning* is the acquisition of facts. Knowledge is a noun—it's the stuff you possess after the learning has taken place.

In the life of faith, I can try to actively be sure of what I hope for, and I can try to be certain about what I do not see. That's a verb. It's action. When I achieve that state of being where I am positive of what I hope for—when it's absolutely as real as if it were sitting on the coffee table in front me, and when the things that I cannot see become absolutely as real as anything in my physical life—then I can say that I possess faith. The noun. The *substance*. The *assurance*. The *hupostasis* and *elenchos*.

I think it's important to realize that these terms are not just metaphorical. Faith *is*. These are descriptors. And if faith is a noun, then it's something we either do or don't possess. If I am holding an avocado in my hand, would it make sense for me to say, "I wish I had this avocado more strongly"? I either have it or I don't. It's a thing, a noun. Many times Jesus said, "Your faith has made you well." He talked about faith the size of a mustard seed (see Luke 17:6), emphasizing the fact that all you need is a speck of evidence that you have it. Whether I have one tiny sliver of chocolate or a whole box of Godiva truffles, I *have chocolate*.

The Difference Between Doing and Being

The apostle James argues: "... *'You have faith; I have deeds.' Show me your faith without deeds, and I will show you my faith by what I do"* (James 2:18). There is a profound truth in this statement. All of Christian life hinges on the difference between *doing* and *being*. Jesus condemned the Pharisees because their entire life and religion was only and ever about doing. They prided themselves on obeying the law, faithfully tithing, and praying their prayers regularly. What accolades could they possess? What *things* could they be credited with? But Jesus understood that they were empty on the inside, because all their focus was on doing, not being. God is more concerned with who His children are becoming. It's more about who we are than it is about what we do. If we take care of the former, the latter will come. This verse from James says in effect, "I will show you my faith by what I do, because my actions originate in who I am as a person of faith." He puts the noun (*faith*) in a place superior to the verb (*doing things* or *deeds*). He puts the being in a place superior to the doing.

It's very encouraging to me to know that I am judged not on the basis of what I do, but on the basis of who I am and what I possess. I am a child of God (see Rom. 8:16). I am a joint heir with Jesus (see Rom. 8:17). I have been placed *in Christ* (see 1 Cor. 1:30) so that everything that is promised to Him, I receive as well, and everywhere and everything He does, I do as well. And, as if to put an exclamation point on the fact that it's not about what we do, God tells us in Romans 4:8 that God does not even take our sins into account!

So if faith is a noun, a thing, a supernatural entity, then it is a power source that shines out from the unseen realm of existence we have been talking about and provides the power and authority to affect reality in the physical world.

Jesus' statement, *"Daughter, your faith has healed you"* is profound (Mark 5:34). It's a line right out of the old "spiritual truths have physical consequences" book. As a result of this woman's faith (her desire to simply touch the hem of Jesus' cloak for healing), Jesus healed her physical infirmity.

Did you notice the spin I just put on that story? Just wanted to make sure you're paying attention! I wrote "as a result of this woman's faith," but that's not what the Scripture says. It says, literally, that it *was* her faith that healed her. This is not a cause and effect kind of thing. Her faith was the force that actually caused the healing. Jesus did not necessarily know that it was this particular woman who touched Him. He only noticed that the power had gone out of Him. He clearly said that her faith was the healing mechanism at work that connected with His unlimited, supernatural power source and caused the healing.

The same thing happened with the ten lepers who were told to go show themselves to the priests (see Luke 17:11-19). It is curious that Jesus did not heal them right then and there. The Bible tells us that they were healed *"as they went"* (Luke 17:14). An act of spiritual faith on their part (appearing before the priest, even though they had not yet received the healing) resulted in a physical miracle. What if they had just stood there and demanded that Jesus heal them right on the spot? Would He have healed them anyway, knowing they had just directly disobeyed Him? We really can't say for sure, but I have my opinion. Very often in Scripture, we are commanded to obey first, and then the provision comes. God's love may be unconditional, but His promises and His provisions are at times very conditional.

Faith and Miracles

How is it that faith has anything at all to do with physical miracles? The standard Christianese answer is that when God sees our faith, He acts to perform the miracle as a result of that faith He sees in us. We good evangelicals seem to believe that if we muster a faith that is large enough in *quantity*, God will respond. But this sounds woefully inadequate to me. There are miracles of healing where the one being healed had no faith or was not even asking to be healed. And this is consistent with James 5:15 that says, *"the prayer offered in faith will make the sick person well...."* In this verse, it is the faith of elders who are praying, not the one being healed, that causes the healing.

But must faith—whether on the part of the one praying or the one receiving prayer—always accompany a miracle? I don't think it's necessary, but in the Bible it seems more common than not, and the Bible is completely full of exhortations and examples linking faith to miracles and implying that without faith the miracles won't happen. Perhaps we could make the argument that faith always precedes a miracle if we define faith as the actual power that heals, in which case God's faith (His power to heal) always precedes a miraculous healing. Now we might be getting somewhere. But what do I mean when I talk about God's faith? Can God have faith? Why not? Remember Hebrews 11:1: *"faith is the assurance of things hoped for..."* (NASB). God is probably quite sure of the things He hopes for, so He probably has a perfect faith that we ought to emulate.

Just think if you had this same perfect faith that God has about things. What if you were as sure as God is that your future is in His hands? What if you were as sure as God is about the fact that He has promised to care for you? What if you were as sure as God is about His own promises to heal, to bless, to guide, and to impart wisdom to you? What if you were as sure as God is about the depth of His love for you? That kind of faith would turn our world upside down. And that's exactly the same faith—the same stuff, substance, and power— that God offers freely to us if we will simply believe Him for it. Those who do not trust God are limiting His incredible power in their lives because of their inability to just accept this free gift!

This definition of faith (the power that heals or achieves what- ever goal we're talking about contextually rather than a decision or force that we conjure up within ourselves) could be consistent with the quantum realities of miraculous healings. We have all heard that the mind is the human being's most powerful healing force. The existence of psychosomatic illnesses is a real phenomenon, and it has been proven that one can sometimes simply will oneself to be sick or conversely to be healed. Norman Vincent Peale's book *The Power of Positive Thinking* is not a gimmick; it's a belief system that actually works to manipulate thoughts and intentions into physical reality. The phrase "mind over matter" has been familiar to all of us since our childhoods, yet do we really stop to think of what it implies?

We are confronted with biblical stories that corroborate the link between faith (a choice of the mind) and physical miracles of all fla- vors. Perhaps there really is more to faith than just God waiting to see if we possess some particular belief before He intervenes. Per- haps there is more to faith than just a quality of someone's person- ality. Perhaps faith and the power of the mind to heal are not just prerequisites for healing or even a quality or achievement that we must obtain before healing can happen, but instead they are the very instruments God uses to heal, just as a crescent wrench is the instru- ment I choose to pound nails.

Think again about God's definition of faith, and consider the depths to which that definition might go: *"the substance of things hoped for, the evidence of things not seen"* (Heb. 11:1 KJV). How have we come to believe faith is some goal to be achieved or some possession that we must strive to have? I'm beginning to believe that faith *("the evidence of things not seen") is* the actual power that causes atoms to re-align and eliminate illness, heals infirmities, prevents car wrecks, saves drowning children, or restarts a stalled heart when prayers are offered. Perhaps faith *("the evidence of things not seen")* in God creates vibes on the spiritual level at which atoms resonate, and these vibes are what rearrange matter according to God's faith/will/desire, exactly like what happened during the creation of the universe (God's will—or faith—organizing physical matter from what cannot be seen). Perhaps in the case where the person being healed is not even a Christian, or the miracle is done on behalf of someone who doesn't even know God, it is God's own faith *("the substance of things hoped for")* that causes the miracle.

Let's do a little mental exercise here. Below are some Scriptures that use the word *faith,* but let's substitute one of the above definitions of faith (either "the substance of things hoped for" or "the evidence of things not seen") and see what we find:

> *Because of [the substance of things hoped for], Abraham went out...* (Hebrews 11:8; author's paraphrase).

> *When Jesus saw [the substance of the things they hoped for], he said to the paralytic, "Son, your sins are forgiven"* (Mark 2:5).

> *Be on your guard; stand firm in [the evidence of the things you cannot see]; be men of courage; be strong* (1 Corinthians 16:13).

We live by [the evidence of things that we cannot see], not by sight (2 Corinthians 5:7).

Let us draw near to God with a sincere heart in full assurance of [the evidence of the things we have hoped for], having our hearts sprinkled to cleanse us from a guilty conscience and having our bodies washed with pure water (Hebrews 10:22).

And where Hebrews lists many heroes of the faith, we could read Chapter 11 like this: "by the evidence of what he could not see," Abraham went out, or Noah built an ark, or Enoch was taken from this life, or Moses' parents hid him. Verse 39 would thus read: *"These were all commended for their* [hope in the evidence of what they could not see]."

Now, keeping in mind that faith is a substance, and faith is power, let me offer a syllogism:

1. Jesus is God and has the power to heal, having infinite faith in Himself as a Healer.

2. We have been put into Jesus, and we have the mind of Jesus and, therefore, the authority of God.

3. Therefore, it's God's faith that is in us and that heals us, not our own!

The Size of Our Faith

Doesn't that totally take the pressure off? We talk about trying to gain faith or grow our faith or make our faith stronger, but then we quote Jesus saying, "If only our faith was as tiny as a mustard seed, we could move mountains" (see Luke 17:6). I almost always hear this Scripture taught as if we ought to keep growing our faith more and more, but it actually says just the opposite. A simple reading of these words from Jesus actually proves to us that it has nothing to do with the size of our faith. He's saying, in effect, "It's OK if you can only muster a tiny little speck of faith, because that's all that's necessary! It's not the size of your faith that matters, but *the one who is the source of your faith!*"

Most of us have faith. In other words, most of us agree that God has the power to heal and to do other miracles. The problem enters when we don't believe He actually will. Often the problem occurs because we are too bound by what we can see with our physical eyes. If we could see into the spiritual, eternal world that surrounds us, like Elisha did when he saw the angel warriors on the hills around him, then we could probably better understand the difference between our faith that God *can* do something and our belief that He actually *will*. But that realm remains a mystery to us because we just can't see into it clearly. Or can we?

In the movie *The Matrix*, there is a scene where Trinity is shot and is dying in Neo's arms. In his mind, since he is beginning to learn to see in the "other" dimension that is invisible to others, he sees the bullet. We are given a view consistent with his, that allows us to also see the bullet. He reaches into her chest with his hand, in a view that looks like electronic or digital reality, and removes the bullet. He saves her life because he could *see* into that other realm and actively participate in it, separate from the physical realm that most of us only see with our eyes.

Paul prays for his readers in Ephesians 1:18 that the eyes of their hearts will be enlightened. This is the prerequisite for seeing in the Spirit. When we can clearly see in the Spirit, then we can see the effects of faith on the circumstances around us. We can see the needs that faith can meet. We can see the maladies that faith can heal. We can see the emotions that faith can calm. There is no longer an effective difference between the physical and spiritual realms because the two are not really distinct from each other after all. Faith transcends borders, it covers all of creation, it flows freely through the same creation-penetrating realm as God's all-permeating Spirit. It flies right across the borders of the realities of quantum physics to affect the very fabric of life. Nothing is beyond the touch of the power of faith, including the devil himself. Even he must succumb when the power of faith is active in the lives of believers according to the will of God.

Most of us believe that God can do the things we ask Him to do. The next step is to simply learn that He *will*. We must work on our belief system, on the strength of our will, and on the confidence that God is readily handing to us if we will just freely take and begin to appropriate it properly in our lives in Christ. We are *in Christ*. We have the *mind of Christ*. We will do "greater things than these." The faith—the power of God Almighty—is right there for the taking. Let's just reach out and take it as our own.

Endnote

1. Ralph W. Harris, exec. ed., *The New Testament Study Bible* (The Complete Biblical Library, 1989), 134-135.

CHAPTER 14

Quantum Spiritual Warfare

If it is true that faith is the very power that not only heals, but also makes other things happen in the lives of those who love God, then of course it is in our enemy's best interest to negate or somehow subvert that faith. Much of the spiritual warfare we experience from the enemy has to do with making us ineffectual. He's already lost us to the Savior, but if he can make us ineffective, then we pose no threat to him. If we do not understand and appropriate the incredible power of faith, then he has no reason to worry about us, and he will let us go on our merry, ignorant way. But those who do understand the power of faith—the kind of power that, according to Jesus, can throw a mountain into the sea—pose a significant threat to the kingdom and the workings of the enemy.

I suppose the devil must be an expert in quantum physics. He might have been around when God created the universe and was establishing the rules that govern space and time. I've heard it said by many pastors and teachers that lucifer (satan before he blew it) was the second most intelligent and shrewd being ever to exist, which could make him very good at science. Remember the demoniac that broke the chains that bound him? Is not steel stronger than flesh and bone? How did he do that except to deny some law of physics? Perhaps you have heard of stories of demon-possessed people exhibiting superior strength. If reality is fundamentally spiritual in nature, as we've been discussing, then I have no doubt that all of us—God, you, me, the enemy and his devils—have the ability to affect physical reality to some extent through spiritual activities.

So the second most intelligent being in the universe—possibly the second best quantum physicist ever to exist—is our mortal enemy, and he will pull out all the stops when it comes to disarming us in our walk with Christ. By weakening one of the most potent weapons in our arsenal—the power of faith—he can gain a major victory. He wants to discourage us and convince us that faith really doesn't work. He tries to keep us complacent about God's promises and tempt us to provide for ourselves instead of having faith in God. He tries to convince us that our prayers are not going to be answered, and he plants seeds of doubt about who Jesus is and what He wants to do for us. He wants to keep us in the dark about the true meaning and incredible power of God's grace (please read John Piper's *Future Grace*), and if he succeeds, then he has cut us off at the very root by undermining our faith and its explosive power—the power to alter the very reality that surrounds us.

But I hate giving him too much credit. Compared to the power of God at work within us, the power of the enemy is of no consequence whatsoever if we follow and obey God's leading in our lives. Our enemy works on that level of the unseen. He understands the power of words, thoughts, and intent to change physical realities, but his power is absolutely infinitesimal and inconsequential compared to the power God has placed inside His children. He seeks to subvert that power within us simply by hiding the truth from our hearts and minds. Aside from lies and deception, the enemy has absolutely no power in our lives.

An effective weapon against this kind of subversion is to live as if God coordinates every event in our lives. In Oswald Chambers' devotional, *My Utmost For His Highest*, Chambers states that, "There is no such thing as chance in the life of a saint."[1] Since God is always actively and purposefully bringing us into situations and in front of people with whom He wants us to have contact, we must be prepared and trained to always contribute in the way He expects us to. This contribution may be a spoken word of encouragement, the meeting of a physical need, a healing prayer, or a word of prophecy, each equally supernatural in its own way and each affecting reality on a subatomic level. Remember, thoughts have physical consequences. The fabric of reality is knit together by the unseen. Physical change can be brought about by spiritual revelation and action. How unbelievably exciting life will be when we learn to approach each circumstance that confronts us with the mentality that we are about to change the universe and eternal reality in some irreversible way!

So we see that faith goes far beyond just believing and trusting in something. Faith says to those who wield it:

> You are about to affect the very reality that surrounds you. You are about to change the life fabric of the people around you. You have the power (through the power of Jesus working through you) to change reality to match what God wants—to bring the Kingdom of Heaven to Earth in the place and time where you are now. You are about to wield a power that the devil himself has no power to stand against if it is used according to the will of God the Father. The very atoms that constitute the physical matter around you will submit to the power of God flowing through you.

This is a power that God wants you to use, but He must know that He can trust you with it. A shotgun contains a power that would be dangerous and deadly in the hands of a child. So we start with what we know, and soon our faith begins to grow a little stronger. After a while, we see things actually being affected by our decisions made in faith. Perhaps some of us are fortunate enough to witness healings or what we consider "miraculous" events, but we just smile, knowing that it's not so miraculous after all. It's just God rearranging atoms and electrons to suit His desires, all activated on a quantum level by the faith God has given us.

We Bring Heaven to Earth

For some reason, God has chosen to do His work primarily through His children on Earth. Why He trusts a clown like me with that huge responsibility I don't know, but nevertheless, it is an awesome power that He has entrusted to those He calls His children. In a sense, we are partaking in the actual creative process of God Himself, the same power that created the universe we live in today. God did not stop creating on the seventh day of creation, because every day I see flowers blooming, and babies being born.

In the case of physical miracles, I have seen new flesh being created where disease once was and a leprous hand being made whole. I have also observed the most brilliant, ongoing act of creation—unsaved souls being born again. God says a new creature is created when a soul is saved, a creature that did not exist before. Yes, God continues to create today in a million different ways. These are all literal acts of creation, and by exercising our faith and working to hone it and perfect it, we will be participating together to create the Kingdom life God is creating.

Our enemy understands this and will do anything he can to prevent us from helping God in His creative processes. Because God has chosen to do His work through His children, these children become the primary target of the enemy. What can we do to protect ourselves? In short, take God's advice. I'm reading for the second time an excellent book on spiritual warfare entitled *Winning Your Spiritual Battles: How To Use The Full Armor Of God* by Gary Kinnaman. This book focuses on putting on the armor of God described in Ephesians 6, and does an admirable job covering the basics in some depth. All of the pieces of armor are presented as metaphors, but the metaphors are powerful and necessary because in our discussion of quantum realities, these spiritual pieces of armor are every bit as "real" as the clothes I put on every morning. Truth can be put on like a belt. Salvation can be put on like a helmet. The sword of the Spirit can be taken up like a metal sword, because in the metaphysical/spiritual/physical world we inhabit, these are literal weapons that affect spiritual and physical reality.

The shield of faith is able to quench the fiery darts of the evil one. These fiery darts are as real as the bullets our brave soldiers fire in combat. We have all had these fiery darts thrown at us, and they have physical consequences. Remember when some tragedy befell you: a loved one involved in an accident, a divorce, a child diagnosed with a disease, the news that the World Trade Center had been hit by terrorists? Do we not feel physical reactions? Do our guts not turn over inside us? What better example is there to demonstrate that the mental, emotional, and spiritual realities are intimately intertwined with the physical?

Spiritual Deception

Naturalists, who believe that we are solely physical beings and that all emotions are only chemical reactions in our brains, have to deny the truth about ultimate reality. They scoff at those who believe in the supernatural, but just think of what they are missing! They are missing an entire realm of existence upon which everything we see, smell, taste, touch, hear, feel, and believe is based. They live in the yin, but ignore the yang, to their incredible detriment. I can't imagine how empty and futile life must be with the perspective that what you see is all you get. The apostle Paul said that if this physical life is all we have, then we, of all people, are most miserable: *"If only for this life we have hope in Christ, we are to be pitied more than all men"* (1 Cor. 15:19). I believe that when Paul talks about "this life," he not only means our life on earth prior to our journey to eternity, but he also means this spiritual unseen life that we are to be partaking of here and now.

Regarding the unsaved, it seems the devil either wants them to deny spiritual realities altogether or send them on some tangent that sounds spiritually attractive, but is empty of power and truth. Cults and false religions abound, presenting every imaginable sort of spin on the truth, and people pursue these things in ignorance because there really is a God-shaped hole in each human being that begs to be filled with something. Some of them come close to the mark, thereby fooling lots of people into thinking they are doing what God wants. Regardless, the end result is millions of people who are blindly following some wayward teaching rather than God Himself, which results in a worldview that is devoid of spiritual power. By *spiritual power* I mean power that it is able to affect reality simultaneously on the physical and spiritual planes.

For God-followers, it seems the enemy's most common tactics (at least for western Christians, which is the only perspective I feel qualified to speak about) are complacency, greed, and legalistic religiosity. Complacency comes about when we are satisfied with where we are spiritually, smug in the opinion that we're pretty good Christians and living a good life is what it's all about. One of the roots of complacency is laziness, an unwillingness to *"work out our salvation,"* as Paul instructs us in Philippians 2:12. Greed keeps many of us busy as we work harder and longer for more stuff, looking and acting no differently than our unsaved counterparts. Who has time for God or the miraculous with that kind of schedule?

Perhaps the most dangerous tactic our enemy uses against Christians is legalistic religiosity. By this I mean a spirituality like that of the Pharisees, based primarily on what I do—in others words, earning my way into eternal life. The problem is that the people who are caught in this kind of behavior are the ones most likely to be blinded to it. Spiritual pride is commonplace, often exhibited in an attitude that says, "I know God, I know the Bible, I know God's will, so listen to me! It's either my way or the highway!" These folks are not open to revelation from God. They often take strict biblical literalism to an unhealthy degree, putting the Bible on a pedestal higher than Jesus.

Idolizing the Bible

Graham Cooke echoes that sentiment in *Developing Your Prophetic Gifting,* where he mentions that some people want to make the Bible a fourth member of the Trinity. Cooke then rightly states that "the Bible is not God's Word. Jesus is God's Word. The Bible is Scripture."[2] Christians often act like their lists of rules and regulations for how we all must live are all-important. It seems that they sometimes believe it's their God-given responsibility to make sure everyone toes the line according to their interpretations of Scriptures. When people make the Bible more important than Jesus, we have Pharisees doing the work of the devil. Jesus identified the greatest commandment for us. It is *not* to obey the Bible. It is *"Love the Lord your God with all your heart and with all your soul and with all your mind"* (Matt. 22:37).

How does religiosity affect the life of faith on a quantum level? Once again, let us remember that the enemy is extremely shrewd and will strive to make Christians ineffective in any way he can. He knows each of our weaknesses better than we do and will use them against us. For many, this spiritual pride speaks to something missing inside our souls, and satan will use that when he can. He has no problem letting us focus all our attention on the Bible, as long as we never really understand it and put it to use. He may even help us memorize the whole of Scripture if he knows he can use it to build our pride and ego to a point where we cause dissention and strife within the Church. And when we are involved in this kind of strife, we know it on a gut level. I mentioned that physical feeling most of us had when the Trade Center was attacked. Have we not also felt something like that when we saw Mr. So-and-So or Ms. Busybody coming toward us in church?

Our enemy uses these circumstances to disarm us, to keep us off balance, and to prevent unity, love, and peace in the Body of Christ, because he knows that if our minds are preoccupied with trivial garbage, we will not be focusing our energies in the realm where he primarily exists and does his best work. The Bible says that there is great power where two or three agree on Earth in prayer (see Matt. 18:20). Our enemy knows that power and authority are multiplied where there is unity, to the point where the whole becomes greater than the sum of the parts. In other words, where an individual Christian working and praying in isolation has some power, this authority is exponentially multiplied as we live and work as a Body, united in purpose, held together by love, governed in peace, agreeing on Earth with God's will, and praying and doing His work accordingly. The whole is indeed greater than the sum of its parts! Anything the enemy will do to keep this from happening can advance his cause.

The Power of Unity

This multiplying of effectiveness (when Christians act together in the unity of love) has a very good analogy in the world of physics. Laser is an acronym for Light Amplification by the Stimulated Emission of Radiation. A laser begins with some kind of lasing medium— either a gas like carbon dioxide or a solid lasing medium like a rod of glass—surrounded by powerful flashing lights. As these lights excite the lasing medium, a fascinating thing happens. The light begins to bounce back and forth inside the medium, being reflected off the ends of the chamber by partially reflective surfaces. Soon all the photons of light inside the medium line up with each other and are being bounced back and forth in perfect unity and harmony. They are then emitted out the end of the device and focused to a very narrow beam of incredibly intense power. A laser can cut through solid steel and it provides a perfect, high quality cut in the process. These are the same kinds of photons that shine on us from the sun and cause the grass to grow and that shine in the evening, their wavelength lengthened and turned red by the atmosphere. The same photons that reflect off a beautiful work of art in the museum are used to slice through solid steel. A miracle!

I can be effective in the Kingdom of God by obeying God's commands and learning to really love Him with all my heart, soul, mind, body, and strength. But there is a reason why God forces us into situations where we must rely on one another and why He urges us to come together in unity of intention. In precisely the same way as a laser, Christian brothers and sisters acting in unity can focus the power of God into a situation to make drastic changes both on the physical-quantum level and on the spiritual level. These changes actually work across that boundary between the seen and unseen to work a kind of holistic good in the lives of people. This happens as a result of our cooperating in the Spirit and all learning to move in the same direction (like the laser) to line up all of our individual powers, talents, and gifts for the most effective end result.

That's why we're described as a Body, many units functioning as a single organism—some are eyes, some are feet (I often feel like I'm a spleen or a little toe)—so that the whole body will function as it's supposed to. The whole is greater than the sum of the parts, just as the cutting power of a laser comes from more than just a piece of glass and a flashing light. I've driven my car past highway construction zones, and stopped beside a flashing caution light. That flashing light coming through the glass in my car's windshield did not produce a laser beam! It's the wrong glass, the wrong light, and the wrong materials at the wrong time. Individual Christians operating alone out of distaste for Body life will not produce laser beams like Christians in unity will. Our enemy knows this. That's why we must fight his efforts to separate us.

In a laser, when the photons begin lining up, and the parallel light begins working together, it is called *coherent*, which in scientific terms means "having a constant phase relationship." When the light becomes coherent then the process of *lasing* begins. As a group of like-minded believers begins to align with the Spirit of God and with each other, the *lasing* begins. Coherence is established, which can also be defined as "united as or forming a whole," precisely as the Bible describes the Body of Christ. This lasing action is completely unaffected by the boundary between the visible and invisible realms of existence. Anything is a target, any affliction can be healed and any condition improved, whether mental, emotional, spiritual, physical, temporal, or eternal. The lasing action of the Body of Christ working in unity is a power that transcends life on earth. It transcends any physical or spiritual boundary that the enemy might try to put in the way, and it achieves the perfect will of our eternal God in the lives of the one on which we are focusing.

When a bunch of Christians gather for prayer, I almost always envision a beam of intense light emanating from the group, and being focused upon the person or situation for which the prayer is being offered. This lasing light is, of course, the power of Almighty God, and it can cut through anything in the universe, *"even to dividing soul and spirit, joints and marrow"* (Heb. 4:12). With such an incredible power at our command, why should we ever desire a life outside of the Body life that God has designed for us?

Endnotes

1. Oswald Chambers, *My Utmost for His Highest* (Uhrichsville, OH: Barbour Books, 2000).

2. Graham Cooke, *Developing Your Prophetic Gifting* (Ada, MI: Chosen Books, 2003).

CHAPTER 15

Science Vs. Faith

Two Necessary Revelations

I enjoy meditating about and discussing the topic of science vs. faith. It seems common among many of my Christian brothers and sisters to pit them against each other, at least when it comes to things that are difficult to understand, but it doesn't have to be this way. If we have trouble grasping the scientific validity of some particular topic, especially those topics that have to do with the age of the Earth, origins of the universe, a universal flood, and so forth, then we tend to believe it is more spiritual to put our trust in blind faith rather than the facts of science. For many, this seems like the more spiritual or godly route, because it seems on the surface to rely more on Spirit sense than common sense.

The rationale goes something like this: If there seems to be some contradiction between the Bible and scientific discovery, we must choose the Bible because we are called to have faith in God. Faith is devalued if we wait until we understand something before we choose to have faith in it. If we choose only to have faith in those things that we fully understand, then of what use is faith? By definition, faith has become the belief in things we do not understand. Our language is even replete with evidence of this with sayings like, "I just had to take it on faith," and "I was just exercising blind faith."

What if, when confronted with a seeming controversy between the Bible and science, we are not required to choose the Bible over science? What if our understanding of God's truth as revealed in the Scriptures is evolving just like our understanding of the physical universe? What if the science that allows us to translate ancient manuscripts into modern languages is developing and improving as time goes on, just as the science that allows us to discover ever-greater and deeper truths about the created world? What if it is merely our understanding and interpretation of both the biblical texts and scientific discovery that needs to be challenged, not the truths and principles illustrated therein?

I believe we are creating a completely unnecessary dichotomy when we pit the Bible against science. It is not unlike asking me if I want steak or potatoes for supper, when I know both are already cooked and sitting on the table, steaming and delicious and nutritious. It simply is not necessary to choose between the two, because there is room in my stomach for both. I need both starch and protein in my diet, so it behooves me to eat both. I don't even have to have a preference of one over the other. They are totally different. I'm a protein boy, and my mom will tell you that when I was young, I would finish off an entire chicken if the carcass were left on the table after dinner. This is literally true, because I love meat. But in the right context, I also love potatoes, especially when they're mashed with lots of butter and cream, and maybe a little garlic. Although I may occasionally prefer one over the other, protein and carbohydrates serve entirely different purposes in my body, and I need them both.

There is plenty of room in our stomachs for the revelation of the physical universe as revealed by modern science *and* for the written revelation of God in the Scriptures. Nowhere is it implied that it is necessary to choose between the two. Nowhere is the Bible identified as a definitive science textbook. Nowhere are the cosmos identified as the definitive proof of God's love for us. Nowhere is the Bible identified as the only viable revelation to us about God. In fact, the Bible encourages us to use the revealed universe as proof of God's glory and power and majesty. Both revelations of God are absolutely necessary.

Studying Science Honors God's Creation

Some may insist that the Bible is the only authority we need, but this makes the words of God meaningless when He says to us that:

*Since the creation of the world God's invisible qualities — His eternal power and divine nature — have been clearly seen, **being understood from what has been made,** so that men are without excuse* (Romans 1:20).

We are actually meant to study *"what has been made"* and make it known to others, with the specific goal of making *"God's invisible qualities — His eternal power and divine nature"* known to those around us. True, there are things in the Bible that natural revelation cannot teach us. There are also things in nature that the Bible cannot teach us.

In the simplest terms possible, I want to suggest we simply stop setting up science as if it is in competition with the Bible. The two are totally different; they are complementary; they comprise two of the most significant revelations of God that have been provided to us; and they stand side by side in their importance as beacons guiding us toward the incredible God we serve.

Recently, I repaired my car with a little JB Weld, a two-part adhesive with amazing bonding power. As long as the two parts, sold in two separate tubes, stay apart, then they both stay soft and squeezable. But when the two parts are mixed together, you have only a limited amount of time to glue your parts together before it sets into a permanent bond of incredible strength. Let's look at our understanding of the Bible and our growing scientific knowledge of the physical universe as a two-part epoxy that will glue together our understanding of God Almighty more strongly than either one could do by itself. But only if we mix them together!

Now we have a strong foundation to build on!

The Bible Is Not God

We shouldn't equate the Bible itself with God Almighty. Before you dismiss that as a silly or unfounded notion, just read the critiques put forth by many advocates of a young Earth, who insist that the universe was created literally six to ten thousand years ago and made to look old. I'm not criticizing the ideas they hold. I just see too much evidence that they often believe and teach the fact that those who disagree with them are heretics. Those who disagree with them and believe that the universe could be billions of years old are sometimes accused of believing in a different God. Why? Because if you don't believe in a literal translation of the first Book of Genesis and the literal six-day creation of the cosmos, then you cannot believe the rest of the Bible. Therefore, you cannot trust in the God who supposedly wrote the Bible or in His plan of salvation, or in the historical accounts about Jesus, or in any other part of the Bible.

This argument is fundamentally flawed, and it looks to me like it is representative (I take no pleasure in saying this) of a lack of faith in God's power to sustain His truth. The argument is flawed in that the Bible is actually only one of God's revelations, and it has only been in existence a minority of the time that humankind has existed on this planet. As Roy Hershberger writes in *A Religion of Irrelevance*, "We must be careful not to put the Bible on a pedestal."[1] God, yes—on the highest pedestal we can find! But let's keep the Bible in its rightful context where God put it. We should not worship the Bible.

To state that a belief in our particular modern translations of the Bible is necessary for salvation ignores the millions of God-lovers who lived before the canon existed, as well as believers today who have no Bible or a very limited version of it. To state that belief in a literal translation of Genesis is necessary in order to literally believe any other part of the Bible ignores the plentiful use of metaphors, similes, poetry, apocalyptic language, sarcasm, and wit that fills the Bible and the significant possibility that Genesis may fit one or more of these above categories.

It is entirely possible to be a lover and follower of Jesus Christ, and yet have legitimate questions and skepticism about the accuracy of our modern translations of the Bible. Certain assumptions have been made for decades or centuries about the Bible that affects the contextual meaning of biblical principles for today's Christians, given that the books were written in an incredibly different cultural climate. This does not in any way endanger the Gospel, as many would claim, but in fact it serves to strengthen it. The apostle Paul himself congratulated the Bereans for testing what he told them to see if it really was the truth (see Acts 17:11).

I want to be careful that I don't give the wrong impression. I strongly believe that the Bible is God's revelation to humankind. I believe it is full of invaluable truth and is infallible and perfect regarding the *principles* that it teaches. There is no doubt in my mind that life and Christian culture would be sorely lacking without the canon of Scripture to help guide us. As Second Timothy 3:16 says, the Bible *"is useful for teaching, rebuking, correcting and training in righteousness."*

However, we must be careful that we don't discredit ourselves to the world. Those around us read the Bible, and they find inaccuracies, discrepancies, and downright contradictions. By denying that these exist, we show the world that we can't even read and understand our own guidebook, so how can they possibly trust our interpretation of it? It is in fact true that some do not accept the Christian faith because of the way some overly religious-minded people rigidly and legalistically interpret questionable passages of the Bible.

There is a very simple solution. Let's begin to accept the Bible for what it is: primarily a gathering of historical documents, guided by God's mind and will, but written by men of His choosing, designed to teach us about God's dealings with humankind and His desires for us regarding how we are to live and love. They contain the fulfillment of verifiable prophecies, which thus establishes their supernatural source. These historical documents have been subjected to our best scientific effort at translating the language and more importantly the thoughts and meanings of the writings into our modern language and cultural paradigm.

This science is no more complete or foolproof than the science that teaches us about the cosmos and the age of the universe, allows us to build cars and aluminum cans, helps us heat and cool our homes, and brings us such modern miracles as fluoride toothpaste and iPods. I hope and pray that our science of translation continues to improve and teach us more about biblical texts just as much as our science of the cosmos teaches us about how God created this incredible universe.

Yes, we can love the Bible and honor it as the greatest book ever written. We can honor it as the words of God translated into our modern languages. We can trust that the principles it teaches are good principles, and we ought to live our lives accordingly. But we must be careful not to exclude all other revelation as some are in the habit of doing, and we must be careful that we are actually allowing the words of the Bible to lead us into a personal relationship with God Almighty and not just teaching us stuff about Him.

Translation, Archaeology, and Astrophysics

The cumulative knowledge of humankind is indeed evolutionary in nature. If an inventor has an idea that changes and improves over time until it finally becomes a viable, marketable product, then we rightfully say his product has evolved. "Evolution" should not be a dirty word; it is a law of life that God has put into action. So if our knowledge of the translation of ancient manuscripts evolves, and our knowledge of God's revealed truths need to be taught and expanded upon by those among us with the gift of teaching and prophesy, then why do many Christian teachers reject what our evolving knowledge of the universe says about our infinite God?

In their inspiring book, *The Privileged Planet*, authors Guillermo Gonzalez and Jay Richards present hundreds of pages of evidence that the world we live in is perfectly positioned, perfectly designed, and perfectly aligned to provide not only an ideal environment for life but also for observation and discovery of the universe around us. A recurring theme in the book is the myriad ways we have of gaining specific information about the universe that all corresponds with one another. God did not leave us to guess at His handiwork, but He gave us many methods of discovery that corroborate one another.

For example, in dating certain geological features of the planet, the authors describe how a huge variety of clocks exist to tell us the age of the earth and record events long past. These clocks include ice cores, ocean sediments, and growth rings on very old bristlecone pines (some of which live several thousand years). A dry season identified by growth rings from three thousand years ago on a pine tree may be correlated to the same phenomenon witnessed in ice core samples. A similar set of tools exists for the study of the age of the universe. Scientists use several different methods to measure distances to extremely remote objects, and when these very dissimilar methods corroborate one another, then we have much more accurate and trustworthy proof that the universe is indeed very old.

We ought to trust in the basic tenets of scientific discovery. We all trust in the hydraulic braking systems in our cars, even though few of us understand how it really works. Jet engines, life-saving medicines, and skyscrapers are all marvels of engineering and science that require thousands of experts and cumulative centuries of knowledge to perfect, yet we fly in planes, undergo complex medical treatments, and ride elevators to the tops of buildings without questioning the science that made it possible.

My purpose here is not to make a definitive statement about the age of the universe or any other scientific quandary. It's to point out that we can learn, and ought to be continuing to learn, about the incredible God who created us, the universe, and the awesome system of interpersonal and cultural relationships that lend an infinite variety to this incredible life we live on this incredible planet. Science and quantum physics have their places and are major players in this book and in our lives, but make no mistake—it's all about Jesus Christ and the unfathomable existence He has planned for us. Now let's dive in a little deeper.

Endnote

1. Roy Hershberger, *A Religion of Irrelevance*; http://kbproweb.com/gel/aribook/introb.html; accessed August 18, 2011.

CHAPTER 16

Evolving Theology

Our theology ought to be evolving.

The word *evolution* has unfortunately become a dirty word because of its association with Darwinian naturalism. But it's a perfectly useful word. Henry Ford's Model A is different from today's Mustang, because cars have evolved. *Evolution* is a useful word to describe the process of development, normally toward a more complex and useful state of being, so let's consider how our theology has evolved and ought to continue evolving, probably throughout all eternity.

Many Christian teachers I listen to seem to hold up our modern systematic theology as virtually as important as the Bible. For many preachers and theologians, to question modern Christian theology is to question the legitimacy of God Himself because, after all, the Bible is God's Word right? (Not really. Jesus is the Word; the Bible is Scripture.) We human beings are very fond of systematizing everything we touch, like our efforts to catalog every one of the millions of insects on the planet. Nothing wrong with that. It's just a revealing fact about human nature.

Ever since the dawn of humanity, we have been striving to categorize everything about life and spirituality, probably because we find security in what is known and familiar. When some loud mouth (like me) comes along and says our theology should also be improving, changing, and evolving as time goes on, maybe some of us get a little uncomfortable with that. But I surely hope that we don't believe that our knowledge of God is so complete that we no longer need to study Him. Very few would come right out and say that, but unfortunately some of us live by just such a notion. I know that simply suggesting that our theology is incomplete, or that it needs updating, or that some new angle on God's character is being revealed to us could cause an outcry from the most conservative among us.

Open Theism

We have just such a case study in our midst that we can scrutinize: all this talk about open theism. Let me quickly elaborate so we are all on the same page. Open theists argue that God can actually change. He is touched by events and has emotional reactions to the good and bad things that happen in His universe. A corollary to this is that God has in some ways made Himself vulnerable to the decisions and whims of human beings. In other words, God has left it to the human race how certain things will turn out, and He has chosen not to interfere in many (perhaps most) of these decisions. The natural laws and the spiritual laws He has put in place are allowed to run their course, and it doesn't always turn out like He wants it to. For example, God is not willing that any should perish (see 2 Pet. 3:9), yet many do. God does not always get what He wants. When things don't turn out like He wants them to (for example, when God said He repented that He had made Saul king), then He begins plan B.

I am not going to attempt to debate the validity of this viewpoint of God. My point in bringing it up is to discuss this evolving theology idea and to use this debate as an example. My first question is why is this viewpoint of God's character being met with such strong opposition from conservative Christian theologians and teachers? The first knee-jerk reaction to that question will undoubtedly be "because it's heresy!" Those who disagree with the notions of open theism have been very quick to disagree with it and very vocal in their defense of descriptions of God that satisfy traditional theology. This is all legitimate, if indeed traditional theology contains the truth and open theism does not.

But here is the point I would like to make about this whole controversy: those who disagree with open theism have a very difficult time simply debating the issue. Many of the critiques that I have heard and read also attack the individuals who hold these views. Christian brotherhood and acceptance are sometimes as lacking in this debate as they are in the debate about the age of the universe. Some of the pundits espousing this "new" theology are being called heretical or guilty of teaching a false Gospel. And the accounts that I am familiar with seem to expose the fact that the traditionalists are attacking on the grounds that this is a new theology, that the Bible has spelled it all out clearly and God will not change, that the thick books of systematic theology that our seminaries hold in such high regard are as authoritative as the Bible itself, and that anything suggesting that God can learn or change or be affected by emotion or pain or happiness somehow detracts from His infinite nature, even if the open theists claim that this is what Scriptures clearly support.

The reason I am bringing up this example is to prepare you to think. It's OK for us to disagree with one another, as long as it's not on the fundamental issues like salvation through Christ. But we can all grow and benefit from some open-minded conversation about the way things might be.

Open to Changing Our Minds

I believe that we should not be satisfied with our existing "theology" (as if God, an infinite and eternal personality with emotions, character, personality, and charisma could ever be boiled down to 1,200 pages of ink and paper) as a static entity. If we as a human race continue to experience God in differing and evolving ethnic and cultural arenas, surrounded as we are by an incredible boom in technology and all the ramifications that these changes hold for life in this century, then perhaps we should remain more open to discussions on the changes to our theology—our knowledge of God—that might be required.

Let us agree at the outset that God's truth is strong enough to withstand some honest questions, especially when the questions are asked for the specific purpose of getting to know Jesus better. If we are seeking God's truth and are asking for and expecting the Holy Spirit's guidance during the process, then we can be at ease because we know we won't be causing damage to the Gospel.

So now that we're not afraid of damaging the Gospel, please allow me to ask a question: What if theology really is undergoing the very process of evolution?

What is theology after all? The best working definition I can come up with is this: Our theology comprises our cumulative knowledge about God and the way He interacts with the human race. Now, since God is infinite, and humans are finite, is it not an incontrovertible truth that we can never know everything about God? And is it not true that in most categories of knowledge, humankind's cumulative knowledge is constantly increasing? So why not allow that our knowledge of God can also increase?

If our knowledge of God is increasing, then by definition our theology is evolving. Not only do we know more about God as time goes on, but we know more about how He interacts with human beings because our statistical sample continues to grow as more human beings come into existence. And I would hope that this change in theology is not only quantitative, but also qualitative.

I can imagine that one argument against theological evolution might go something like this: "The attributes of God are unchanging, and we know about those attributes through Scripture, so we must chisel it in stone."

While I would agree with the statement that God's attributes—His love, perfection, infinite kindness, and purity, for example—never change, this does not automatically mean that our knowledge of Him or these attributes of His never changes. It is one thing to receive knowledge or revelation of God's kindness through Scripture, but to fully understand all the expressions of this attribute worked out in the daily lives of several billion people on this planet is altogether different.

I think this is one reason why Christian philosophies and arguments are often losing meaning to many in the Church: while some insist that the Bible is the only authority on the planet, others may believe that God has provided other meaningful revelations of His truth and beauty. Some may come across as belligerent about their stance on what they deem are moral issues, while others may emphasize grace, forgiveness, and acceptance toward those who don't act or talk the way they do. Some insist on an interpretation of Scriptures that seems narrow and constricting to others, creating unnecessary and divisive arguments, while other segments of the Church are experiencing new revivals, unique experiences, and fresh revelations about God's love and power. It seems to me that any time a fresh power of God is revealed, traditionalists tend to stand up and shout, perhaps even blogging feverishly about how this fresh "move of God" is actually a heresy designed by the devil to take unsuspecting Christians straight to hell. When did the Gospel of Christ become so fragile?

Of course we have to be careful. The Bereans were commended for testing everything against the Scriptures (see Acts 17:11). We too are in the habit of checking everything against the Scriptures, but I think we often have a mistaken goal, and therefore come to the wrong conclusion. Often, we may see a particular thing happening in some church or during some revival, and we then search the Scriptures for an exact duplicate of that thing. When we don't find it in the Bible, we declaim that it must be of the devil, and we post our opinions on YouTube and write books about all the dangers.

What if the primary lesson we are to learn from the Bible is not about the specific ways in which God has interacted with humankind in the past, but the fact that God actually acts in totally unpredictable ways? We fail to find evidence of certain things we are seeing in the Church today, and we freak out about it, but from cover to cover, the Bible is full of God being completely unpredictable and unique in His ways and methods.

Am I suggesting that we should accept any old wacky behavior that comes into our midst? Of course not. Every authentic move of God has its excesses, because the enemy is there trying to confound it. But as Patricia King says, when there is an excess in a new move of God, for example the outlandish behaviors seen during the Toronto and Lakeland, Florida, revivals, we just need to pastor it, discern what is good and what is deceptive, and keep the good so God's will can be done. Christians tend to be overly conservative when it comes to new moves of God, but would it not be a refreshing change to err on the side of God's unpredictability rather than being so overly cautious that we completely miss His outpourings of provision?

Graham Cooke is fond of saying that we ought to be bumping up against the line of presumption when it comes to the upgrades God has planned for us, rather than being way back in unbelief. If we risk our lives out there at the front lines of the battle, we are sure to gain far more victories than if we cower behind the hills waiting for Jesus to return. The life of abundance involves risk. But it's a perfectly safe risk as long as our hearts remain true to God's Spirit.

With risk comes victory, because it's guaranteed in Christ (see 1 Cor. 15:57), and with victories come increasing knowledge of the way God interacts with us both individually and corporately. In other words, our theology evolves. It keeps life interesting. Whoever thinks the life of a Christian has to be all boredom and drudgery has no idea of the incredible, life-giving, freedom-loving God we serve!

CHAPTER 17

The Bible and the Language of Quantum Physics

Henry and Hugh are relaxing on the back porch after dark. The breeze is warm, the iced tea is cold, and the conversation is stimulating. Henry's rocking chair creaks against the wooden porch floor. Hugh is puffing contentedly on his pipe in which he is burning a delicious Balkan blend. The humid Louisiana air is condensing on the tea glasses, and the occasional droplet drips onto the arm of Hugh's wicker chair, where the surface tension created by the love affair between oxygen and hydrogen atoms cause the water to stretch, cling, quiver, and dance the molecular rumba called "capillary action."

Henry: I say, Hugh, what a spectacular display of stars tonight!

Hugh: I could not possibly agree with you more, my friend.

Henry: I must admit to a certain restlessness when I gaze at the Heavens. When I die, I shall very much look forward to exploring the universe and alas, now I am reminded that God's Word tells us everything will be destroyed in the end. Hmmm...perhaps God's new universe will be even more spectacular!

Hugh: Well, I suppose if this were only the prototype, the real deal would be something to behold.

Henry: What do you think the new Heavens and new Earth will look like?

Hugh: Well, I'm not so convinced all this will be destroyed.

Henry: No?

Hugh: Nope.

Henry: Umm...well, how do you explain Peter's second book where he says...

Hugh: ..."*the Heavens shall pass away and the elements melt with fervent heat*"?

Henry: Well, yes, good fellow!

Hugh: You remember some of our past, well...our past *animated* discussions. You know, that I don't necessarily interpret Scriptures quite like you do?

Henry: Well, of course old chap, but surely when the Lord's Word says *"the elements will melt with fervent heat"* perhaps He really meant it that way!

Hugh: Well, I was paging through a Greek lexicon one day and learned that the Greek word for *elements* is also translated elsewhere as, for example, "principles," as in *"you died with Christ to the basic principles of this world,"* which is in, I believe, the second chapter of Colossians. Or how about in Galatians where it says *"when we were children, we were in slavery under the basic principles of the world?"*

Henry: Well, uhh...I must admit I was not aware of that peculiarly interesting fact.

Hugh: Also, the writer of Hebrews was not so happy with the progress of his readers, so he told them that they needed someone teach them *"the elementary truths of God's word all over again."*

Henry: So am I to understand that these terms "elementary truths" and "basic principles" are the same Greek word for our elements that will be destroyed?

Hugh: Yes, sir; you've got it!

Henry: By Jove, I'm going to have to mull that one over a bit...

Hugh: Would you like...

Henry: Yes, I am certainly going to have to assimilate this little tidbit.

Hugh: Umm...earth to Henry! Come in Henry!

Henry: I will have to locate my concordances and of course brush up on my Greek, and talk to Dr. Smith about all this and...

Hugh: Henry!

Henry: Oh! So sorry, I must have been a bit lost within my own gray matter.

Hugh: Just wanted to ask if you were ready for some more tea.

Henry: I could scarcely refuse a refill since I happen to know that your darling wife makes the best sweet tea in the south!

Hugh picks up the pitcher from the old wooden

table, and as he refills Henry's glass, an ice cube tumbles out and splashes tea onto Henry's shirt sleeve.

Hugh: Oh, I am so sorry, Henry!

Henry: Think nothing of it, my boy. I should think the basic elements of tea should easily come out in the wash!

* * * * * * * * * * *

Language is a funny, and at times, unruly beast. When we take into consideration the myriad languages in the world, each one intimately interwoven with the culture and history of its people, each one continuously evolving over the centuries and millennia, it's a wonder that we can know anything at all of each other, let alone of ancient civilizations. Much more amazing than mere historical facts is our ability as moderns to surmise the thought processes and intentions of ancient people groups based on our understanding of their languages and idioms.

Math, too, is a language, perhaps the only true universal language. Anyone from any culture on this planet can agree that if I have one apple in my hand and someone gives me another, then I have two apples. Each language is specific to its intentions and needs (I've heard it said that the Eskimos have myriad words in their vocabulary for "snow," hardly useful to those living in the Sahara), but still contains principles that allow intelligible communication between human beings.

Is it possible that the very reason we have such trouble intuitively understanding quantum physics is that we are trying to express spiritual truths with the language of mathematics? Could that be what quantum physics really is? Believe me, I'm the first to put the brakes on when we start equating quantum physics with spirituality, but there very well could be some deeper truths being expressed through our science than purely physical realities. There are plenty of people out there trying to bestow upon quantum physics some spiritualized or religious authority that it doesn't have, so please work with me here. I'm not trying to say that science is religion, and I'm not equating physics or science with God. But the presence of God is interwoven throughout all of creation, so there must be more to quantum physics than simply a method of describing physical reality. Whoever said that the physical sciences must be limited to expressing truths only about things we can see or touch?

What if your math teacher in high school handed you your final exams at the end of the semester, and all the questions had to do with history? I think that might be a very confusing test to take. We might rightfully ask, "I thought this was a math class!" Perhaps we could make a concession, and by describing in painful detail the historical assumptions and conclusions that history has made available to us, we could possibly come up with some roundabout answers to the math questions couched in the language of historical events ("Ugh chiseled a wheel out of stone and then he married Ooph who already owned a stone wheel, so together how many stone wheels did they have?"). The bottom line is, expressing mathematical truth in the language of history is not the most efficient means of communicating.

So if quantum physics contains or hides some kind of spiritual truth, I imagine it would be difficult to express these truths with mathematical language. We have tried, and done an admirable job, but the results reveal a strange world indeed. It looks like quantum realities are too different from our familiar Newtonian world. It looks too random. Remember Einstein's skepticism about the realities of quantum physics? Yet, our mathematical language continues to evolve in an attempt to embrace quantum reality, and we can't avoid using some metaphysical nomenclature. It's almost like it's necessary. And Albert finally came around, admitting that his rejection of quantum physics was a blunder.

I believe that quantum physics—and math and science in general—are languages that can express realities that are not strictly physical in nature, but at the same time, let's maintain a realistic view of what they can really tell us about spirituality. Spiritual truth is discerned in the heart. One cannot easily describe the process of salvation through the blood of Jesus Christ in scientific terms. We have myriad examples in the Bible and in history to prove that God does not often follow a logical (or scientific) path. But while some Christian teachers completely reject the value of science and logic in a life of faith, and others demand a logical, pragmatic view of Christianity based on lists of dos and don'ts and outward appearances, the truth actually lies somewhere in the middle (isn't that the way much of life works?).

To those who demand strictly pragmatic interpretations of Scripture and reject anything that doesn't fit their preconceived notions based on strictly literal interpretations of Scripture, I would point to the countless examples in Scripture of God doing things that are completely illogical and non-sensical. Seizing a city by walking around it and blowing trumpets? (See Joshua 6.) The least shall be the greatest? (See Luke 9:48.) Reducing Gideon's army to 300 so he can conquer an army with tens of thousands? (See Judges 7.) God is not bound by logic and predictability, and those Christian teachers who demand that God will only work according to logical and literal interpretations of Scripture severely limit God.

I believe they will never see the true extent of God's power and provision because they believe that any information, methodology, or experience not specifically and overtly described in the Bible cannot be from God. These folks need to learn that the Bible is not all-encompassing. Just because the Bible does not mention animals that look like beavers, but have duck's bills does not mean that the platypus at the zoo is fake.

On the other hand, those who seek strictly experiential faith and insist that God *never* uses logic or common sense may be equally misguided. While the Bible is full of examples of God being unpredictable, it is also populated with stories and statutes that are wholly based in logic. Those who are hired to work in the vineyard get paid for it (see Matt. 20:1-16). Mixing leaven in your dough makes the whole loaf rise (see Matt. 13:33). New wine should not be put into old wineskins (see Matt. 9:17). As in most aspects of life, the truth is somewhere in the middle of the two extremes. Quantum physics is one of many languages God uses to speak to His creation, but it's not the only one. It just so happens it's one that can shed some fascinating light on the life of the Spirit if we look at it all in the proper context.

Supernatural Phenomena and Quantum Physics

How might we explain what really happened when Jacob wrestled with God in Genesis 32? It was so real that his hip was put out of joint, and he actually had a limp the next day. Or how about the demon-possessed man in the cemetery? (See Mark 5:1-20.) The people talking to Jesus shared how the man had broken the chains that constrained him. Chains are stronger than flesh and bone. There had to be something happening there that was beyond the natural, because pulling hard enough to break chains would have broken and destroyed the man's flesh, not the chains. Perhaps the molecular bonds that hold flesh and bones together were temporarily made stronger than the molecular structure of the iron of which the chains were fashioned. There was some bona fide, subatomic, quantum physics hocus pocus going on there. It seems that for a moment the laws of quantum physics and the behavior of matter on a subatomic level were subverted so that flesh became stronger than iron.

The Bible is full from cover to cover of stories demonstrating the intimate relationship between the science God has put in place and the miraculous things that happened. Even the demons, to some extent, seem to be able to manipulate scientific constants to their advantage. Our enemy certainly has the power to manifest in physically "miraculous" ways. How much more should we, as children of the Creator, have power to change the physical realities that we are confronted with? This is how Jesus could tell us that we will be doing greater works than He did. His power, the same power that raised Him from the dead and created the known universe, is ours for the asking, so that we may do good for those around us and bring the Kingdom of Heaven to Earth.

This power includes not only purely spiritual authority, but also the authority to change the physical things around us through the miraculous manipulation of matter and energy on a quantum level, including healing from diseases and protection from physical harm. God accomplishes a lot in this world through the language and the methodology of quantum physics. It is the actual power behind many, if not all, of the physical miracles we read about in the Bible and continue to experience today. God uses science. It's an important tool in His toolbox. And as we study science and better learn His methods, we will become better and better at healing the sick, solving world crises like hunger and pollution, and promoting health and prosperity for all peoples in every nation.

* * * * * * * * * * *

I can sense some religious folks at this point becoming uncomfortable. "God has given us all the information we need in the Bible," they might argue (and I've heard this rationale a thousand times in a thousand different forms), "so we don't need to speculate on whether He communicates through the language of quantum physics (or insert here your chosen scientific endeavor, or unexplainable supernatural event, or new revelation from some gifted teacher or prophet). The Bible is the only revelation we need. The Bible supersedes everything else."

To these brothers and sisters, I would provide a gentle reminder very similar to the one I give the scientific community elsewhere in this book: if we concur that God is infinitely knowledgeable, infinitely intelligent, and infinitely capable, and we are not, then how can we make any absolute claim concerning His chosen methods of doing anything? Are we going to insist that God works only in ways that He has shown us in the Bible? The point of all the Bible stories that showcase God's incredible imagination in dealing with human beings is not to define the specific ways He works in this universe, but precisely the opposite: they are to prove to us that He is completely sovereign and totally unpredictable. The whole idea is not to demonstrate exactly how God works, but to show us that *we cannot know* how He's going to work. This is precisely the opposite of the way many believers treat the Bible. "If it didn't happen in the Bible then it can't happen today." Sorry. That's just not true.

A Balanced View

How can we insist that physics and science are *not* touching upon God's truth if we do not know everything there is to know about God? Again, God is infinite; we are not. By the very definition, we cannot know as much as He can nor can we know everything about Him. In fact, we all agree that we can only know a tiny fraction of what God knows. Therefore, is it not intellectual arrogance to proclaim that we know what is *not true* about God? We often proclaim that "God's ways are so much higher than our ways; we can never understand how He works," yet we demand that our theology is complete. Both of these things cannot possibly be simultaneously true (see the chapter entitled "Evolving Theology" for more on this topic).

While we can definitely re-state what the Bible says is true or not true about God ("God is love," therefore we can conclude that God is not hate), yet we must not limit our theology to only what the Bible says. We can look at events like some of the modern revivals that draw a lot of controversy because of the unorthodox things that happen. We can insist on our own interpretation of these revival events and the people who lead them—whether in support or in criticism. But what can I say to someone who went to one of these wacky-looking revivals, was genuinely healed, found Jesus Christ, and is now living a life of faith? While we must obviously be on the lookout for false teachers, false Gospels, and apostasy (and there's plenty of that out there), we must be careful when we say things like "God is not there—it's all deception and lies." God can choose to work in any situation and through any messenger He chooses. God used Moses. *He also used Pharoah.*

We can have our thick books on systematic theology on our bookshelves, and we can even memorize them from cover to cover. We can scold one another for not having as firm a grip on theology as we should, or for believing that the Bible is only one of many important revelations God has given us about Himself, and it may or may not be most important. We can gasp in horror as we are presented with arguments that our theology cannot be fully systematized, but ought to be evolving, because it is merely a statement made by finite people at a particular finite time in history about an infinite God.

But until each of us has a personal relationship with the God of the universe, and His son Jesus, and their partner the Holy Spirit, and understands how to receive encouragement, love, revelation, strength, and passion from Them, and have seen Them heal people and deliver them from dark unseen powers, then we might as well sell that three-volume set at our next rummage sale, because it's only good use is as a door stopper. Those who teach about strict theology, but do not possess a living and dynamic relationship with God, often come across as cold and legalistic, and it's difficult (if not impossible) for them to transmit the love and grace of Jesus Christ.

Christians are often characterized by the world as rigid, not willing to think, believing for the sake of believing, and choosing blind faith over fact when the two are juxtaposed. No doubt there is a time to act in faith on the facts of what we know about God, but there is wisdom and maturity in determining a healthy balance between faith and fact. In the movie *Bruce Almighty*, a truck hits Bruce when he kneels in the middle of the street, in the middle of the night, in the pouring rain to cry out to God in desperation. God later tells him, in essence, "What did you expect? You were kneeling in the middle of the street, in the middle of the night, in the pouring rain! Of course you're going to get run over!"

I believe what the Bible says. To put it more accurately, I believe that the Bible is an accurate historical document and is inspired by the Holy Spirit to communicate all kinds of truths to us. Those non-religious and other skeptics that doubt this are encouraged to study the manuscript evidence for the Bible. The Bible has several thousand physical manuscripts supporting its authenticity and dating. The next closest body of work in number of manuscripts is the works of Homer (author of *The Iliad* and *The Odyssey*) numbering in the hundreds of manuscripts.

The Value of the Bible

The Bible is the most reliable and authentic historical document known to humankind, but I believe that mainline Christianity often interprets part of it in a way that is damaging to God's cause. Sure, it's supernatural. It's mere existence and preservation attests to that. It is God's words and advice to humankind. But it's also much more than that—and, perhaps at the same time, somewhat less than what some may think.

The Bible is a collection of books containing:

- Poetry
- Prose
- Historical records of ancient Hebrew life
- Storytelling (which, before being written down, existed for possibly centuries or millennia as oral tradition)
- Apocalyptic language
- Letters from the early Church apostles to various churches
- Historical accounts of the life of Jesus, some of His followers, and early organized Christianity

What the Bible *is not* also makes an interesting list. I think the Bible is not:

- A science textbook (where is the speed of light defined in the Bible?)
- The only revelation of God to humankind
- The only spiritual authority in the lives of spiritual people (I believe that God's other revelations—the physical creation, the Body of Christ on Earth, and the Spirit of God speaking directly to the hearts of His people—are also valid spiritual authorities for authentic followers of Jesus)
- The fourth member of the Trinity

The Bible is a tool that did not exist until recent history. The apostle Paul probably did not have access to all the books of the New Testament since many of them were letters to churches from other apostles, like John and Peter. The Bible will no longer be needed when we are face–to–face with God Himself. It is crucial that we read it and study it and live by its principles, but we must understand it in its broader context. The Bible is not really "the Word of God." The Bible is Scripture. The Word of God is Jesus (see John 1). The Bible is not Jesus. It tells us about Him, but we must not put the Bible on the pedestal where Jesus Christ actually belongs. Knowledge about the Bible is not a substitute for relationship with the Person of the Bible. The difference is like night and day.

I would suggest an idea that you may either find compelling or heretical. I have gained a greater appreciation for the Bible by considering it as follows:

Let's assume that, instead of the Bible being the definitive resource that describes to us all the attributes of God, the deep truths about life and the universe, and the way we ought to act in certain situations, it's more like this:

There are fundamental truths that exist—and have always existed—in the universe. For example, God is love; God loves me; I am to love others; God created everything. These truths have existed long before the Bible even existed. Early people of God knew these things about God even before the Bible existed. God wants these fundamental truths to be learned and followed by all people everywhere. God has put in place *several* revelations of these truths; *all* are important and beneficial to us. The Bible is but one of these revelations.

In other words, rather than the Bible being the first go-to source for all matters relating to life and love, we understand first that life and love exist; therefore, I will go to the Bible to learn more about them, as well as to all the other revelations of truth that God has provided for us. These other revelations include the Body of Christ on Earth (the gathering of all individual believers together in unity), the created universe, prophecies spoken to me from men and women of God, and my own spirit interacting with God's Spirit within me, to name a few. When a gifted Christian teacher speaks a truth to me that deeply impacts me, causes me to fall on my face in adoration of an infinite and powerful God, and moves me to the point that it creates lasting positive change in my spirit and personality, I consider that this speaker is altogether as "inspired" as the Scriptures in the Bible.

Heresy? Why would we consider that the speakers and writers in biblical times were more inspired than those today? Do we actually believe that God is not able to supernaturally speak His truth into our lives through the people that He has chosen to be His mouthpiece today? What makes the Spirit of God speaking through Moses any more or less trustworthy than the Spirit of God speaking through C.S. Lewis or my pastor, Dennis, in Greenwood, Louisiana?

I know some readers may believe I am diminishing the power and authority of the Bible, so let me assure you that I am not. The Bible remains our best revelation about certain aspects of God's truth, perhaps the best revelation of God among all those I've listed. Yet, I don't believe that the Bible is meant to be our only authority. Jesus Himself did not command us to follow the Bible at all costs. He told us to follow Him. We are not first and foremost to obey the Bible; we are called first to love God, then love others, then to live justly in this world. Of course, the Bible helps to guide us in this effort, and certain truths only appear in the Bible. In that sense, it is an incredible and necessary revelation of the true heart of God toward His people.

* * * * * * * * * * *

So, of course, the Bible is trustworthy and we ought to learn from it in its proper context. We see some strange things as we study it— things that can't be explained by mere Newtonian physics. Miracles happen, strange occurrences strike fear into the hearts of people (the fire of God consuming Elijah's sacrifice, stones and all; see 1 Kings 18), and scientifically unexplainable things are described that just cannot be logically explained (the sun standing still, the darkness and earthquake when Jesus died; see Josh. 10:13; Matt. 27:45-54). Unexplainable, that is, without quantum physics. We discuss elsewhere in this book that the miracles of Jesus required some awesome displays of molecular and subatomic science (for example, expanding a few loaves of bread enough to feed thousands, and healing incomplete limbs). The Bible talks very simply about these things, as if we ought to easily accept them. If we listen with our hearts, we can, but not if our understanding is limited by that which is merely physical.

- With quantum physics, things don't always make sense.
- With quantum physics, things happen on a subatomic level and are not logically intuitive.
- With quantum physics, things happen that are not necessarily predictable.
- With quantum physics, things happen that seem to defy common sense and the experiences that our five senses can absorb.
- With quantum physics, things can be explained that previously were considered mysterious or unknowable.

Interestingly, this list is equally adequate to describe God's modus operandi. Leaving everything else the same, let's replace "quantum physics" with "God" in the list above and then reconsider each item in the list:

- With God, things don't always make sense.
- With God, things happen on a subatomic level and are not logically intuitive.
- With God, things happen that are not necessarily predictable.
- With God, things happen that seem to defy common

sense and the experiences that our five senses can absorb.

- With God, things can be explained that previously were considered mysterious or unknowable.

Is quantum physics *the only* language of God? No, but it's one of them. Is science the only way to understand God? Of course not, but it is one expression of His character. Is mathematics the method God uses to communicate truths to us about the physical world? It's one of His methods, but intuition plays a larger role than most probably realize.

Once again, is it possible that the very reason we have such trouble intuitively understanding quantum physics is that we are trying to express spiritual truths with the language of mathematics? I suppose there is some of that going on. But we cannot afford to take it to either extreme. On the one hand, we have a segment of the Christian community that insists the Bible is the only thing we need, that everything is spiritualized, and that if it's not in the Bible then it's not true. At the other end of the spectrum are those who put *all* their eggs in the basket of scientific discovery, strict biblical literalism, or logic. The truth, as always, is in the middle of a path that is straight and narrow, but leads to a gate that is wider than imagined. On one side of the path is what we see, feel, touch, and experience pragmatically. On the other side of the path are mystery, quantum physics, dreams, and intuition. We walk steadfastly down the center and use it all for God's glory.

CHAPTER 18

The Incredible Spiritual Brain

*T*he Wisdom Paradox is a book by Elkhonon Goldberg about how the brain becomes better at such things as wisdom as time goes on, even while the brain itself suffers loss and shrinkage and becomes intellectually "less capable" as we age. The superstars of physics that we read about—Albert Einstein, Richard Feynman[1]—accomplished their greatest work in their younger years. The brain simply isn't capable of maintaining its highest level of raw horsepower into our later years. However, the acquisition of wisdom is something that can continue to grow all our lives, and it is a quality that the Bible heartily recommends, especially in the Proverbs.

Goldberg primarily ties acquiring wisdom to pattern recognition. Pattern recognition in turn is brought about by a particular repeated stimulus that causes the synapses in our brains—the connections between our billions of brain cells—to hard-wire themselves into specific patterns that enhance our memory. Our brains are incredibly complex, to the point of being perhaps the most complexly constructed object in the known universe. Stars are simple, huge, burning masses of hydrogen and helium. Your brain has as many individual cells as there are stars in the Milky Way galaxy (billions!), and each individual cell may be connected by its synapses to as many as 100,000 other cells. These synapse connections re-organize and re-wire themselves as we live life, and the more often we undergo a specific experience, the stronger and more numerous the synapse connections become that deal with that particular life experience. For instance, if you are an actor in a community theater and you need to memorize lines for a two-hour play, then you will probably have to study and rehearse for quite some time to get all the lines committed to memory (unless you are one of an extreme minority with a true photographic memory).

As you read and repeat and rehearse your lines, the intimate connections in your brain between millions of brain cells (the synapses) are re-arranging themselves to help complete a circuit for the memory of your lines. These circuits are enhanced each time you exercise them, and they can become so ingrained that you never forget certain lines for the rest of your life. I remember dialogs from my high school German class from almost 30 years ago because those synapses have not only been re-wired, but super-glued together:

"Guten tag, Louise, wie geht's?"

"Danke, gut, und Dir?"

"Prima!"

Goldberg makes an interesting comment at one point in his book: that he is an agnostic with atheist leanings. Nevertheless, he quotes the wisdom of Solomon, and he has made me think very deeply and at length about what exactly wisdom really is and about the interface of spiritual with physical. The brain itself obviously has a lot to do with it. Goldberg (a renowned brain scientist) proposes that the brain and the mind are inseparable—you can't have one without the other. What he believes happens when a person dies and the brain turns to dust is another issue, but he makes an interesting point. The brain seems to be the link in the chain that enables the person's will and spiritual values to be changed into physical actions and, therefore, physical reality. When the brain dies, the person dies.

Brain Waves and God Vibes

We know that the brain is made up of molecules and atoms, so it also obeys the same theories I'm trying to define; that is, on a sub-atomic level, it has a lot to do with God vibes! And if this is true, then the human brain is the pinnacle of communication between physical and spiritual. Or maybe I should say it's the quintessential example of a material thing operating on a spiritual level. Brain waves create moral decisions. Brain waves and the resulting decisions and physical realities are precisely what contribute to sin, love, wars, hate, intelligent conversation, the composition of prayers, the groans resulting from my stupid jokes, and the interpretation of emotions on another's face. The brain waves themselves are being informed by a deeper mechanism—either the spirit or the soul, depending on whether a particular individual has been regenerated by the Holy Spirit. But the brain is what makes these deep-down decisions real and brings thought and intention to physical reality.

This physical reality is merely one of several possible manifestations of the brain/mind/will, since other non-physical manifestations could also result from activities of the brain/mind/will (a thought, an emotion, and so forth). So it seems that the line between brain/mind/will/mental/spiritual/physical reality is not at all a clear one and that it is sufficiently blurred to conclude that all of reality is at least incredibly closely connected, perhaps too closely to delineate one state of being from the next. This is consistent with the idea elsewhere in this book that all aspects of our lives, whether washing dishes or preaching from the pulpit, can be seen as holy and redemptive (see also the chapter "Viva La Sparks!").

The process of becoming like Jesus relies strongly on pattern recognition—in other words, wisdom—which is one reason that God seldom subverts *process* in our lives. Rarely do we instantly and freely receive the spiritual upgrades we seek. God just does not like to do it without *process*. Process is the tool that God uses to grow our faith, to teach us to rely on Him, and to show us the inadequacies of our old mindsets, because without process, synapses cannot be re-wired and lasting change cannot happen.

Learning from pattern recognition requires lots of time and lots of experiences that we can compare one to another. As we experience life—a very time-consuming process—we learn which *causes* trigger which *effects*. This kind of wisdom can only come from a statistically large number of experiences, which requires years of living in and amongst the people and circumstances that trigger these learning events. Eventually, we begin to notice patterns—a soft answer, for instance, can turn away wrath. A loving touch can bring peace to a troubled soul. A certain word of encouragement at just the right time can bring out the hero in someone. A large number of experiences can teach us much about life, people, God, and eternity. But there is a caveat.

We must be attentive. Intentional. We must be watching and looking for the lessons as we're in the middle of them. We must be cognizant of the fact that God *is*—present tense, right now—in the process of teaching us something. So what is the lesson we're supposed to learn? In this way, we can actually accelerate our spiritual growth. If we remain ignorant of the fact that our entire life is about gaining a large sample of experiences from which to learn and gain wisdom and become more like Jesus, and therefore remain ignorant of the lessons we are to be learning, then all those life experiences that require years and years of our precious time may be wasted. It's like not paying attention in class. After class is over, it's too late to get the knowledge you need since you blew your chance when the opportunity presented itself.

One more caveat: in addition to being attentive and watching for learning experiences, and intentionally seeking the wisdom and knowledge that God would have us gain in the process, we must also tie our experiences and wisdom into a spiritual viewpoint of the world that surrounds us. Nothing is merely physical. Everything has at least some spiritual component in it. Sure, we can be intentional about learning from our experiences, but unless they are understood in the context of God's eternal perspective, we will not really gain the benefit we ought to gain.

We will end up translating our new wisdom into a "what's in it for me" type of soulish, self-centered thinking. Wisdom can certainly lead to knowledge or self-preservation, but more often than not, God has ideas about what's best for the other person. As the apostle Paul so clearly describes in First Corinthians 13, it's all about love. The kind of wisdom that comes from years of experiences, with our minds and hearts intentionally focused on what God would have us learn, and our wills actively pursuing Christ's character through it all, is the kind of wisdom that can change lives and the world for the better.

The Wisdom Paradox

The wisdom paradox is that as our brains—and by extension our physical bodies—become less capable as we age, our level of wisdom and the strength of our will ought to rise steadily and even exponentially as we learn to more and more focus on God's will for us. This creates in us an ability to literally see into the immaterial realm upon which all of reality is built and make decisions that have long-lasting, positive, eternal effects. I have been talking about years of experience and the necessity of a statistically large sample of circumstances from which to learn, but this also can be affected by the spiritual realm, because God is able to *"restore to you the years that the locust hath eaten,"* (Joel 2:25 KJV) to restore you to a place you should have been had you been obeying God and living for Him all along. These eternal and spiritual effects of increasing wisdom can be accelerated, and of course, we all know young Christians who are particularly precocious in their levels of wisdom and spiritual maturity.

God is the God of miracles, and this does not only include outwardly manifested physical miracles. We know that Jesus rearranged physical material when He healed lepers and turned five loaves into a meal for 5,000. So too He can rearrange the material in your brain—the synapses, the chemical composition of your brain matter, the physical synaptic connections between brain cells—to accelerate your growth or to restore the growth you may be lacking due to the mistakes you've made in your past life or some type of abuse or neglect that stunted your spiritual growth or knowledge of Jesus.

Quantum Physics and Prophecy

There is a type of spiritual gift called prophecy. This is not simply the ability to foretell the future. It may involve that at times, but prophecy is really about speaking out the innermost, loving heart of God to people in the context of their everyday lives and struggles. Those who operate effectively in this gift have the ability to see things that may be hidden from the rest of us, namely, the struggles an individual is having and/or the gift that God is holding out to that individual that will help them rise above and conquer the circumstances that are weighing them down. It could take the form of problem solving, or a message about a behavior that needs to be worked on or changed, or simply a blessing or a big upgrade that will take the beneficiary to a new level of relationship or victory in the Christian life.

At some point in this process of prophecy, the prophet has to experience brain waves that allow him or her to form the thought that needs to be heard by the recipient. These waves will turn into words and be spoken out loud, and these spoken words and intention will have the authority of Almighty God behind them. From where do these thoughts originate? Across that boundary between God's eternal immaterial plane and our physical existence of brain chemicals and cells comes a message. This message is an ethereal, immaterial substance, an entity as real as the book you're holding, but as fleeting and ghostly as the human spirit. It literally becomes one of those statistically measurable experiences that we can add to our large wealth of experiences that, in turn, will cause new synaptic connections in our brains or re-enforce existing ones, thus causing an increase in wisdom.

For this to happen, the physical synapses in the prophet's brain must somehow be stimulated in such a way as to form a thought that is consistent with the heart of God and can be transmogrified into a meaningful message that will subsequently cause the *hearer's* brain synapses to fire in such a way as to receive a message that will make a significant change in their attitude, outlook, or persona. Whew! We're talking about an incredibly complex cycle that moves from Spirit life, into the prophet's mind and brain, out his or her mouth, into the ears of the recipient, through the synapses of the recipient's brain, down into his or her spirit, then back again to change behaviors, attitudes, or mental composition (whatever the need of the moment might be). What an amazing quantum-spiritual-physical-and-back-again dance! The process might be viewed like this:

Recipient recognizes a need within or desires input from prophet.

Recipient's request could be instigated by a merely physical need (requiring quantum rearrangement of physical particles in the recipient's body), an emotional or mental need (synaptic re-wiring of the brain), or spiritual need (solely in the spirit level of existence)

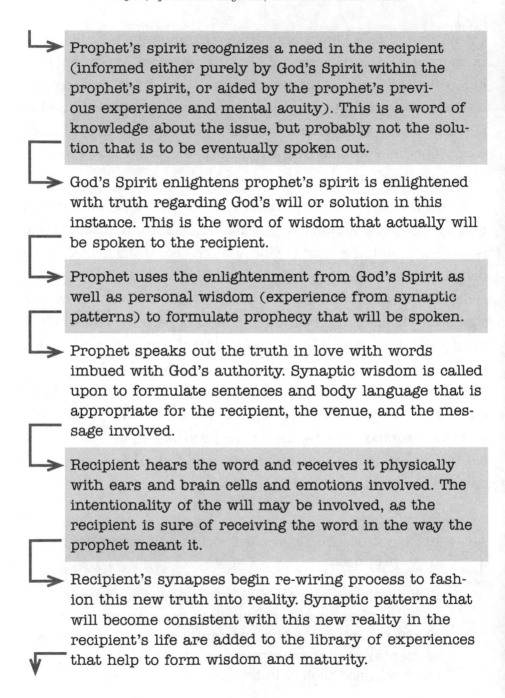

Prophet's spirit recognizes a need in the recipient (informed either purely by God's Spirit within the prophet's spirit, or aided by the prophet's previous experience and mental acuity). This is a word of knowledge about the issue, but probably not the solution that is to be eventually spoken out.

God's Spirit enlightens prophet's spirit is enlightened with truth regarding God's will or solution in this instance. This is the word of wisdom that actually will be spoken to the recipient.

Prophet uses the enlightenment from God's Spirit as well as personal wisdom (experience from synaptic patterns) to formulate prophecy that will be spoken.

Prophet speaks out the truth in love with words imbued with God's authority. Synaptic wisdom is called upon to formulate sentences and body language that is appropriate for the recipient, the venue, and the message involved.

Recipient hears the word and receives it physically with ears and brain cells and emotions involved. The intentionality of the will may be involved, as the recipient is sure of receiving the word in the way the prophet meant it.

Recipient's synapses begin re-wiring process to fashion this new truth into reality. Synaptic patterns that will become consistent with this new reality in the recipient's life are added to the library of experiences that help to form wisdom and maturity.

→ Prophet learns from the experience and the prophet's synapses are also re-wired/strengthened from what was learned, which results in a stronger prophetic gift/understanding for future similar situations

This is an incredible tango between the Spirit of God, the spirits of people, the subatomic chemical and electrical reactions in the synapses of the brain, the tongue and lips forming the words, the vibration of air that transmits sound waves to the hearer, the vibration of the ear drums, the communication of these minute vibrations to the brain, further synapses firing and interpreting the message, into the spirit of the recipient and back to the heart of God.

This is an excellent example of the apostle Paul's description of life in the Spirit: *"For from him and through him and to him are all things..."* (Rom. 11:36). The message, gift, or encouragement first comes from the Father, through His Spirit in us, is passed amongst us in one of many different forms, then returns to the Father from whom it began. Given the incredibly complex interactions of physical, chemical, electrical, mental, emotional, and spiritual dynamics at work here, how can we possibly draw a line between where the "physical" and "spiritual" realms begin and end?

As you already know, I believe that we can't. It is really not possible to separate one realm of existence from the other. All things are holy; all things are permeated with the presence and life force of God's Spirit; all things can be redeemed for physical, mental, emotional, and spiritual good; and all things are eternal in nature. Let us live our lives in such a way as to appreciate and optimize the value of the incredible, spiritual brain God has given us.

Endnote

1. Richard Feyman (1918-1988) was a Nobel Prize winning physicist who was very influential in modern physics. He helped popularize quantum physics for the public by his affable and easily accessible writing style.

CHAPTER 19

Over The Airwaves

Television astounds me. Ever since those old black-and-white episodes from my childhood, I have witnessed the miracle of transmitting people, words, and emotions through the air. Today we have high definition and Blu-ray, making the images we see on the television amazingly lifelike. But it's not really a person in there. Or a penguin. And that's not a real pastrami sandwich on that cooking show. They are just images.

Yes, total common sense, I know. Please realize I'm not trying to insult your intelligence. I only want to point out that in our electronic world, the things, places, and people we see on television are more real to us than we may care to admit. These moving images make us cry, make us angry, make us laugh, and cause us to think. We see personalities on the screen, and we think that we get to know them, empathize with them, hate them, or love them. But those are not really people in the television. It's not even images of people. It's a bunch of tiny little dots of various colors that, when combined in the correct fashion and viewed from a distance, resemble those things, places, and people with which we are familiar.

Look at a television screen up close. Not for too long, because it's probably not good for you. You'll see either little dots on a conventional tube television or tiny little squares on an LCD. Even high definition television betrays the little bits of color and light that make up the image you're enjoying. Television broadcast technology allows us to view a scene somewhere—with today's machinery, anywhere in the universe—and break it down into its color constituents at a resolution only practically limited by bandwidth and the number of transistors that can fit onto a chip of silicon. Then it is translated into a format that can be beamed through space for what is probably an infinite distance on invisible electromagnetic waves. Then that electromagnetic radiation is collected, re-assembled as the original scene, and the television is instructed to put a dot of a particular color at a particular place on the screen. Televisions do this with millions of different dots of color, and they re-write the entire screen fast enough—many times per second—to give us the illusion of a natural scene moving in natural time. We see a lion stalking its prey or Rachel Ray pouring a little EVOO into her saucepan, and it looks exactly like real life.

Is this not itself a miracle?

We can talk with loved ones on the phone and laugh and cry at the sound of their voice. We can take it a step further and email a video, or post it on YouTube, showing our facial expressions, our pain, and our joy to the rest of the world. We can communicate with loved ones via webcast, the next best thing to being with them in person since it allows real-time access to facial expressions and all the nuances that friends or lovers enjoy about each other. Imagine a soldier on duty overseas, communicating with his wife and child in real time over the Internet. That image of Daddy is real. It's really him on that computer screen! We don't stop to think that this image is only a bunch of dots arranged on an LCD screen. It's Daddy! And he's talking to us from 9,000 miles away!

This is a precise example of how the physical world of electronics, wires, and plastic interfaces with the immaterial world of emotion, thought, and intention. We do not distinguish between the technology and the actual object. We really are talking to Daddy, just as if he were here, face-to-face. The only difference is we cannot touch him.

The emotions are just as real though, and this leads us into a reality in which the unseen is as real as the seen.

As you sit reading this book, there are an untold number of electromagnetic signals passing right through your body and brain. But none of them register on your radar unless you have the correct machine available to gather and translate the signals. Every electromagnetic signal for every television signal, every radio station, every shortwave communication, even gamma rays and other signals emanating from deep space, are all flying right through your body. If you're talking on a cell phone, and you turn such that your body is between your cell phone and the cell tower, it doesn't matter. You can be inside a building with concrete walls and the signal still gets to your cell phone.

Immersed in the
Invisible Wavelengths of God's Blessings

The Kingdom of God is like that. Ephesians 1:3 tells us that God has blessed us—past tense—in the Heavenly realms with every spiritual blessing in Christ. Second Peter 1:3 tells us that everything we need for life and for godliness has been (past tense) given to us. All the provisions, all the growth, all the maturity, all the gifts, all the fruits of the Spirit that we will ever receive are ours right now. Just like those ubiquitous electromagnetic waves that surround us everywhere we go, so we are immersed in all the blessings of God in real time. If you are His child, then you are part of His Kingdom, and in His Kingdom there is no lack. We cannot escape the provisions and the abundance of God, but it is quite easy to overlook them. It is altogether possible to be immersed in God's favor and never use it or gain the advantages of possession.

How can this be? Let me tell you a story.

Imagine a young man living under the freeway in Los Angeles. Let's call him John. John's bed is the cardboard he scrounges from behind the supermarket. His pillow is the abandoned t-shirt he found beside the highway. His food comes from restaurant dumpsters and garbage cans. John does not like his style of living, but circumstances have forced him into it. Yet he is heir to a massive fortune. A distant relative has passed away, leaving tens of millions of dollars, mansions, and a life of luxury to John, who is the last living member of the family.

He is an heir. He is rich beyond his dreams. He actually owns everything he could possibly need for many lifetimes. Yet, his circumstances define that he is homeless, hungry, and dirty. He does not actually enjoy the fruits of his riches. He does not actually participate in the lifestyle that such fabulous provisions offer. His time on the streets has taught him that he will always have provisions — he knows where the good leftovers are, and he actually can choose every night between Italian, Mexican, or seafood. He does not have to pay rent, and there is always something over his head to keep him dry in case it rains. He is surviving.

What is the primary factor keeping John from living the life that is rightfully his? Knowledge. If he only knew that he was an heir, and how to contact the people who are desperately searching for him, then it could all be his. His riches come through the knowledge of who he is and whom his inherited estate appointed as the executor or provider of the fortune.

If we take another look at Second Peter 1:3, we will learn that not only has God given us everything we need for life and godliness, but we are instructed on the method of obtaining those riches — *"through our knowledge of Him who called us."* Consistent with John's circumstances, we too stand to gain an unfathomable inheritance through knowledge, in this case knowledge of who Jesus is, who He wants to be for us, and the fact that we are joint-heirs with Christ and have the right to accept the awesome privileges and inheritance He has to offer. Knowledge that Jesus is the One who has called us and offers us these riches is paramount.

Now imagine that John has been found. The executors of the estate somehow located him under Highway 101 and explained the whole story. This is where the rubber meets the road. We could imagine a number of scenarios taking place, some making a lot more sense than others:

1. John does not believe that the fortune is actually his. He says "I don't believe a word of it. It's not for me, and I think you're scamming me." This would be a ridiculous thing for him to say, even if it was true. At least he ought to take a shot at it. What's to lose? The chances that these folks took all that trouble to find him and think up such a story is itself intriguing enough to at least pursue it to see how much of it is true. The downside is that his circumstances don't change. But the upside potential is huge!

John's response here is akin to the many who have been confronted with the reality of God's Kingdom, but refuse to begin walking with Jesus. The inheritance is there for them if they would simply accept the free gift from God, but they miss out due to skepticism, doubt, stubbornness, or ignorance. Not a very smart thing to do, but very common in today's world.

2. John might feel that he doesn't deserve this lifestyle that is being offered to him. He may very well believe the whole story, but feel that his past behavior has been so atrocious that no one would actually allow him to step into this position of wealth and authority that is being offered him. Pre-Christians, in other words, sometimes feel that the deeds they have done will prohibit them from ever entering Heaven. Once again, hogwash. This is the whole point: you *can't* get your life together by yourself. That's

precisely why we need God and why He tells us to come as we are. If we wait until we "get things cleaned up" in our lives, we will never come to Him.

3.   John tells the executors, "No thanks, I have food to eat and a place to sleep at night. I believe that the inheritance is mine, but I just don't have the motivation to pursue it. Besides, think of all the responsibilities, the work I would have to do. I would have to learn to live in polite society. I would have to take a shower every day!" This is the response of some Christians who hear all their lives about the inheritance that can be theirs in Jesus, but do not have the motivation or discipline to pursue it. The status quo is always easier. It might be embarrassing to get into some Christian circle and feel like I don't fit in. Besides, I just don't really know how to take the next step! These folks are into Christianity for the fire insurance, but don't value personal relationship with God, which is really what it's all about.

4.   John could also accept the invitation, move to the compound in Beverly Hills, but live down the street in the guesthouse, never actually entering the mansion or driving the Maserati, or even seeing his new house! He knows it's there right behind the stone wall, but he will not look at it, enter into the gates, or enjoy the silk sheets. When asked why, he stammers a bit and finally replies, "Well, I guess it's just too good to be true. How can it really be that fabulous? How can it actually be mine? What did I do to deserve this? I've got it pretty good right here anyway."

I believe this is where many Christians are living right now. The guesthouse is nice, it's secure, we're being provided for, and it's really all we need to survive, even with some style. But it's not the whole inheritance. We haven't actually seen the mansion. We're pretty sure it's there behind the wall, but we're apprehensive about actually walking down the street and entering into the gate. This can't possibly be all mine! And it can't possibly be this easy! Just turn the knob and walk in?

What if the guard doesn't recognize me? What if the guard dogs eat me? What if the hired help curse me? What if there's some condition attached? What if I have to act a certain way to make it all work? What if I won't know how to act in certain situations? What if others criticize me or think I've taken advantage of the system, accepting things that weren't mine, owning things I did not buy or work for? What if it's not really true? What if I walk into those gates and there's just another cardboard box for me to live in? It's comfortable where I am. It's nice here in the guesthouse. Do I really need more? Don't I have it made for the rest of my life? If these people are real and this inheritance is real, then I'm taken care of right where I am. Is there really a need to pursue all of that mansion-riches-wealth stuff? *Is it really worth the risks?*

5. John could dive in with both feet, claim all the riches that are rightfully his, begin studying how it all works—how to drive the Maserati, how the security system in the mansion works, how all the accounts are set up—and start responsibly dealing with his riches in ways that will honor the memory of his loved ones who left it to him. He could provide for the needs of some chosen charitable organizations and enhance the community in which he lives. This is the only proper response.

It is possible for John to be immersed in the favor and riches of inheritance, but remain in the guesthouse for the rest of his life. Why he would want to do this, I can't imagine. I think one of the most important things the Church needs to learn today is the truth about the depth and richness of the inheritance that surrounds us if we are walking with Christ. Like electromagnetic waves, these provisions permeate every part of us; they surround us, and they are immediately available to us if we simply have the right receiver to interpret them with. They are not visible to us where we are.

It is necessary to grab that handle, twist it with conviction, walk through those gates, and march confidently by faith into the things that have been promised us. The step of faith always precedes the provision. Otherwise, faith would completely lose its meaning. If we waited until we were sure about everything before we stepped out into our inheritance, then faith would not be involved at all. There's no faith in accepting things that we clearly see. Faith is exercised when we act in belief on what we cannot see, and this is what demonstrates to God our surrender to Him and our complete confidence in His ability to provide. Yes, there is risk. But who better to trust than the One who created you and put those desires in your heart in the first place?

Like electromagnetic waves, these provisions are invisible until acted upon by certain interpreters and tools. We can't see television signals drifting through the air, but we know they surround us, and we simply need to turn on the television in order to see the information that those waves are carrying. As children of promise, we need to turn on the switch to start the flow of provision and inheritance in our lives. How?

First, we must understand the inheritance God is holding out to us, which is intimately tied to our identity in Christ. This is unique for each individual. It's about what you were designed to do, what you love or hate, what you must fight in this life, what you must champion and support. It's about your deepest desires, the things that make you groan, make you cry, that affect you deep down in your gut, the thing that C.S. Lewis describes this way:

Even in your hobbies, has there not always been some secret attraction which the others are curiously ignorant of—something, not to be identified with, but always on the verge of breaking through, the smell of cut wood in the workshop or the clap-clap of water against the boat's side? Are not all lifelong friendships born at the moment when at last you meet another human being who has some inkling (but faint and uncertain even in the best) of that something which you were born desiring and which, beneath the flux of other desires and all the momentary silences between the louder passions, night and day, year by year, from childhood to old age, you are looking for, watching for, listening for? You have never *had* it. All the things that have ever deeply possessed your soul have been but hints of it—tantalizing glimpses, promises never quite fulfilled, echoes that died away just as thcy caught your ear. But if it should really become manifest—if there ever came an echo that did not die away but swelled into the sound itself—you would know it. Beyond all possibility of doubt you would say "Here at last is the thing I was made for." We cannot tell each other about it. It is the secret signature of each soul, the incommunicable and unappeasable want, the thing we desired before we met our wives or made our friends or chose our work, and which we shall still desire on our death beds, when the mind no longer knows wife or friend or work. While we are, that is. If we lose it, we lose all.[1]

These signals that surround us and permeate us every day must be translated in the context of our relationship with Jesus Christ, the work that the Holy Spirit is attempting to do in our lives, and the people that God the Father wants us to become, which is consistent with the deepest desires God placed in our hearts. We were not designed to remain static in our lives, but to continue growing and maturing until the end. We must pray, we must discuss these things with trusted Christian advisors, we must get prophetic words about our future and our inheritance, we must introspect and ask the Holy Spirit to reveal to us who He wants us to become. When we figure out what our true identity is in Christ, then we can begin pursuing it.

The pursuit is primarily about obedience. We are right to believe that God's love toward us is unconditional, but His promises of growth and abundance are very conditional. The Bible is clear that *if* we ask, we will receive. *If* we knock then it will be opened up to us. *If* we seek then we will find. First John 5:14 says *"This is the confidence we have in approaching God: that **if** we ask anything according to His will, He hears us."* We can be Christians and disobey God. We can be swamped in lack and mediocrity and still make it to Heaven. Those who want to excel in life and experience the fullness of God must learn to be more and more obedient to His calling as we grow and mature.

This growth and maturity is contextual with the deepest desires that God has put in each of our hearts. We can get clues to what that life calling is through careful prayer, attentive listening to the Holy Spirit in our lives, and joyful obedience to the things He has called us to do, but we must then be obedient to the calling He has given us. Then these invisible signals that surround us can swell into the sound itself, and we will have at last found the reason we were placed on this Earth at just such a time as this.

Endnote

1.   C.S. Lewis, *The Problem of Pain* (New York: Harper One, 2001).

CHAPTER 20

The God of Physics

Tao, God, and Spirit are just a few words that appear in book titles in the physics and science section of the local bookstore. Many titles have strongly spiritual implications, which is actually quite surprising given the naturalistic bent of much of modern science. As we study the world of the incomprehensibly small or the infinitely large, we can't help being drawn toward the conclusion that there is more here than meets the eye. Quantum physics is one of the languages that describe this invisible world to us and at times its practice and conclusions border on the mystical. Even secular scientists and authors suggest by their book titles and content that there is some metaphysical aspect to what they are writing about. This just seems natural given the questions of ultimate origin that we are discussing.

Some scientists and laypeople strongly reject the concept of "mystical" or "metaphysical" or "spiritual." They reason that the material world is all there is because only the material universe can be scientifically studied and quantified. But theirs is a frail and faulty argument. Any honest thinker or scientist will admit that of all possible knowledge that can be known, we have discovered only a tiny part. The vast majority of what *can be* known remains to be discovered, so it seems rather intellectually arrogant to state conclusively that there can be no spiritual reality or to insist that God cannot exist.

If we've only discovered one percent of what can be known, how can we know what is not known? If we admit we don't know 99 percent of what can be known, how can we know what is in that 99 percent? What if someone had said to Galileo hundreds of years ago "There are no galaxies"? Making this statement would not, of course, cause galaxies to stop existing. It's just that they had not yet been discovered. If a scientist insists that the existence of God cannot be empirically proven, could we not respond in the same way? There was a time when Galileo was ignorant of the true nature of the universe. Knowledge is cumulative. Eventually the true nature of the physical universe was discovered. Why not eventually the existence and true nature of God?

These same scientists who claim that God cannot be empirically proven to exist believe that there must be such a particle as a graviton even though it has not yet been empirically proven to exist. This also seems somewhat duplicitous.

The Building Blocks of Scientific Inquiry

One of the building blocks of the scientific method is hypothesis. We first hypothesize about what we believe is true based on our experience, evidence, and previous knowledge. Then we construct experiments to validate our hypothesis. If the experiment fails to support the hypothesis, we start over or go a different direction. If it corroborates our hypothesis, then we get peer reviews, or move on to more in-depth experiments for further validation, or write articles, or all of the above. Then, and only then, may our hypothesis possibly become what we know as *fact* or *law,* and even those words are suspect at times.

Physicists hypothesize the existence of the graviton based on observations of the universe, from which they conclude there must be some kind of particle through which the force of gravity works much like photons are the particles through which electromagnetism is transmitted. Funnily enough, the same argument is used for the existence of God—observations of reality that lead to the conclusion that He must exist. But by insisting that anything spiritual or unseen cannot exist, modern naturalistic science eliminates the discoverability of the spiritual realm simply by the way they frame the discussion.

If I sit down across the table from you and we agree to discuss birds (ornithology), but I state before we begin that there is no such thing as pileated woodpeckers and we are not allowed to discuss them, then what chance do we have of learning about pileated woodpeckers? We have no chance at all, because the discussion was framed to eliminate the possibility of discovery. And it's important to realize that this decision is completely arbitrary. What possible reason could I have to eliminate pileated woodpeckers from the conversation, given the extensive evidence that they're out there, except that I *don't want to learn about them*?

What possible reason could there be for eliminating the possibility of the supernatural from the discussion about ultimate origins? It's arbitrary, and I believe it's born out of a fear that if we allow the possibility of God into scientific discussions, and we happen to prove that God really does exist and really did create the universe, then we must become accountable. It would be very difficult to remain atheistic or agnostic after someone scientifically proves the existence of God!

Now, I'm the first to admit that scientifically "proving" that God exists could be difficult. We can point to a billion effects that required an intelligent cause, but that's not the same as proving the existence of the cause. To prove the existence of something, we need to achieve a few particular milestones. We see the effects of gravity, but no one yet has seen a graviton. If the graviton exists, there will have to be some empirical proof beyond just the effects it causes, because we might discover that gravity is caused by some other force or entity.

To prove that God exists, we would have to prove that all the effects we see require a specific kind of cause that only God could fulfill. Exclusivity can be a tough nut to crack. If I want to read a book in my house at night, I can obtain reading light by a number of different causes that are quite distinct from one another. I could light a candle, providing photons for reading via the burning of a substance. I could turn on the light, which provides light from the glowing of a resistor being electrically overheated by electrons moving through a tungsten filament. I could walk outside, and if the moon is full and bright, I could use sunlight reflected from its surface. I could break a glow stick, which uses a chemical reaction to create light. Considering all these sources, can I scientifically and empirically answer the question, "What is the source of light?" Not at all! The question is incomplete, and there are too many answers. Exclusivity is elusive, but it all depends on how we frame the question.

We can view all the seeming effects for which we believe an intelligent Creator must be the cause, but in order to convince those naturalistic scientists we would have to prove that God must be the *only* cause. For us believers, it's not a problem believing that God is the prime mover. Even if we don't understand the science of it all, we still believe by faith. Intuition is actually a better way to understand God and His ways than pragmatism. We see into the spirit realm with our own spirits, our hearts speak to us as clearly as our minds, and we are convinced. We are convinced of the supernatural to such an extent that we see it manifested in physical ways, for instance in miracles of healing. For us, the faith and belief comes first; then it is often manifested in the physical realm. But for naturalistic scientists, it's the other way around—they want to see the physical evidence first.

Scientific Inquiry and Creationism

This is why I believe this study and conversation are so important. Different people respond in different ways to the move of God upon their hearts and minds. The apostle Paul wanted to approach the Corinthians with displays of power (see 1 Cor. 2:4), not with mental or spiritual arguments. He knew that this particular people group would respond to a display of God that spoke to their logical minds and emotions. Jews looked for miraculous signs, Paul said in First Corinthians 1:22, while Greeks looked for wisdom. If we approach the scientific community with the language that they speak, perhaps we can make some inroads.

Reasons to Believe, the ministry of Hugh Ross, is in the business of studying the universe and publishing evidence for design, specifically design by the loving Creator God of the Bible. He is now making it possible for scientists to believe in both an ancient universe *and* the God of the Bible. And he's doing it by appealing to their brains. God is quite clever—He'll take whatever path is necessary to invade the soul, psyche, or spirit of an individual. Then He'll work on balance. If a particular scientist is too pragmatic and logic-oriented, God will begin to move him toward an emotional, intuitive, spirit-based center. If a particular individual has too weak a foundation in reality and logic, then God will move her toward the center by emphasizing more left-brain theology. A good balance of left and right brain is needed, and the scientific community needs to learn this more than most.

God is indeed the God of physics, the God of the universe, and the God of science. He is the one responsible for dreaming up the resonance of the carbon atom and the precise speed of light. God is the one who determined the unfathomably fine-tuned scientific constants by which the universe continues to operate. He is also the one who gives us intuitive spirit-level input into our lives and attitudes. He operates freely across the boundary between the seen and unseen as if it weren't there, which then theoretically obviates its existence.

As we've already discussed, perhaps this boundary is simply a tool, or dare I say a crutch, we use to delineate two seemingly different ways of interfacing with reality. If we begin to view all of reality as an unbroken continuum between what we can physically see and what we cannot, and God is equally active in and concerned about every point on that continuum, then perhaps we can accomplish a lot more for His Kingdom in that we will:

- present a unified message about Jesus across all human disciplines,

- present this message as relevant to all types of thinkers, from creative non-linear types to strictly pragmatic scientific types,

- present a tenable spiritual alternative to the mystics among us, a lost method of spirituality that I believe was the original intended form of Christianity (study Christian Orthodoxy for a more complete revelation about the crucial role mysticism can play in our relationship with God),

- make a lot more sense of the quandaries we face when studying the true spiritual/natural/physical/ mystical nature of the human creature,

- and become equally relevant to technologically advanced cultures as to spiritualistic and technologically undeveloped ones.

If we can succeed in expanding our thoughts about God and His Kingdom across any perceived boundaries of technology, visibility, invisibility, culture, language, descriptions, and science, then we have taken a quantum leap forward in our understanding of the amazing God who both transcends and permeates all of creation. Someday, Paul tells us, we shall know fully, even as we are fully known (see 1 Cor. 13:12).

CHAPTER 21

Jehovah Rascal

Given the correct information about initial conditions, I could very accurately predict what will happen when a cue ball strikes another billiard ball (let's say the eight ball) at a known angle and a known velocity. This math, while intimidating to some, is actually quite straightforward and understandable. Even if you can't do the math, you can still logically understand the science. For instance, the harder you hit the eight ball with the cue ball, the further the eight ball will travel. This is very logical. We also know intuitively that as we hit it harder with the cue ball, the eight ball will not only travel farther, but will also be launched on its trajectory at a higher speed. All of this is relatively logical and predictable, and the science that proves and predicts what happens is easily understood. This is high school physics, or Newtonian Physics, named after one of the founding fathers of modern science, Isaac Newton.

Problem is, none of this is real life. Well, at least on a subatomic level.

Real existence is rooted in Quantum Physics, which states specifically that we cannot precisely know the outcome. Uncertainty is actually part of the equation. The math is not always predictable. In fact, in some cases it is never predictable. We make estimates and best guesses about the behavior of what we know as matter, and the outcomes are predictable enough on large scales that we can build computer chips, pacemakers, and personal computers. But on the level that we're talking about—at the core of the existence of all reality—we just don't know exactly what's going on. There certainly is an element of faith involved in all of this, but it's based on provable assumptions. Most of the time a silicon circuit wants to do such-and-such, so we can build a computer to do millions of mathematical operations per second and rely on its results. But the electrons moving around to make all this happen are as unpredictable as the Day of Pentecost.

Much of spirituality today is based on logic and predictability. Cause and effect are common indicators of life in Christ. For instance, *if* I do something wrong, *then* I expect to be punished or to suffer some consequence. *If* I read my Bible and pray every day, *then* I am assured wisdom and eternal life. If I interpret the Bible precisely literally and follow every command, *then* I will be pleasing to God. Once again, the math is very easy. These known conditions bring forth those predicted results that are by the book.

While the most common forms of Christian spirituality are based on strict cause and effect logic, biblical reality much more closely resembles the seemingly random world of quantum physics. And why should it not, since God's unpredictable and often clever schemings permeate all of what we know as "physical reality." God is certainly not predictable in any common sense of the word (study the stories of Jericho, Gideon, and Moses to get an idea of the surprises God has up His sleeves), and since His presence is woven throughout all the created order, it follows that this created order must exhibit some of that unpredictability. God has many names, like Jehovah Jireh (God as Provider: see Gen. 22:14; 1 John 4:9; Phil. 4:19), Jehovah Elyon (The Lord Most High: see Ps. 38:2), and Jehovah-Shalom (Lord of Peace: see Isa. 9:6; Rom. 8:31-35). But have you heard of Jehovah Rascal? This is the manifestation of God that sneaks up on you and throws you such a curve ball that it can change your perception of Him forever. And usually for the better.

Jehovah Rascal is the one who allows you to get down to the last day of the month with no money in the bank to pay the bills, then gives you $500 more than you actually need. He's the one who pulls you close to His chest when you've done something really stupid and says, "Let me tell you about all the ways that I am hopelessly in love with you." He's the one who lets you stew in your own juices for a while and then, with great humor and sensitivity, helps you laugh at yourself and fall in love with Him all over again. And you won't see it coming. He'll just knock you off your horse like He did Saul (Paul) and will love you until you can't resist Him. Then you'll laugh.

This is Quantum Physics. This is the unpredictability of an amazing, loving, personal God. This is why we must learn the crucial lesson of letting go of our own understanding. When you're driving down the highway in your car, of course you must hold onto your logic and reasoning, but when you're dealing with the God of the universe and His Kingdom realities, then you must take Proverbs 3:5 to heart: *"Trust in the Lord with all your heart and **do not lean on your own understanding"*** (NASB). It can't get any more black and white than that. Even now I hear people saying, "Surely God does not mean that we let go of our own reasoning! He gave us brains for a reason!" Read it again. *"Do not lean on your own understanding."* There is only one way to understand that statement. We must not rationalize it away. We simply need to learn to trust in the still, small voice of God no matter what our circumstances are screaming at us.

For those of you who need more convincing, there's more. You are not the one clearing your own path: *"In all your ways acknowledge Him and He will make your paths straight"* (Prov. 3:6). You are not the ultimate arbiter of your own purpose on this planet. *"Many are the plans in a man's heart, but it is the Lord's purpose that prevails"* (Prov. 19:21).

So am I encouraging you to dispose of all reason and logic with reckless abandon? Well, not so fast. Just like a 6-year-old driving a car is dangerous, action without equivalent experience could backfire. In Quantum Physics, even though results can be unpredictable, the science that tells us that the results are unpredictable comes from much observation, study, and experience and is based on identifiable laws. Scientists understand what that unpredictability looks like so they can identify the processes at work. If you simply stop paying your mortgage, insisting that God promised to provide all your needs, you may find God providing you a cardboard box to live in. God is a God of the mind and the Spirit. We must have renewed minds, but we must also have renewed spirits. Where is the line drawn between pragmatic knowledge and spiritual sensitivity?

I have come to believe there is no line. Just like we are blurring the line between physical reality and spiritual reality, so there really is no line between logical knowledge and spiritual intuition. We have developed this defining line between the two as a crutch to help us understand things more clearly, but I believe that as we come to know Christ better and better and become more sensitive to the voice of the Holy Spirit within us, then we will come to understand that revelations of all kinds are simply us communicating with our Loving God. We have the Spirit of Christ within us, we are one with Him, and we have His mind (see 1 Cor. 2:16), so we no longer need to distinguish between spiritual and logical thought. We need both, and we can freely float between them because we are learning that all of physical reality is founded upon unseen spiritual truth, so it's all part of the same dimension of existence.

When Jehovah Rascal sneaks up on you and allows some curve ball to throw you way off course (or what you have pre-conceived as your course in life), you can step back, chuckle, ask Him for wisdom and strength, and become a better spiritual person through the physical things that you are suffering. In God's world, the cue ball strikes the eight ball, and chocolate cake is formed! And this whole process is completely consistent with classic Newtonian Physics, with Quantum Physics, and with God's spiritual truth. Oh, and by the way, it's probably the best chocolate cake you have ever tasted!

CHAPTER 22

Supernatural Life

The origin of the word *super* is from the Latin for *above* or *beyond*.[1] When we talk about the supernatural life, we normally have in mind the idea of a life that is "above and beyond" the one we typically experience. I would argue that, for Christians, the supernatural life is the one that ought to seem normal to us, which would thus make the word *supernatural* mean something completely different!

I think it's important that we discuss what this supernatural life in Christ is about. The Bible makes it clear that none of us will ever figure it out completely (*"We see as in a mirror, dimly..."*; 1 Cor. 13:12 NASB), but we ought to at least agree on the lifestyle that God has clearly called us all into as it's defined in Scripture. It's not healthy to have an overly pragmatic view of life in Christ, in which one's entire belief system—and the way they choose to judge the behaviors and belief systems of others—is based on a strict, literal interpretation of the Bible, leaving no room for God to operate outside of the examples we can read about and study verse by verse, jot by jot, tittle by tittle.

I'm not suggesting we shouldn't study the Bible. In fact, I believe we don't study Scripture enough, because if we did, we would realize that God is totally unpredictable and can't be nailed down to a predetermined set of behaviors that we read about in the Bible. If there is any key lesson for us to learn from the stories in the Bible, it's that we cannot and must not think that we have God's methods all figured out.

Most Christians agree that God's methods cannot be fully understood or predicted, yet we tend to act like any Christian behavior not specifically discussed in the Bible must be from the devil or at the very least heretical or misguided. We see news of revivals and the unusual behavior that sometimes accompanies them, and we immediately declare that this cannot be from God. Sure, there are some strange things going on, and sure, the enemy can and probably does infiltrate and cause confusion. But we certainly must not throw the baby out with the bathwater. Of course there will be excesses and of course there will be enemy deceptions during effective workings of God's Spirit. We need not reject these moves of God, just pastor them! When did we start limiting God so severely, insisting that anything we haven't seen before is sinful?

Exploring Our Relationship with Jesus

We can sometimes be so incredibly cautious that we miss the best things God has on offer. We are already forgiven. Jesus paid the price for all the sins we will ever commit. No matter how many times we mess up and drop the ball, it's already forgiven and paid for. So why are we so paranoid about crossing the line? How did we ever become so fearful of going too far into what we consider "inappropriate behavior?" I would much rather be accused of trying too hard than never trying at all!

Obviously, I'm not talking about pushing the line of blatant sin. I'm not talking about taking sex as far as I can without crossing over into "inappropriate." I'm not talking about taking unjustly from others and trying to stop just short of causing harm. What I'm talking about is pushing the limits in our relationship with Jesus Christ. Do you think He would rather see those He loves pushing the envelope of blessing and inheritance, or sitting back being so overly cautious that they never cross the line into risk concerning what He has on offer for us? Isn't the whole parable about the talents about action and risk?

The servant who received one talent hid it in the ground. He did nothing. He was very careful. He was overly cautious. I Ie admitted that he did not want to risk losing the money and receiving punishment. The other two servants took a risk and invested the money, thus gaining a return. Aphorisms like "nothing ventured, nothing gained" have withstood the test of time for a reason. I can guarantee that you will never hit the target until you pull back the bow and release the arrow. More often than not, blessing requires risk. While God's love is unconditional, His promises are not. The promises of God are often very conditional:

- First, we must seek God with all our hearts, *then* provisions will come (see Matt. 6:33).

- Knock, *then* it will be opened; seek, *then* you will find; ask, *then* you will receive (see Matt. 7:7).

- Cry out for wisdom and understanding, seek for them as for silver, *then* they will be given (see Prov. 2:1-5).

The conditional nature of God's promises forces me into a decision: will I trust God or will I not? Can I, in spite of what my circumstances are screaming at me, put my faith in God for a different outcome than what I can logically calculate? Are the promises that God made to me in Scripture literally true or are they not? If I truly decide to trust in God with all my heart and *not* lean on my own understanding, will I fail or succeed?

The very discovery of quantum physics illustrates this concept. Remember Einstein's initial rejection of the science and implications of quantum physics? Apparently, he was either extremely skeptical or just not willing to take the risk associated with this new way of understanding ultimate reality. Either way, he lived to regret his initial decision and changed his mind as he risked a move forward into a new science, a new way of describing the world that he studied.

And it paid off for him. Not only did he recognize the validity of quantum physics, but it helped him further develop his science and theories, because, as it turns out, it's real. It works. The risk was well worth it, because it paid off in spades. It changed his most fundamental viewpoints about reality, and the same should be true as we approach the depths of God's truth for us.

In other words, are the spiritual principles upon which the unseen realm is based trustworthy and capable of changing my physical reality? If I answer "yes" and actually choose to live that way, then I am agreeing with the conclusion that all of reality is actually and literally built upon that which cannot be seen and that which was previously not understood. And is it not then logical and even wise to build up and exercise that part of my being rather than the physical stuff that I can see and touch?

Trying to Change Our Own Behavior

No one said it would be easy. Most Christians will admit that the Christian life is not easy. But most of them see it as a struggle to change their own behavior. Of course that's not easy. In fact, it's impossible! That's because we're not meant to undertake that kind of battle. We can concentrate on trying to kill our old way of living—the fleshly desires that spring up constantly and that are so difficult to control—*or* we can choose to concentrate on knowing Jesus, communing with Him, becoming like Him, loving Him more, worshiping Him more, and just let those old ways dry up and fall away because of our proximity to the healing light. These two methods of Christian living are exact opposites.

The first method (trying to change our behavior to fit an envisioned outcome) is like trying to cram the realities of quantum physics into the old framework of Newtonian physics. It simply can't work. The math that describes quantum interactions is actually as different as a foreign language. To force the wrong methodology (me trying to change my own behavior) into the framework of "Jesus does it for me" requires fantastic fortitude of character that most of us lack. I'm speaking from experience here. This is a very difficult process, and I suppose not even possible for most people. Our old habits, environmental influences, and our own weaknesses and liabilities all work against us, and it often ends up being just too difficult to "stay on the straight and narrow."

But the second method (striving to know Christ and letting His presence in us melt away what does not belong) seems much more effective and permanent. It is also a difficult task, perhaps even more difficult, but not so painful as the first method. Just like quantum physics, the math is exceedingly difficult to understand, but the results have incredible power to describe life in its fullness. It's tough because we are not accustomed to thinking this way, and changing one's thinking is often one of the most difficult tasks we will ever undertake. But it's good work. It's fun. It's encouraging because you can actually see the progress. Maybe not today, maybe not tomorrow, but next year you will be able to look back and see the progress you made, and it will be significant and good.

Measuring Progress

What does this "progress" look like?

Well, we know we can't judge our progress by physical indicators. We are instructed *not to* lean on our own understanding, because when we pray for change and then experience some kind of challenging trial, then by all *outward* appearances we are being defeated.

It may look to others like you are utterly failing (like the disciples felt when Jesus was killed, before they realized the larger plan). Even in your own eyes, you may feel totally defeated and wonder why life just isn't working out the way you dreamed it should. But God does not judge by these outward appearances.

God judges the heart, and He is especially concerned about things like your levels of patience, the strength of your faith, your ability to maintain your level of peace in the midst of trouble, and the progress you're making on the specific challenges that plague you. In a manner of speaking, the outward appearance of how things are going in your life is completely irrelevant, because it is in the very heat of these battles and heartaches that the best work inside your heart gets accomplished. In fact, it's almost a rule of life with Christ: things are *never* as they look on the outside.

When we get things backward in our walk of faith then we may struggle to come into the wonder and fullness that God has planned for us. Sometimes in the heat of battle we tend to rely on what we see, but not on what God says. If our circumstances make us uncomfortable or cause us pain, our first reaction might naturally be to try to get out of it, not realizing that God may have just invested a lot of time and effort to get us into this predicament in the first place in order to teach us some important lessons! We may even rush off to prayer, alerting the "prayer chain" that they ought to dive into intercession, when God's real motive is to let us stew for a while so we can learn some lessons about who God wants to be for us in this particular snafu.

We often put too much emphasis on what others say about us, and often forget to pay attention to what God says about us. We allow the opinions of others, past wounds inflicted by others, and present broken relationships with others dictate how we feel when we really need the grace to live above emotional knee-jerk reactions.

We should practice submitting our feelings to the strength of our will and to the healing power of the Holy Spirit.

We worship the Bible, yet in our daily walk with God, we may forget who Jesus really is and how to relate to Him intimately and personally. We study our thick books on theology and strive to know more about the Bible, when sometimes God simply wants us to just love Him and love each other (see Matt. 22:37).

When we begin seeing things the way God sees them—which, by the way, is very often opposite to the way we interpret things—then we are beginning to participate in bona fide supernatural life. Our responses must become responses of the Spirit, whose first concern is "How can this circumstance be used to bring glory to God and to touch and help the persons involved?" This kind of intentional focus on what lies beyond the natural does not come about accidentally. It results from a personal agreement between you and the Living God in which you actively pursue obedience to Him while He actively pursues blessing you with deeper insight, wisdom, and love.

Once again, we see that the primary influence comes from that which is not seen, that invisible world where ideas and thoughts trump physical reality. The supernatural life is one that is built upon a foundation that exists in a realm we cannot see with our eyes. This foundation is unseen, yet is more real than any physical reality in our lives, and from this invisible place flows all the power and change we need to upgrade our physical lives in ways that honor God and fulfill His plans for us and the people around us.

Endnote

1. *Online Etymology Dictionary*, s.v. "super"; http://www.etymonline. com/index.php?search=super&searchmode=none; accessed August 19, 2011.

CHAPTER 23

We See Dimly, but We're Not Blind

At one time long ago all of creation was perfect. Then sin crept in. Adam and Eve walked and talked with God, and all things centered on their relationship with Him. I believe Adam and Eve originally had no concept of a division between what was spiritual and what we now deem as non-spiritual, because walking and talking with God was just as real as working in the garden. Since God permeated all of creation, and it was created in perfection, everything was considered holy and consecrated for Him, from the dirt Adam tilled to grow food to the words and concepts shared in the cool of the garden between the man and his loving Father.

Sin changed all that, but it did not obliterate our understanding of reality. Sunsets are still beautiful. Roses still smell lovely and sweet. Chocolate (my weakness) still tastes Heavenly. Love and relationship and good discussion and great wine and delicious food still feed our souls and cause us to give glory to God. We can still study the universe and experience it through all of our senses; we can grow delicious produce in the garden; and we can learn in-depth and complex subjects like music and literature and science. But it all takes more work now.

I suppose it's not as easy to understand things now as it was in Adam's day. Our knowledge continues to evolve and our understanding gets a little clearer as time passes, but as Paul says in First Corinthians 13, we see things dimly now, but some day we shall see all things clearly. We don't see things as clearly with our "fallen minds," right? Hmm...that doesn't sound quite right.

The "Fallen Minds" Argument

I have heard many Christian teachers who insist that our "fallen minds" simply are not capable of understanding things clearly and completely. One of the realms in which this argument repeatedly surfaces is that of the young-Earth vs. old-Earth debate. Some of those who believe that a "literal" translation of Genesis insists on a young universe (roughly, less than 10,000 years old) reject the ancient universe of modern science. Although the young-Earth crowd has many reasons for this, one of them is their suspicion of science being performed with "fallen minds." They argue that these fallen minds cannot understand clearly enough to make decisions on important things like the age of the universe. This is discussed in more length elsewhere in this book.

This kind of thinking presents lots of problems. First, these same fallen minds are translating our Scriptures from ancient texts, a discipline just as reliant on science as the study of the universe. To be consistent, we would have to suspect the accuracy of our Scriptures just as much as we suspect the accuracy of science's claims about the age of the universe. Second, the "fallen mind" theory contradicts the clear scriptural teaching that we have the mind of Christ (see 1 Cor. 2:16). Third, the same fallen minds that study the age of the universe also have successfully designed airplanes, cars, computers, and robots, all of which are reliable enough to entrust our lives to daily.

So, the concept of Adam falling from grace and having to struggle and work harder than he did before must be tempered by New Testament revelations about what we have received as a result of being placed "in Christ." Paul spoke in First Corinthians about seeing in a mirror darkly, but we ought to think about the additional 2,000 years of revelation we have received since his day. He did not have access to the whole of the New Testament like we do. He did not have our knowledge of the universe, of science, of human and biblical history. He did not have access to modern science and all the things it teaches us about God's languages of math, science, and quantum physics.

We may be limited in what we can understand merely by virtue of the fact that God and His reality are infinite and we are not. Of course there are things we cannot know now. If we did know it all, we would then be omniscient. However, we do know a lot more than Moses did about the structure of the universe. I would dare say we also know more about God and Jesus than Moses did, because we have much more biblical and historical revelation. We know more now about the structure of the universe than Albert Einstein knew, who knew more than Copernicus did. We may see dimly as in a mirror, but we're not blind!

The "poor me" attitude of the ascetics is not the Gospel of Christ. Jesus calls us to love ourselves ("...*love your neighbor as yourself*"; Matt. 22:39). Do you love yourself? There's no reason not to. The God who created the universe loves you to distraction. If He can find something in you to love so deeply, so thoroughly, so completely that He was willing to sacrifice His own Son for you, then certainly you must find it within your being to love yourself.

If you are worth something, and if you are important enough that God made a plan *"before the creation of the world"* to redeem you personally (Eph. 1:4), then you have some significant things to add to the human race in spite of what you think you can see in this world. You don't understand everything clearly, but as you act in faith, the invisible realm will open up to you, and you'll begin to more clearly understand—here and now, in this life, in your present physical body—the extent of the authority that God has granted you through Jesus.

God Has Revealed Things to Us by His Spirit

As we learn that skill of walking in the supernatural light beside Jesus, the latent power in the invisible realm becomes a tool in our hands. We learn, very literally, to wield the power of quantum physics to change the world around us. We may not see it as such (we won't have to learn differential equations or graduate-level calculus), but we will see the physical results: prayers for healing answered, body parts made whole, hormonal imbalances fixed, and brain chemistry altered. We may not even recognize that there is any science at all involved in what's happening before our eyes, but nevertheless, there will be and in a big way.

We are truly capable of understanding much of God's truth. I'm not saying we have the ability to understand everything that He does, but we ought to give ourselves credit and permission to know more about God and His plans than we typically do. A good example of how we mess this up is a common interpretation of First Corinthians 2:9-10:

> *No eye has seen, no ear has heard, no mind has conceived what God has prepared for those who love Him—but God has revealed it to us by His Spirit....*

We have historically done a huge disservice to this verse by quoting only the first half and leaving off the *"but God has revealed it to us..."* part. I have typically heard this Scripture used to indicate that the mansions in Heaven that God has prepared for us are so far above and beyond us that we can never comprehend them.

However, that has nothing to do with this particular piece of Scripture. The whole point of these verses is to make a distinction between the perceptive abilities we have in our eyes, ears, hearts, and spirits. The first half *("No eye has seen, no ear has heard, no mind has conceived what God has prepared for those who love Him")* tells us that we can't perceive these things with our eyes, ears, or minds. Our souls and bodies cannot perceive the things of God. That's why these methods of perception are identified early in the verse as being unable to conceive what God has laid out for us. The eye, the ear, and the mind are not capable of understanding the deep things of God. Paul speaks in detail about the perceptive abilities of those who do not know God, those who only use their eyes, ears, and minds to perceive life and not their spirits. He further says they have no hope or ability to please God:

> *Those who live according to the sinful nature have their minds set on what that nature desires; but those who live in accordance with the Spirit have their minds set on what the Spirit desires. The mind of sinful man is death, but the mind controlled by the Spirit is life and peace; the sinful mind is hostile to God. It does not submit to God's law, nor can it do so. Those controlled by the sinful nature cannot please God* (Romans 8:5-8).

While the eyes, ears, and minds of people cannot fathom what God has prepared for us, the spirits of people are completely capable of understanding these things because Paul continues *"...God **has** revealed it to us by His Spirit"* (1 Cor. 2:10). For many years, I understood that we should always include the second half of the verse with the first, and I took issue with folks who always cut if off early, but now I know that it goes even deeper than I realized: it's really about the distinction between our ability to gain revelation through our body and soul versus through our spirit.

If we listen to the whole second chapter of First Corinthians, it becomes clear. Verses 7 and 8 talk about those who crucified Jesus; if they had understood the mystery of Jesus, they would not have crucified Him. Then Paul goes on with verse 9 above. What he's talking about, in the context of the letter he wrote, is that the rulers who rejected Christ cannot understand what God has prepared for those who love Him, which is a Messiah! Forgiveness! Grace! A life of love and grace through Christ as opposed to the oppression of the law! This is a huge theme throughout Paul's writings. If they had understood all this (the specific shortfall of the Pharisees, that is, their rejection of Jesus as the Messiah), they wouldn't have killed Jesus. Eye has not seen, ear has not heard, it has not entered into the heart of unregenerate humanity how God has prepared the gift of salvation and the amazing supernatural life that is now made available through Christ for those who love Him. *But* God has revealed it to us who love Him through His Spirit.

The whole passage is talking about the gift of salvation made available to us through Jesus, and it cannot be understood in terms of mind and body and logic. It has nothing to do with the mansions of glory prepared for us in Heaven or the fact that we can't understand or fathom them. While it may be true that what God has prepared for us in the afterlife is unimaginable, I believe that these verses simply do not address that, and by understanding this we gain access to a far deeper and more profound truth.

If we read the first three chapters of First Corinthians consecutively, we find that it's all about comparing the natural mind to the spiritual mind and their ability to comprehend God's truth. That's the entire topic of the beginning chapters of the book. It puts the verses above squarely in the middle of the first three chapters and squarely in the context of the discussion about the natural mind versus the spiritual mind. Chapter 1 talks about how God has made the wisdom of this world foolish:

Where is the wise man? Where is the scholar? Where is the philosopher of this age? Has not God made foolish the wisdom of the world? For since in the wisdom of God the world through its wisdom did not know Him, God was pleased through the foolishness of what was preached to save those who believe. Jews demand miraculous signs and Greeks look for wisdom, but we preach Christ crucified: a stumbling block to Jews and foolishness to Gentiles, but to those whom God has called, both Jews and Greeks, Christ the power of God and the wisdom of God. For the foolishness of God is wiser than man's wisdom, and the weakness of God is stronger than man's strength (1 Corinthians 1:20-25).

Chapter 2 talks about how the natural mind cannot understand the things of God and compares this with the insight we have when we are enlightened in our hearts and minds by the Holy Spirit:

The Spirit searches all things, even the deep things of God. For who among men knows the thoughts of a man except the man's spirit within him? In the same way no one knows the thoughts of God except the Spirit of God. We have not received the spirit of the world but the Spirit who is from God, that we may understand what God has freely given us. This is what we speak, not in words taught us by human wisdom but in words taught by the Spirit, expressing spiritual truths in spiritual words. The man without the Spirit does not accept the things that come from the Spirit of God, for they are foolishness to him, and he cannot understand them, because they are spiritually discerned (1 Corinthians 2:10-14).

Chapter 3 continues the same topic:

Do not deceive yourselves. If any one of you thinks he is wise by the standards of this age, he should become a "fool" so that he may become wise. For the wisdom of this world is foolishness in God's sight. As it is written: "He catches the wise in their craftiness"; and again, "The Lord knows that the thoughts of the wise are futile" (1 Corinthians 3:18-20).

I believe these passages address truths far deeper than we sometimes think. We are often far too easily pleased with a shallow surface rendition of God's truth.

So we are learning that everything about Kingdom life with God is geared toward increasing our levels of knowledge, wisdom, and insight. God promises to give us insight, wisdom, and shrewdness if we search diligently for them (see Prov. 2:3-5). He tells us that we have the mind of Christ (see 1 Cor. 2:16). We are God's ambassadors on this planet, and as such, we obviously need to know some of the things that God knows. God does not intend for us to remain ignorant, and He wants us to know the same things He knows. He's not threatened by our knowledge since He is quite secure in who He is! One of the primary principles of life with God is becoming like His son, Jesus—learning how to think with His mind, learning how to operate in His realm of thinking and existing. It's true that we may see dimly now, simply due to our lack of experience, but we're definitely not blind.

CHAPTER 24

Virtual Reality

As computer technology advances, the line between physical reality and virtual reality is blurred. Video games, movies, and other types of graphics become increasingly lifelike, and it will soon be difficult (if not impossible) to distinguish between what's "real" and what's not. In fact, the very definition of *real* is being challenged. If it looks like a rose and smells like a rose...

The video game industry is one of the leading-edge venues for virtual reality devices. There is one game where the user grabs a pair of boxing gloves with sensors in them and stands in an area where proximity sensors know the position and movements of the player's body. You can actually have a boxing match with a virtual boxer, but the advantage is you don't feel the pain when you get punched! When you're in the thick of the battle, you're really not thinking about the fact that you're boxing with a machine. You duck and punch and get lost in the reality of a real fight. Someone watching from a distance might believe you're in a true boxing match, except they see no opponent. It's only a matter of time before the graphics are good enough to truly blur the lines between "real" and computer-generated. Add the science of holography and three-dimensional images to the mix, and we are on the cusp of a reality revolution.

The question of what's real and what's not will give way to debates about the very definition of the word *real*. In the movie *iRobot*, Will Smith's character begins with an innate mistrust of robots.

By the end of the movie, he's calling the protagonist robot "friend." Along with the humanoid shape of robots (an already well-advanced technology), artificial intelligence further muddies the line between human and machine. Machines are capable of conversing with humans, including recognition of speech, decision making, expression of emotions, and responding with lifelike voice inflections.

The relationship between what we know and accept as "real" and the technological marvel of virtual reality is a perfect parallel between what we normally see as physical reality and spiritual reality. When does the robot become real? When do its thought processes and its programming, that can uncannily match the appearance of true emotions, become real enough for us to attribute to this machine some kind of human worth? When the robot's brain becomes as sophisticated as ours, and the only noticeable difference between the robot and the human is the material of which it is made, then what? The atheistic humanist ought to be ready and willing to grant human rights to such machines, considering that they see the human being as nothing more than a machine, a meaningless mass of cells on a meaningless planet lost in a meaningless universe. The ghost in the machine (the human spirit) is fiction to them, so they must base the worth of an entity on other criteria, namely, its worth in society.

Those who personally know the God who created the universe know that there is a ghost in the machine. Those who have been reborn by the grace of God have a new life within them. They are literally new creatures. There is a new person there that did not previously exist (see 2 Cor. 5:17). This new person wholly exists within that unseen realm we have been talking about, but is manifested through a physical body and controlled by the soul. The soul—mind, heart, emotions, will—is the part of us that animates the physical body and is the link between what is seen and what is unseen.

Contending for the Promises of God

Our spirit self is united with God's Spirit, and as such, has access to all the promises God has ever made and will ever make. We are in Jesus and are heirs with Jesus (see Rom. 8:17), and we currently possess all the power, inheritance, and eternal character that He possesses. But while all these things exist right now in our spirits, they are often not manifested in physical, visible reality. Why? That's where the whole process of becoming like Jesus comes in. It's called maturity. We are not in a battle to gain eternal life, the precious promises God has made to us, or to achieve the riches of our inheritance in Him, because we already have been given all of these things. Our struggle is to make them physically manifest and visible in our lives.

In the language of virtual reality, our spirit life is the programming. Everything we will ever need or inherit from God is there, but it's not necessarily visible to us right now. The computer—the soul, comprising the mind, emotions, and will—has been programmed with every possible scenario and is ready to deliver it to us. We simply need to develop the hardware—the boxing game with its screen, position sensors, and boxing gloves—to allow us to bring the programming into a physical manifestation. The ducking and punching is the real stuff of life, but it would not exist without the invisible programming and behind-the-scenes engineering that has already taken place.

We have already been placed in Christ, and a whole lifetime of tasks has been pre-programmed for us: *"For we are God's workmanship, created in Christ Jesus to do good works, which God prepared in advance for us to do"* (Eph. 2:10). This pre-programming contains experiences far above and beyond our wildest dreams: God is *"able to do immeasurably more than all we ask or imagine..."* (Eph. 3:20). God's plans for us are far greater than our own—far brighter, far richer, far more influential:

"For I know the plans I have for you," declares the **Lord,** *"plans to prosper you and not to harm you, plans to give you hope and a future"* (Jeremiah 29:11).

These incredible plans of God for our lives are all there in Christ, and our primary job is to bring them to reality. How? Now that's a great question!

Unlike my opponent in the boxing game, who can never step out of the screen and become a real person (that is, a person who is manifested in physical reality), the virtual reality of the spirit world is designed to become real in our lives. We should see physical manifestations of this spiritual reality, in the form of miraculous healings, daily physical provisions, and even the "soft" realities of emotions and peace and love. The way we accomplish this is by cooperating with God's plan for us. His plan includes the introduction of these spiritual blessings into our physical lives, but only according to His schedule. I think we can have some effect on the speed of our own advancement, but God will not eliminate process from our lives, because we need to learn that process is actually the destination we are pursuing.

All these physically manifested experiences and provisions that God promises are not in themselves the goal. The goal is to experience the process necessary to bring these things to fruition, because it's in the process that we experience God Himself. We will not experience the personhood of God if He just hands us everything we need. But if He walks beside us, teaching us reliance upon Him and faith and confidence that He will provide, then we get to know Him personally. This can only take place through the process of the journey. In the words of Martin Sexton, "It's in the journey that we see there's no destination...it's in the journey that we find our true love...."[1] If God automatically gave us everything we needed and wanted, we would have no need to seek Him, to have relationship with Him, to learn from Him, and faith would be obsolete. To immediately arrive at the goal requires no faith, no persistence, and no character. It's in the journey that we learn these very important character traits, and they become second nature to us.

The virtual world of the Spirit is invisible to us and often simply off limits. God does not show us everything at once—our whole future, all the upgrades that are coming or all the pain that we may experience. This is because, more than anything else, He wants us to completely trust Him. When we don't know what the future holds, when everything in this physical world seems to be going wrong, when the challenges and confusion begin to mount, that's when He wants the virtual world to overtake our visible world. He wants to teach us to rise up to a higher elevation where we can look down upon our circumstances rather than be smothered by them. When we have that kind of perspective, then we are no longer subject to the impact circumstances can have on us. We actually live outside of them. The programming—our experiences with God and the resulting faith and knowledge of His Kingdom that develops within our hearts—takes over, and what is real is defined by the rules of the game, the invisible rules that govern the programming, the unseen realities of God's eternal Kingdom, not the physical things that surround us.

I watch my nephew Paul play video games, and in some games there is a mode where you can push a button and get a bird's-eye view of the entire playing field. The player can see his own position, and also the position of all his opponents. He can see obstructions, which rooms are occupied and which are empty, and he can see what resources are available. It's a sort of God-like perspective on the whole virtual game world, and it's very similar to the viewpoint that God has of our lives. However, although in real life we often flounder around, stumbling over what's in front of us and rarely getting a glimpse of what's coming, God wants us to learn to rise above and get His view on things. He may not let us see the next 20 years, but He may very well allow us a snapshot of the immediate future so that we can learn to cooperate with the direction that He's taking us.

All of this requires a perspective that is not limited by our five senses. We must learn to see in our spirits that unseen dimension where God likes to operate. That dimension is fundamental—it's the foundation upon which all else is built, and as we become more mature in Christ, we are better able to operate, think, and react in that realm. It really is like a virtual reality game, except truthfully it's more like the spiritual realm is the real deal and the physical realm is the virtual one. Ten thousand years from now—when we have a firm grasp on what the eternal reality really looks like—I'm sure you will agree.

Endnote

1. Martin Sexton, "In the Journey," *In the Journey* (Kitchen Table Records, 2004).

CHAPTER 25

Water Into Wine

Henry is at Hugh's house, having accepted a dinner invitation, and is sitting at the kitchen counter watching Hugh prepare steaks for the grill.

Hugh: Henry, would you like a little shot of wine? I'm opening a really good Dry Creek Valley Zin.

Henry: Well, um...As you know, my dear friend, I don't normally imbibe. However, a very modest serving may help me sleep tonight. I seem to be suffering lately from a peculiar kind of restlessness.

Hugh: Well, red wine is very good for you, and I suppose it—along with the tryptophans from the mashed potatoes—may very well help you relax tonight.

Henry accepts a glass of wine from Hugh.

Henry: Thank you, very kindly. Mmmm. This is quite tasty. You know your wine, don't you?

Hugh: Well, yeah. I'm no expert, but I know a cab from a sauvignon blanc.

Henry: What exactly makes a really great wine?

Hugh: Boy, that's tough. If anyone on this planet knew the definitive answer to that question, they would be rich. I can tell you what I like about a particular wine, but I certainly can't tell you what's happening to my taste buds to bring me to that decision.

Henry: It must be an extraordinarily complex formulation!

Hugh: Yes, and this all-natural red beverage, created by God's own process of fermentation, continues to amaze the medical community with its significant health benefits.

Henry: I have heard a bit about that myself.

Hugh: Wanna know what I find the most interesting?

Henry: What's that, old chap?

Hugh: God made stuff taste good.

Henry: OK, I agree with your conclusion, but what exactly are you getting at?

Hugh: God could have designed us so that we just plugged our belly buttons into a tree to get our nourishment. Why not? That's about as random as taking stuff in our mouths, chomping on it until it's all mushy, and then feeling it travel to our stomachs!

Henry: I cannot argue that God could have done it differently.

Hugh: But He didn't! He loves us so much that He made stuff taste good! Isn't that cool? He created us with taste buds for the specific purpose of tasting things. And some of the finest things in the world—a great glass of wine, a really sweet and ripe orange, a cup of roasty, toasty strong coffee—are all purely natural, all created by Him to specifically give us great pleasure in eating them!

Henry: You are quite passionate about this, Hugh.

Hugh: Sorry. I guess I am. I just think it's amazing that God gave us all these incredible pleasures in our lives, and he designed our bodies specifically to enjoy them. Food, sex, rock and roll, beautiful sunsets—the chemical composition of our bodies, along with the sensations that are picked up by our brains, conspire to make these things extremely pleasurable.

Henry: And God did not have to do it that way.

Hugh: Right! He chose to. And the science behind it all is overwhelming. Did you know that your sense of taste is sensitive to a few parts in a million?

Henry: I have to admit, my good friend, that these are all quite interesting points. I guess I have never taken such effort to appreciate the finer things in life. Like that beautiful steak you are about to grill...or those amazing garlicky mashed potatoes!

Hugh: God paid some amazing attention to the details when He created us.

Henry: And out of the dust of the earth no less!

* * * * * * * * * * *

What would it take to turn water into wine?

A random U.C. Davis student might answer, "Well, you just squish some grapes and let them ferment and a thousand different chemicals all work together to cause fermentation, and the alcohol and tannins and fruit and flavors all meld in a really complex interaction, and you get wine, with a bouquet of black cherries or currants and a long, complex finish of smoke and fruit."

Sounds tasty, but that's not really what I meant.

What actually happened when Jesus turned water into wine? What exactly is a miracle? Do miracles really happen?

Here is a topic where the naturalist would strongly disagree with a believer in God, stating that there is no such thing as miracles. But this is simply not true as there are countless examples of medically documented miracles. An X-ray shows a tumor. The biopsy confirms it is cancerous. A bunch of people pray for healing. The next day there is no evidence anywhere of the cancer. The non-Christian doctor is amazed and admits he can't explain what happened. Miracle!

Quantum Physics and Miracles

This happens a lot, and to deny it is either simple ignorance or a concerted effort to squelch the truth. For those reading this book who do not believe in healing miracles, I challenge you to reconsider in light of all the pragmatic evidence for miraculous healings. They happen regularly, and there's too much proof to conclude otherwise. I believe the very advancement of medical science could be accelerated if we were to study how these miracles happened, so we can learn how to emulate the process and apply that knowledge for the betterment of humankind.

Typical of Jesus, He wasn't satisfied to simply turn water to wine, but He made really good wine (see John 2:10). He liked to do really good miracles. He had to make some significant changes on a quantum level in order for this to happen. Wine has hundreds of complex chemicals that all need to be finely balanced, especially if the wine is to be "good" wine. I wonder to what level Jesus participated in creating the molecular matter that made up this really good wine. Did He simply command the water to become good wine and it was done? Did He determine during the miracle what type of wine He was going to create? Did He have to have knowledge of the chemical composition of wine? Probably not, since they just didn't have the instruments back then to analyze all those chemicals. Regardless of the answers to these questions, the fact remains that the wine was good, and those flasks contained thousands of chemical constituents that were not in there when the servants brought them to Jesus full of water. Quantum physics!

Some believers in God tend to separate the miraculous from the physical world they see with their eyes. When there is a miracle, they seem to simply believe that it was miraculous, and there needs to be no physical explanation. They may even feel it betrays a lack of faith to try to figure out what physical processes must have been used to make the miracle happen (including the creation of the universe). "God just did it!" they reason, "He didn't have to rely on science. He's all powerful, and He can do things any way He chooses!" While it may be technically true that God can choose any method He chooses to do miracles, we can't deny that a miracle requires some significant changes to matter on a quantum level—it has to involve science. There's no other way.

Consider a different miracle that to me seems even more amazing than turning water into wine. Jesus healed a man whose hand was withered (see Mark 3:1-5), and at another time, He healed two guys with leprosy (see Matt. 8:2-4). Just think of the physical changes that had to take place when healing the man with the withered hand:

New flesh was created—molecules of skin, its several layers, its pigments, and its follicles.

New veins, arteries, and capillaries were created, and filled with blood.

Every new cell that was created had DNA (an exceedingly complex molecular construction) that matched the rest of the man's body.

We don't know this for sure, but the physical reconstruction (size of the bones, color of the flesh, size and shape of the muscles and tendons) probably matched the other hand so it looked natural.

Nerve endings were created and distributed and connected to the rest of the man's nervous system (and I would imagine that the process of making a new hand would be quite painful, so the nerve endings were numbed until the process was finished—but this also is just speculation).

There was a phenomenal amount of activity on a cellular and subatomic level to make that hand new again, requiring lots of molecular re-organizing of matter and energy. And it all happened as quickly as the man could reach out his hand. No matter how we define a supernatural event like this, we have to conclude that something new was created that was not there before. Matter was created out of thin air. New flesh and bones that did not previously exist, and the complex chemicals of which they are composed, came into being. Science was involved. And it's especially interesting to note that creating flesh and bone where none existed is the same type of miracle as creating the universe or creating bread to feed the five thousand—and quantum physics is required to do that kind of thing. Something new was created from what cannot be seen.

When Jesus fed the five thousand, He was creating bread right there on the spot. He apparently had such a command over quantum reality that He could rearrange energy into bread in front of the disciples' eyes. That would have been fun to see. I wonder if the loaf just kind of expanded as He tore pieces off, or if little identical loaves kept popping up? Or maybe He would throw a little bread in a bas-ket, and as each disciple was delivering it to a group of people, the bread would reproduce in the basket. We can speculate, but no mat-ter how we slice it (pardon the pun), bread was created from nothing just like the original creation event.

To create something from nothing requires some interesting sci-ence that we as a human race are just barely beginning to understand and are not yet able to control. We are just beginning to delve into the relationship between matter and energy (Einstein proved they are actually the same thing) and how it may be that matter can be created from little balls of energy sticking together in various ways. It would have seemed that Jesus was creating bread from nothing (baking *ex nihilo!*), but in reality all that is required to feed five thousand people with a few loaves of bread is the ability to manipulate energy into the proper forms. I say "all that is required" as if this process is simple and easy to grasp which, of course, it's not. At least not for us.

In his book, *The Singularity Is Near*, futurist and scientist author Raymond Kurzweil discusses nanotechnology (technology and machinery built at a microscopic level), and provides a very intrigu-ing thought experiment. Nano technology is already a developed technology, one good example being the blood-cell-sized (micro-scopic) bots that can be injected into the bloodstream and which release insulin at a pre-determined rate. Kurzweil imagines the day when a huge pile of nanobots will be programmable, so as to rear-range themselves and reattach themselves to each other into an infi-nite number of recognizable patterns. In other words, a huge pile of nanobots, just like molecules attaching to each other to form some fundamental element, can rearrange themselves and grab onto each other to form a chair, a sheet of paper, or an ink pen.

There are large-scale machines that can do exactly that. I have a video of little electro-magnetic devices that can rearrange themselves and reattach themselves to each other to form different letters of the alphabet. It is all programmable and all controlled by a computer program. It's only a matter of time before we are able to do this on a microscopic level, thus imitating the miracle of creating bread from *"that which cannot be seen."*

The fact that Jesus started with five loaves and two fishes is actually inconsequential and seems to serve more of a poetic cause than a scientific one. He could just as easily have turned Peter's sandals into bread, but there were other lessons He wanted to teach us. Besides, Peter probably wouldn't have appreciated that (and the bread may have tasted kind of funny). Truth is, it probably worked out the same as the wine miracle—this was probably really good bread. Maybe even the best the people had tasted. Why not? It was Jesus, after all. If you had the ability to create food from nothing, would you make it disgusting and stale? Or would you make it really good? It is God's own principle that whatever we find to do, we ought to do it to the best of our ability. If Jesus were to create the best bread He possibly could have created, it must have been amazing!

The incredible thing about great food and drink is its connection to all aspects of our being. Meals are not strictly for nourishment, but throughout history have also been opportunities for socializing and building friendships and intimacy. This creates a powerful emotional and spiritual connection that is actually enhanced by a common love for wine or appreciation for gourmet chocolate. *Food can actually enhance spiritual connectedness.* Jesus chose the last supper as an occasion to basically say goodbye to those dearest to Him. Jesus chose to honor Zaccheaus by dining with Him. All Christians look forward to an event that will culminate all of earthly human history—the marriage supper of the Lamb.

All aspects of our being—including food and drink, marriage and family life, work and professional activities, prayer and intimate relationship with God, hobbies, and leisure time interests—have an unseen and eternal aspect to them that perhaps we don't pay enough attention to. And every good memory, fun time, fond feeling of nostalgia, and anticipation of making the next great memory are intimately tied to the workings of quantum physics. Why? Because just the simple act of *thinking* about last week's memory or anticipating next week's memory-making event involves massively complex brain functions, all of which rely on complex chemical reactions and activities on a subatomic scale—the scale at which quantum physics operates.

And these complex brain functions are in turn intimately tied to *memories* and *emotions*, which are completely non-physical entities. Wine and cheese cause synapses to fire in my brain, and years later, I can reflect on the humor and warmth I felt as my cousin Karen teased me about my cheese map—the little hand-drawn map I drew that identified each variety of cheese on the plate I had brought to her party. Quantum science, cheese, fun, and love are rolled into one big supernatural package, the quantum dance that helps to bridge the chasm between what we physically experience and what we feel and think, marrying the seen with the unseen in the elegant dance of life!

CHAPTER 26

God's Will, Our Desire

What allowed Jesus to access the power and authority to rearrange physical matter through a simple act of His will? How did Jesus have such an intimate familiarity with that realm of existence that we can't see but seems to be the authority behind every beat of the heart of God? Let's expand the question into this: What will allow you, just as Jesus did, to access that power and authority to change life and reality, accomplishing the things that Christ wants you to accomplish, both for yourself and on behalf of the people in your life? After all, Jesus said we would do *"greater works than these"* (John 14:12 NASB). How do we know what these greater works are supposed to be?

More importantly, let's expand this question yet further into a much more general and broad-reaching one beyond discrete activities, miracles, and daily decisions: What is God's will? This question is one that I think most Christians struggle mightily with. I certainly have.

God's will. Such an elusive topic! We hear sermons, we read books, we accost our friends, family, and pastors, and yet we don't know what God's will is for our lives. We ache and we groan, begging God to reveal to us His "will" because we really are sincere about knowing it and following it. But what we are really asking is, "What job should I take?" and "Where should I live?" and "Who should I marry?" I'm beginning to believe that our primary struggle with finding these answers is rooted in our lack of understanding of how the term *God's will* ought to be used and the fact that we don't realize God has already given us the answers to these kinds of questions.

Allow me to make a suggestion. What if we start using two different terms to create some finer resolution in this discussion? Let's use the term *God's will* to describe the general things that God desires for all of His children, which will be quite specific in nature, but will apply broadly to all Christians—in fact, to all people since we know that it is God's desire that all should come to know Him. And second, let's start using a term like *God's vision* or *God's dream* to talk about His specific plans for your life—where you should go to college, what color socks you should wear today, or where you should live? Now I think we have a more biblically based model for discussing how we should live our lives.

What Is God's Will?

God's will is specifically stated in Scripture: to make us more like Jesus, *"...attaining to the whole measure of the fullness of Christ"* (Eph. 4:13); to bring all things together under Christ's authority (see Eph. 1:10); to show love to His people (see John 13:34); so that none should perish (see John 3:16). All the questions of physical provision are not necessarily specific to God's will, but they are an outworking or result of us following God's will, which has primarily to do with our proper spiritual development. Jesus said that if we seek first His Kingdom and His righteousness, then all these other things that we worry about and strive for would be freely given to us (see Matt. 6:34). God's will is that we should trust Him as our sole source, our strength in trouble, our salvation and confidence, our healer, and our friend. It is God's will that none should perish and that we learn to think and act like His son, Jesus. This is the quintessential example of the spiritual realm impacting the physical: Seek God's Kingdom and

His righteousness—completely non-corporeal entities—and all these things (physical provisions) will be given to you. The cause is wholly spiritual, but the effect is as much physical as it is spiritual.

God's Personal Vision for Your Life

God's vision for your life is a different issue than His general will. It's what He specifically envisions *you* doing, learning, and becoming as a unique individual consistent with the gifts and strengths He has given you. This goes far above and beyond the general knowledge of God's will for all Christians, and I believe these things are not in the same category as the things described in the previous paragraph. God's will has to do with character development and becoming like Jesus. God's vision for you has to do with the things you should do that are consistent with the way He made you individually. God's vision for you flows out of your deepest dreams and desires, the things you love to do, the activities you get involved in that cause you to lose all track of time, the things that you would do as a career for the rest of your life if money was not an issue, the things you never get tired of. It's your inheritance in Christ. It's your very identity.

I believe that many of us never find that thing, that deepest dream, that thing that would deeply satisfy our mind, soul, and spirit. I think of some of the choices I have made, the choice to pursue a "responsible" engineering career out of high school rather than pursue music, the thing I loved most. I think of what could have been, and I question why I made the choices I made. I try to imagine how things might have been if our little high school band had been able to turn our music into a lifestyle. I'll admit that some of this thinking is not beneficial if I allow it to cause regret or sorrow in my life, because I firmly believe that God has worked all the things in my life together for a far greater good than if I had lived a dream life.

But I find some therapeutic value in exploring the motives behind my previous decisions, because if I determine that I made mistakes in the past, I don't want to repeat them in the future. Luckily, I rarely think about the past, even more rarely regret past decisions, because I'm always so busy looking into the future with my millions of projects and dreams that I'll never have time to fulfill. I'm thankful that this is the way God made me, and I love that about myself. But this kind of thinking gives me motivation to continue searching for the one thing, the one thing that Curly talked about in *City Slickers*, that one thing that C.S. Lewis described in Chapter 19.

This is the key to knowing the answers to these more specific questions that we often mistake for God's will: God's vision, His dream, His gift for you is based on the way He created you and is manifested by your deepest dreams and desires, those things that may be nigh unto indescribable even to your closest friends and family. If we can get a handle on what that thing is, if that echo ever "swells into the sound itself," then we will more than likely stop begging God to reveal His will to us, and we'll start living the abundant life for which He designed us. That is, if we have the guts to go for it.

It's God's will that you become like Jesus in your character. It is God's dream for your life that you pursue and achieve your deepest longings. However, typical of the invisible/visible dichotomy we have been discussing, the latter is built upon the foundation of the former. As our immaterial self—our character, soul, mind, heart, and personality—line up with God's will, I believe our material lives—our hobbies, jobs, relationships, means of support, and leisure activities—will line up with the deepest desires that God planted in our hearts and the provisions to make these things happen.

Sure, there are those who seem to be living the dream. They have the secondary material life without knowledge of Christ in their lives. We all know about those who are evil, yet who prosper. But that's short-circuiting the process. We all know and have seen a thousand examples of materially successful people who are "living the dream," but are strung out on drugs, sex, violence, or heartache. That's the quintessential house built on the sand of soulish desires, not on the rock of God's love and desires. There is nothing wrong with possessing stuff, but if it's built on the foundation of selfish pursuit, rather than God's Kingdom, then it's all meaningless and powerless.

What does it mean to *"seek first His kingdom and His righteousness"*? If we understand the answer to that question, we will get a glimpse of how the immaterial realm influences the material realm, which for some will become a dramatic and life-changing revelation of truth.

I'm no theologian. I'm not going to attempt a discourse on the biblical and hermeneutical interpretations of the reality of God's Kingdom (I don't even understand what I just said!). But I do know that all other realities are built upon the unseen reality of eternity, the realm of existence that we cannot see with our eyes, but that is more real than anything else.

What Does God's Kingdom Look Like?

When Jesus arrived on the scene, the Jewish people believed that the promised Messiah would provide freedom from Roman rule. They were living in occupied territory and wanted the Messiah to set up a political kingdom that would give them political and cultural independence. Little did they know that the Kingdom that was promised them from ancient times was not a physical kingdom, but a spiritual one. The only physical manifestations that they were going to see from this new Kingdom would be the good things done in love by those who lived in the Kingdom, who had learned to love God and love their neighbors.

But even though this Kingdom was to be a strictly spiritual one, it would have profound effect on all of physical reality. Look at what happened previously when God intervened in the lives of the Jewish people. They had been slaves in Egypt for more than 400 years. What they had to look forward to every day was making bricks for Pharaoh. Through a promise based on the love of God for His people, the dream of freedom and independence became reality, wherein the Egyptians showered the Jews with gifts, gold, and booty as they walked out of Egypt on their way to their promised land. A promise became physical reality in the form of gold, camels, and fabric, all popular currencies of their day.

Building upon the foundation of the promises of God—how ethereal and non-corporeal can you get?—causes physical change in the circumstances of our lives. We get food, shelter, clothes—all those things that others seek after—if we simply seek first God's Kingdom and His righteousness (see Matt. 6:31-33). Jesus began to usher in God's Kingdom during His life on this Earth. Prior to the coming of Jesus, the only way we could approach God was through the intercession of the priests, who alone had authority to enter the holiest place in the temple and commune with God on behalf of the people. When Jesus died, that veil prohibiting access to the holiest place was torn in two, establishing a Kingdom in which we are free to approach the throne of the King with confidence (see 1 John 5:14-15).

As we approach the King as His children, He showers us with His unconditional love and His acceptance of us in Christ. What does it mean to be "in Christ"? It means that in that unseen realm of existence, we are literally put in a place by God in which He only sees the perfection of Christ when He looks at us. All your sin has already been paid for. All your shortcomings already have provision placed next to them so you can become like Jesus. *"Blessed is the man whose sins the Lord will never count against Him"* (Rom. 4:7-8). What an awesome way to live! Could it possibly be true that God doesn't hold our sins against us? This is a truth that faithful fundamentalists—preoccupied with sin as we are—need to carefully consider. We read these things in black and white in the Bible, but how deeply do we really believe them?

So we've stumbled upon one of the primary ways we are to seek His Kingdom — we simply believe. This Kingdom of Heaven is governed by spiritual rules that are more consistent and reliable than the rules of gravity or electromagnetism, so we need a thorough and well-implemented system of belief. The first rule is that it's not about what you do; it's about what you believe.

Modern Christianity is primarily built on just the opposite assumption: it's all about what you do. That's where Fundamentalism got its bad rap, and some of it is justified. If you don't obey this list of rules, then you are going to end up in hell. Many of us have learned in church: "It's just that simple: Don't drink, don't chew, don't date girls that do." And the world gets the unfortunate impression that the only thing that matters is your actions. If you're losing the battle with homosexuality, abortion, divorce, drugs, alcohol, pornography, or lust, then you are just not going to make it to Heaven. Sorry.

Nothing could be further from the truth.

We can't afford to continue living primarily in the physical world of pragmatism. We need to become intimately familiar with the immaterial reality of Spirit-led intuition where Jesus lives. Of course, it's not good to practice these things, but don't we all have our struggles? Don't we all have thorns in our flesh to deal with? Don't we all have those things that keep us humble before God and require us to daily submit to Him so that He can help us overcome the wrong things we do and their consequences?

If you are receiving condemnation for the things you do, then come to Jesus instead of to church people who are condemning you. Jesus was presented with a woman who was caught in the act of adultery, an offense punishable by death back then. He had no words of condemnation for her (see John 8:11)! Also consider the story of the woman at the well who was "living in sin." He simply offered her living water. He did the same thing with Zacheus. Jesus simply told him that He wanted to have supper together, and that was enough to cause a complete change of heart in old Zack, and he blessed the entire town with his generosity. No words of condemnation. No list of dos and don'ts, just love and acceptance and encouragement to live a better life, and gifts of grace to help the people do just that.

What Should We Believe?

So if it's primarily about what we believe, then what exactly should we believe? Complete volumes have been written about this, but I can offer a few suggestions:

- Believe that you have been forgiven, past tense. Every sin you have ever committed as well as every sin you will ever commit, has already been forgiven. I don't like starting right off with a sin-forgiveness thing because I believe the evangelical church already puts too much emphasis on perfect behavior, but I want to slay this religious dragon before it does any more harm. If you are a Jesus follower, you are forgiven. God does not hold your sins against you, and He sees the perfect cleanliness of Jesus when He looks at you, not your sins, baggage, and shortcomings. Sure, He'll work on those things with you, but never, ever in a condescending or condemning way. He will gently help you rise above where you are now, to ever-increasing heights.

- Believe that God has an incredible plan for you. You may not be seeing it right now, and I think this is quite common because of the poor quality of our thought life. Nevertheless, it's true that God has plans for you, *"plans to prosper you, not to harm you, to give you a future and a hope..."* (Jer. 29:11). His plan is far better than anything you could dream up on your own, and it is more consistent with who He made you to be. God's dream for your life is not dependent on what others think you ought to be doing or what you feel obligated to do because of some opinion about responsibility or sacrifice.

- Believe that God's dream and vision for your life are consistent with your innermost dreams and desires, those things that are almost unexplainable, as C.S. Lewis described, those things that cause you immense joy and fulfillment. God is the one who created you to love what you love, to be captured by what fascinates and feeds you. He made you very good at something, and there is a specific place in the Body of Christ for you that no one else on the entire planet can fulfill as well as you can.

- Believe that God wants you to achieve that dream, that passion, and He wants you to learn to use it for the benefit of the people in your life. Everything must be about the only two real commandments in the Bible: in the words of Jesus Himself, it all boils down to love God and love others (see Matt. 22:37). Your dream will have a component to it that will bless others. This does not necessarily mean that you will overtly talk about Jesus every time you strum your guitar or do your needlepoint, but it will mean that the *shekina* sparks of God's glory (see the chapter "Viva la Sparks") will fly when you are lost in the

middle of your passion and that it will be a reflection
of His creativity, His power, or His provision, or
perhaps a combination of all of these.

How can it be as simple as "just believe?" *Surely there must be more to it than that! Surely there must be some behavior modification I have to go through to achieve this abundant life we are talking about.* While it's true that some behavior changes may be necessary, it's not you who is going to make them. How many of us have things in our lives that we have struggled with for years, or maybe decades, and still haven't learned to rise above? We have tried every conceivable way to get rid of some bad habit, or tried to institute some new good habit, but it just doesn't work. It's because you cannot make those changes. Only by submitting our wills and spirits to the Spirit of God within us can we hope to change. And then it becomes less about us changing or eliminating the baggage from our lives and more about that stuff just drying up and falling off as God's Spirit within us gradually makes us more like Jesus.

Once again, the invisible realm controls and changes the visible. Belief, intention, and the spoken word—all unseen and admittedly mysterious concepts—inform and affect all that is seen. If we really believe this and live like it's actually true then I know things will change dramatically for the better. Your God-given dreams can happen, that deepest passion within your heart can begin to manifest, that habit you have been fighting will begin to melt, and those worries that plague your mind will give way to confidence.

You are presented every day with thousands of choices. You have the choice whether or not you will worry about something. Anxiety does not force itself into your life. You allow it. You invite it in. You nurture it by giving it words that further enforce its negative influence in your life. You actually give it muscle by devoting words and time and mental energy to it. It is just as easy to reject worry with words and the strength of your will. Just don't give it a voice. Kill it immediately so that it cannot take root and gain a life of its own. Speak out a curse against it, then praise God for a few minutes, and your anxiety will fade away, all by the power of your choice.

You have a choice whether or not to allow the driver who cut you off in traffic to make you angry. It's a very simple choice. Just don't get mad. That's all there is to it. If an ambulance cut you off in traffic, and you knew it was because the person in the back was desperately fighting for life and depended on getting to the hospital within the next five minutes, you probably would not have an issue with that. What's the difference if it's an irresponsible driver eager to see his girlfriend? Physically the two events are precisely the same. In the natural, the price you pay in either circumstance—having to step on the brakes or swerve to get out of the way—is identical. The only difference is your knowledge of the circumstance. If simple knowledge can cause you to make one of two wildly different responses, then so can your brain and the authority of your will. Just choose to not let it bother you and it won't.

This life in the Spirit is also a choice. There are things that you simply must choose, and they have to do with authority and development of your mind and soul and heart in the unseen realm of the spirit. Choose to believe the previous list of things we ought to believe. Choose your responses beforehand; choose to live according to Philippians 4:8:

> *Finally, brothers, whatever is true, whatever is noble, whatever is right, whatever is pure, whatever is lovely, whatever is admirable—if anything is excellent or praiseworthy— think about such things.*

Choose to believe that your choices are powerful to make permanent change in your life and in the lives of those around you, and your life will change. Choices made in the unseen realm will change physical reality. *"So we fix our eyes not on what is seen, but on what is unseen, for what is seen is temporary but what is unseen is eternal"* (2 Cor. 4:18).

CHAPTER 27

Sintropy

We have discussed the ideas that *God's will* is common to all people and is clearly described in Scripture, and that *God's dream or vision* for each of us is unique and comes through further revelation beyond what is simply found in the Bible. I believe that sin could be construed as disobedience to either God's will *or* God's individual vision for us: "*...Whatever is not from faith is sin*" (Rom. 14:23 NASB).

Keeping that in mind, let's talk about *entropy*. It's a technical term derived from the second law of thermodynamics, which states that a closed system will always lose heat or energy—or energy can only move from a state of more usable to less usable. What it really means is that matter or energy or buildings or gardens or the paint on my house or anything will always go from more orderly to less orderly if left alone. Things naturally will decay and become less useful. In fact, they can become liabilities.

Cars burn gas, changing a substance with a lot of potential energy (gasoline) to a substance with very little potential energy (exhaust and work, or moving the car forward at great speeds). My firewood pile outside decays if I don't burn it, and rotten wood burns much more poorly than dried, hard firewood that is in good condition. Every physical, chemical, and biological process on this planet suffers entropy, because it is not possible to create energy from nothing or to create something of value without a greater loss in "value" (or available energy).

I was thinking about sin and entropy one day. We know that sin can cause all kinds of damage, both in the physical realm and the non-physical. Sin can cause property damage, injury, death, heartache, sadness, pain, horror, regret, depression—and all these things are consistent with the idea of entropy. We tend to wander in our lives if we do not put intentional and purposeful effort toward our spirituality, mental development, and relationships. In other words, our natural tendency is toward selfish and pleasurable things, and sometimes downright damaging things, which are not the things we ought to be doing at the moment.

Our tendency to drift—to slide toward the wrong rather than the right—is a perfect analogy to the concept of entropy. I call it Sintropy.

What Is Sintropy?

It's actually more than just an analogy. Sintropy is as real a phenomenon as entropy. God tells us to be watchful and to work out our salvation (see Phil. 2:12). Effort is required. Intentionality is necessary. The way we overcome physical entropy is by putting effort and work into the system. It requires a lot of time and energy to paint my house, but if I don't do it, the wood will rot away. It takes time and money to change the oil in my car, but if don't it will break down. It requires an unfathomable amount of energy to launch a spacecraft into space. In the same way, it takes time and effort to remain vigilant in our walk with Jesus. It's not difficult work—in fact, it's downright joyful if we maintain the right attitude. But it's work nevertheless, and it's the only antidote to the damages caused by sintropy.

Andrew Wommack provides a great series of lessons called "Effortless Change." The point he argues is that true, lasting inner change is not really difficult. It's simply a matter of changing our hearts and minds through the study of Scriptures and through the enlightenment of our hearts and minds by the Holy Spirit.[1] Sure, it requires time and effort, so the term "Effortless Change" is not totally accurate. But we seem to believe that the Christian life is tough, that we need to be hard on ourselves and beat ourselves into submission. In certain ways, this is true, but we must understand that the beatings are mostly mental and spiritual. It's our hearts that need to change as much as our minds. Perhaps Christians spend too much beating up on ourselves for things we (and others) do and not enough time working on our thought processes and the things we believe.

C.S. Lewis put it this way in *Mere Christianity*:

> The sins of the flesh are bad, but they are the least bad of all sins. All the worst pleasures are purely spiritual. The pleasure of putting other people in the wrong, of bossing and patronizing and spoiling sport, and backbiting; the pleasures of power, of hatred. For there are two things inside me competing with the human self which I must try to become: they are the animal self, and the diabolical self; and the diabolical self is the worst of the two. That is why a cold, self-righteous prig, who goes regularly to church, may be far nearer to hell than a prostitute.[2]

As I was growing up, I was taught that the animal self is the thing that most needs to be controlled. Don't drink beer, don't go to certain movies, don't go to parties, don't listen to rock and roll, don't don't don't don't don't! But Lewis says the animal self is not the thing God primarily worries about. Those animal priorities are things that can be dealt with easily enough. The diabolical self is the dangerous one. That's the Pharisee, the one who acts like Heaven, but has a heart like hell. The diabolical self is the one Christ is talking about when He says it's what comes out of a person's heart that makes a person unclean, while eating with unwashed hands does not (see Matt. 15:18-20). If Christ can deal with the diabolical creature, then there will be no animal instincts to worry about.

God wants to cut out the root of the weed (our sinful or diabolical tendency), not just trim back the leaves (our specific animal sins or shortcomings). If the root is cut, then the whole weed will die, not because of any effort of the weeds, but *because of the action of the one doing the cutting.* And then the question of whether we ought to go on sinning since we're under grace becomes a moot point. We won't want to. We will have gained something in return that is far better and more attractive.

So the best way to fight sintropy is to attack that diabolical self, the self deep down that is the cause of my distasteful actions. Sometimes we get it backward, thinking, *If I can simply control my actions or behavior then I'll have that godly life our Lord urges of us.* It actually works the other way around. We must first change our hearts; then doing the right things comes more naturally. There is a deeper part of us, deeper than perhaps we realize. I once thought that my life of thoughts and emotions was the deepest part of my being, but there is something more foundational than that:

> *And you, my son Solomon, acknowledge the God of your father, and serve Him with wholehearted devotion and with a willing mind, for the Lord searches every heart and understands **every motive behind the thoughts**. If you seek Him, He will be found by you; but if you forsake Him, He will reject you forever* (1 Chronicles 28:9).

This "motive behind the thoughts" is what informs the words and actions that come from my physical self. That's why Jesus said, *"The things that come out of the mouth come from the heart, and these make a man 'unclean'"* (Matt. 15:18). It is at the level of this internal "structure"—the underlying framework upon which my mental and emotional life is based—that change must take place. This is where the battle against sintropy is won or lost. This is where the world of body and soul meets the world of mind and spirit. This is where the material meets the immaterial and where that unseen world remains a mystery to us. But without change at this intimate level of existence, we will not—we cannot—win the battle against sintropy.

Entropy is ubiquitous. It is everywhere. There is nothing that anyone can do to prevent it. It exists throughout the universe, and it has never been thwarted. Sintropy is the same. It is everywhere. I'm not suggesting that sin is winning, or that it is unconquerable, just that the battle rages on every part of this planet and in the hearts of every human being. The world is full of pain. There is evil on every continent. Good will triumph, make no mistake, and in places it already has. But our enemy is active, so there is evil anywhere you care to look, including acts of aggression against innocents, wars, and hate crimes.

Sintropy Affects Our Lives

Now, just like entropy affects the quality of our physical lives, sintropy has no less a damaging effect on our spiritual lives. If indeed the reality we live in is governed less by physical forces and activities, and more by thoughts and intentions, then these egregious acts of evil, the inflicting of suffering and pain, the acts of hate and aggression and other manifestations of what we all agree to be evil or wrong, must contribute to the quality of the atmosphere surrounding us. Let me give you an example.

My wife was in New York City a while back and had a chance to visit Ground Zero at the former site of the World Trade Center towers. She told me that as she was walking around thinking about what happened, she suddenly felt rather overwhelmed and kind of nauseous. I don't think that was a purely emotional reaction. I felt the same kind of things when I visited the Dachau concentration camp in Germany.

I think these things are expressions and manifestations of this spiritual sub-visible reality we are talking about. If one considers all the suffering, emotion, and trauma that happened at Ground Zero, and believes that the eternal spiritual world that we know exists is all around us and permeates time and space, then there was a major disturbance in this spiritual fabric during the 9/11 tragedy.

Maybe to some this sounds like the disturbance in the Force that Yoda talks about in *Star Wars*. Well, science-fiction writers have often been far ahead of their times. There just might be something to the idea of the Force. Before you write me off as a New Age whacko, consider what I have to say. Jesus Himself stated that He holds all things together (see Col. 1:17). Without Him, nothing that was made would have been made. And this fabric of His Being that holds together the universe is nothing less than a Force, just like in *Star Wars*. We are working out our salvation with His strength. This unseen Force working in and through us is real, and perhaps our fear of looking too "New Age" or "mystical" prevents us from a much deeper life in the Spirit.

Holy Spirit: The Underlying Force in Our World

This spiritual fabric that knits together the universe is none other than the Spirit of Jesus Himself. If His compassion, love, joy, and sadness over the World Trade Center tragedy are real—and of course they are—then we, as His children (filled with His Spirit), ought to be able to feel the same things. Do we assume that God shrugs His shoulders over 9/11 and then walks away? Do we not believe that God is the original territorial Spirit? Does He not care deeply about territory? Did He not originally divide up the tribes of Israel into their respective territories? Does He not, to this day, show up stronger or in different ways in physical places that are devoted to His causes?

Have you ever walked into a church service, or some other spiritual gathering, and immediately experienced a strong perception of the presence of God? While this presence can be felt anywhere, even in the dark places of the world where the spiritual warfare is at its fiercest, there are physical places like that where God prefers to predictably provide us with a greater manifestation of His presence. This is nothing less than the fabric of space-time being invaded and permeated by the unseen world of the Spirit. The Force. Call it what you like, but it can't be described in merely physical terms. It's the Spirit of Jesus Christ Himself.

That pull on your heart-strings for physical places you've been, that overwhelming feeling my wife had while close to the former World Trade Center, that contemplative feeling one gets on a cool fall day when the sun still has enough energy to warm your skin, that flood of memories and feeling of peace I experience while I'm visiting the house I grew up in...these may all have to do with realities that are underlying the actual physical things that are located in these places. What this suggests about this other realm of existence is that it can be torn, and probably healed, but perhaps it also maintains the marks and scars of past quantum fluctuations. Sintropy had its way and the scars remain.

To fight entropy, as we've already discussed, requires intentional input of energy. Entropy is the decaying of useful energy, so an input of energy is required to overcome the level or rate of decay. The key is that the influx of new energy must exceed the rate of decay. When you drive your car, the influx of and rate at which the gasoline enters the engine must exceed that of the engine's thirst. If it doesn't, the car won't go. To fight sintropy, we need to put the same intentional input of energy into the system. This energy is none other than the

Holy Spirit, who enlightens us and strengthens us from within. Second Samuel 22:33-35 states,

It is God who arms me with strength and makes my way perfect. He makes my feet like the feet of a deer; He enables me to stand on the heights. He trains my hands for battle; my arms can bend a bow of bronze.

His strength courses through our spiritual veins, and this influx of infinite power is more than enough to defeat sintropy in our lives.

I believe that this tendency to stray off the path is the real fight in our lives. Sure, we have an enemy, and we do well to remember that we are literally on a battleground; weapons are being fired around us, and we are likely to get hit if we don't realize what's going on. Imagine being in the middle of a physical battle, but not even realizing that there's a battle going on. If you are just wandering around aimlessly out on the battlefield, smelling the flowers in between the two fighting armies, it won't be long until you are hit. We are involved in a war between God and His goodness on the one side and the enemy and his evil intention on the other.

But in my experience, the biggest battle I have in gaining territory is with my own flesh, its limited vision and its undisciplined approach to life. The enemy will certainly try to use my own weaknesses against me, and if I succumb, then sintropy has taken me down a notch. But as the Holy Spirit and I work together on my own character, and develop both my inheritance in Christ and my identity as a much-loved child of God, then I grow to warrior status, and the battles I lose to sintropy become less and less frequent. Those old struggles just melt away because the influx of God's energy through His Spirit is more than enough to conquer: *"We are more than conquerors through Him who loved us"* (Rom. 8:37).

Those physical feelings that my wife experienced at Ground Zero were real. They were a physical manifestation of the rift in the created order that God originally called "very good." This spiritual reality in which we are continuously immersed has real and profound effects on our spirits, minds, *and* bodies. Parallel to the physical entropy that causes our skin to wrinkle and our bodies to tire with age, we have sintropy fighting to bring our spirits down into *"the miry clay"* (Ps. 40:2 NASB). But unlike our physical bodies, our spiritual bodies are being refreshed and in fact are experiencing the exact opposite of aging: *"Though outwardly we are wasting away, yet inwardly we are being renewed day by day"* (2 Cor. 4:16). This renewal is precisely what we have been talking about—the action of the Spirit of God fighting back the sintropy in our lives so that we are presented to Him faultless and spotless, victorious and effective for Him. Let's fight the good fight of faith—the fight against sintropy, apathy, and lethargy, and let's fight hard for the inheritance God has promised us!

Endnotes

1. Andrew Wommack, "Effortless Change," (Tulsa, OK: Harrison House, 1984).

2. C.S. Lewis, *Mere Christianity* (Collier, 1960), pg 102-103.

CHAPTER 28

Holistic Science

If science began to base its foundational assumptions on the fact that this is a highly organized, intelligently created universe, and sought to understand its inner workings and the inner workings and methods of the one who created it, the progress we could potentially make would be astonishing. We might even reach a point where we would achieve what we now consider unbelievable according to our existing paradigms about existence and reality. If we made it a goal to specifically study this interplay between spirit (or Spirit) and body, and be ready to accept the consequences of the knowledge we will gain, life on this planet could improve immensely.

Love is in that place of Interface. Love and grace, kindness and justice, right and wrong, good and evil can all be identified as lurking and ever-ready to make an appearance depending on the circumstances at any particular moment in space-time. We are so earth-bound in our thoughts and actions, and modern science tends to anchor us firmly there, denying us the privilege of discovering exponentially deeper truths about life and existence. C.S. Lewis hit the nail on the head:

> We are half-hearted creatures, fooling about with drink and sex and ambition when infinite joy is offered us, like an ignorant child who wants to go on making mudpies in a slum because he cannot imagine what

is meant by a holiday at the sea. We are far too easily pleased.[1]

Let us expand our vision beyond what only empirical, naturalistic science can teach us. I love science. Science teaches us things that are good, but what science can reveal to us is incomplete. There is much more to life than quarks and gluons and quantum physics. A holistic approach would not only teach us facts, but also purpose. *Why* is the Earth located precisely where it is in the Milky Way galaxy? *Why* do psychosomatic illnesses respond to mental therapy? *How* does the brain handle its millions of parallel processes simultaneously, yet remain able to mix abstract right brain activity with left brain logical activity? Knowing the logic and reasoning behind the design of the universe would be just as useful as knowing the logic and reason behind the design of my car when it breaks down. *Why* are those spark plugs so difficult to reach? Oh yeah, so they can sell me a special tool to get them out!

One's paradigm has a tremendous effect on both a person's ability to discover *and* on the quality of the discovery. Approaching the study of the universe's ultimate origins, the development of plant and animal life on this planet, and interpretation of the fossil record will be dramatically different if the assumption going in is that it is all a product of naturalistic chance processes rather than intelligent design. If the paradigm is naturalistic evolution, then the hypotheses upon which the experimentation is based will bias the results. We all see what we want to see in most situations. For example, if you know someone with a critical spirit, that person will find faults with everyone and everything even if those faults are not there. Every action of every person in their life will be interpreted through glasses that are tinted with criticism. This same type of bias also shows up strongly in the sciences and can cause neutral results to lean one direction or the other.

Thank God there are a lot of scientists today studying the universe and its origins who are believers in a Creator God. These fine folks are doing much to advance truth. The Church at large needs to be supporting these discoverers because an awesome image of our beautiful Creator will flow from them, since His signature and His personality permeate the created order. The more we learn about the universe and its "hows" and "whys," the more we know of the God who lovingly created a most incredible dwelling place for us.

This, in turn, helps turn people toward Him, especially people who are themselves involved in these scientific endeavors. Individuals who are not moved by science and ultimate origins have other means of approaching God—be it through creative avenues like music, art and writing, or through philosophy, psychology, or literature. All of those arenas of study ought also to be redeemed by God's eternal viewpoint. All things are from Him, for Him, by Him, and ultimately belong to Him. This discussion about science is merely one of the discussions that Christians ought to be initiating to turn the thinking of humankind toward our creative and incredible God.

Endnote

1.   C.S. Lewis, *The Weight of Glory* (New York: Harper One, 2001).

CHAPTER 29

Big Bang and Bible Bangers

Henry and Hugh are on the back porch, watching the squirrels compete with the tufted titmice for sunflower seeds. The occasional cardinal glides in with a flash of bright red to steal a seed and carry it away to the nearby bushes before skillfully hammering it open with its strong beak.

> **Henry:** ...and this man actually believes that the universe began in some sort of huge explosion! He calls it the big bang. One would at least hope they could devise a more intriguing nomenclature!

> **Hugh:** Oh? Well, what is it about the big bang that gives you such a cringe factor my friend?

> **Henry:** Well, first of all, I guess it would be that atheistic scientists all demand that the big bang was the way the cosmos came into being! We certainly can't afford to sleep in the enemy's camp, can we?

> **Hugh:** Well, I suppose fraternizing with the enemy could have its dangers...

> **Henry:** Besides, the big bang obviates the need for a Creator. They use it to replace the need for an

Intelligent Creator God.

Hugh: Yes, that they do, my friend.

Henry: These folks are evolutionists who insist that all of life emerged from the primordial soup and that I have evolved from a crustacean!

Hugh: There are those who believe such nonsense, I agree.

Henry: My dear boy, you are looking at me kind of funny.

Hugh: I am?

Henry: I know you well enough, old chap, to know that you're smirking on the inside. What did I say?

Hugh: Listen, Henry, it's not a smirk, it's...well...I'm just trying to hold my tongue about a couple things you mentioned.

Henry: Well, out with it, boy! As delicious as your lovely wife's iced tea is, that's not the only reason I regularly walk all the way over here to your porch!

Hugh: Well, you may be surprised to hear that... well...I think God used the big bang to create the universe.

Henry: The dickens you say! Now, why does that not surprise me?

There are a few moments of silence.

Henry: Are you not going to enlighten me?

Hugh: It's not something I regularly volunteer.

Henry: I am willing and ready, as always, to entertain your interesting ideas!

Hugh: Well, it's just that I don't think it's necessary

to equate evolutionary thinking with big bang theory. Macro-biological evolution and the origins of the universe are two different issues. I think the science that developed the space shuttle is the same science that tells us the universe is ancient. I think the big bang is the best estimate we have right now to describe how God made the universe. I think God wouldn't have made the universe look ancient if it's actually only a few thousand years old; that would be deceptive. And I think…

Henry: Whoa, slow down there my friend, slow down.

Hugh: Sorry, Henry. Maybe you can tell I'm passionate about this stuff.

Henry: Believe me, it shows!

Hugh: Well, I like science.

Henry: This I know.

Hugh: And I trust science.

Henry: No surprise there.

Hugh: I think God is the ultimate scientist. And that He gave us brains that can do science. So He expects us to. And He expects us to look at what we see in the universe and make conclusions about it. That's all.

Henry: Well, I have to admit that your arguments are compelling, but I don't think I'm ready to give up my "on the seventh day God rested" theology. I trust you can overlook that little indiscretion on my part.

Hugh: Henry, you know there is no indiscretion. I would hope that our friendship goes deeper than our agreement on scientific or even theological issues.

Henry: As long as you keep serving me iced tea like this, things will be just fine between us!

Henry holds out his glass with a smile, and Hugh refills it from the pitcher.

* * * * * * * * * * *

A large and growing band of Christians are getting on the big bang bandwagon and preaching that it's OK to simultaneously believe in an ancient universe and a transcendent God, even a God that used the big bang to create the universe. They believe the Bible *and* what their science teaches them about the universe. They believe that if our science tells us that the universe is about 15 billion years old, then it probably is, especially since the Bible really says nothing specific about the age of the universe. And most importantly, they believe that this whole discussion is not crucial for salvation and relationship with Christ.

In other words, it is not one of the pivotal issues of the faith. I like that a lot, because I believe that even though my opinion about the age of the universe really has nothing to do with my level of intimacy with Jesus Christ, I believe it is a very important issue, because the ability of many scientifically-minded people to accept the truths of Christ hinges on what they believe about scientific discovery. The two should not be at odds with each other.

If we think that modern science contradicts the Bible, then the problem probably lies not in our science, but in our interpretation of either our scientific evidence or our biblical translations and assumptions. Some who are adamantly opposed to an ancient universe conclude that our science is not dependable enough to make firm statements about the age of the universe. They argue that the universe, and everything in it, was created six to ten thousand years ago because they believe that a literal interpretation of the Bible says so.[1] They demand what is, in their opinion, a literal interpretation of those Scriptures that seem to talk about creation, and they dissect Bible verses word by word. There are great and famous debates about Hebrew words and verb tenses that even skilled scholars can't agree on.

"Fallen Minds" Argument Still Faulty

Some actually claim that because our science is performed by "fallen minds" (because of the sin of Adam) then this science cannot be trusted. Although we've already discussed this, please permit me to refresh our memories on two very important deficiencies in that argument:

First, these fallen minds that are studying the universe are also translating ancient Scripture. To remain consistent, those who use this argument must mistrust the validity of our translated Bible just as much as they mistrust modern science. Translation of ancient texts is just as much a scientific endeavor as the study of ancient sea deposits or ancient planets. If our minds, having been polluted by the sin of Adam, cannot be trusted with the science of space, then I don't think they can be trusted with the even more important science of translating our holy Scripture into modern languages.

Second, the fallen mind argument is faulty at the outset. The Bible is clear that our minds are renewed (see 2 Cor. 4:16; Rom. 12:2); that we have the mind of Christ, the Creator of the universe (see 1 Cor. 2:16); and that we are new creatures (see 2 Cor. 5:17). We are not performing science with fallen minds (at least, this is true of the Christian scientists who both love Jesus, believe the Bible, and also believe in an ancient universe). There are Christian scientists who believe in big bang theory, or at least believe in an ancient universe, who are studying science with the mind of Christ and concluding the universe is old, and then are seeking to reconcile this with another equally valid revelation of God—the Bible.

The ancient Hebrew language of the Bible had only a few thousand words in its vocabulary while modern English has millions, so of course there will be some discrepancies, some areas where we don't all agree—even some areas where we *can't* all agree. There is simply no way for modern scholars to fully and perfectly understand the cultural mindset and interpretations that led to the writings that we now call the Bible. What are important is not so much the words on the pages, but the principles behind the words, the person they are describing, and what that person expects of us. In one sense, who cares how old the universe is? I love Jesus Christ and want to know Him better every moment of every day. Others can ridicule my belief in the big bang, but they ought to realize that this can only serve to create a barrier between us. What really matters in all of this is our heart relationship with the One who created it all. They don't know my heart or my relationship with the Creator; neither do I know where they are coming from. Therefore, lots of grace and patience are necessary to continue to live in harmony with one another in order to be an effective witness to the world around us.

Let me pause for a breath here. Please believe me, I don't like Christian-bashing. I don't mean to do that here. That is precisely the thing that I am so tired of in these types of debates. I just want to remind us all that Jesus did not focus so much on what people believed about science, what they thought about politics, or even what they actually did with their lives and bodies. The adulterous woman and the woman at the well are two excellent examples. The focus of Jesus was always, always, always on changing hearts and introducing people to the God of all creation. *Jesus wanted to impart living water more than theology or science.* The rest takes care of itself.

Choosing to Love and Unify When We Disagree

You and I can disagree about the age of the universe, about evolution, about a global flood, and a host of other issues, and we can still love each other and love God. In fact, I would argue that these disagreements are what ought to be uniting us. I have very close and dear friends with whom I disagree about seemingly basic things like the rapture and hell. But we love each other dearly and greatly enjoy—even look forward to—our discussions about the things over which we disagree.

Would it not be grand to hear these debates about young Earth versus ancient universe focusing on Jesus Christ and what our opposing viewpoints can teach us about Him? Rather, we hear mostly about how wrong and heretical the "other side" is and how dangerous their viewpoints are. I really don't believe that God's truth and His ability to preserve it are that fragile. So, how about we rethink big bang theory and what it portends for the Body of Christ. Here are a few things we might want to think about and debate amongst ourselves:

First, the Bible says nothing at all about what effects our views of science have on our faith or our relationships with one another. So let's have the confidence and freedom to actually be Berean in our approach and study to see if these things are true. If a better description than the big bang emerges of how the universe came into being, then we ought to gladly accept it if it makes more sense than what our prevailing science tells us. Until then, perhaps we should choose to trust the brains God gave us and commanded us to use.

Second, our interpretations of ancient Scripture probably should not be cast in stone. One would hope that our cumulative knowledge as a human race ought to increase with time, and this includes our ability to understand and interpret ancient texts. As knowledge increases, so should our understanding of Scriptures and their translations and original meanings and, therefore, also our understanding of God. To state otherwise, e.g., that our theology is correct as it is and any challenges to it smack of liberalism or heresy, seems tantamount to claiming omniscience. I don't know about you, but I'm nowhere near achieving that goal.

Third, many of our fathers of science were godly men or at least believed in a transcendent Creator. That tradition lives on, no matter what some hard-core fundamentalists are saying about the modern science scene. There are a great many Christian scientists who believe that big bang theory is presently the best estimate we possess regarding *how* God created the universe. In fact, big bang theory is fundamentally very supportive of, and almost requires, biblical creationism. The more we learn about the big bang, the more we are forced to accept there had to be a Creator involved in the whole thing, fine-tuning the process to an unfathomable degree, designing exactly how things would unfold, and determining the scientific constants necessary to allow life to exist on planet Earth, not to mention being there to start the whole thing.

Fourth, science may not be *the* language of God, but it is definitely *one of* His languages. God is truth. Math is true. God created the principles that cause math to be true. Therefore, certain truths about God's universe and, therefore, about His creative power and His personality can be seen in math and science just as much as through other studies like music, art, literature, and human history.

Fifth, if we can concur that science and math are capable of teaching at least some truth about our Creator, then we can put more merit in the study of quantum science and trust a bit more in its ability to teach us something about the universe and about God's methods of creation. This is a good thing because quantum physics is a newer discipline than many of the other sciences and as such has more room to grow. If we accept it as one of the languages that God uses to communicate with us and we understand that His natural laws and principles are extremely trustworthy and reliable, then we ought to have a lot of confidence that these disciplines will teach us important things about His revelation in His created universe.

The Value of Respectful Debate

I know that big bang cosmology may be a lot for some to bite off. That's OK. I don't actually expect you to change your belief system at all! I'm not at all offended if you continue to completely disagree with me. However, in my life, I want to be sure of *why* I believe what I believe, and I urge others to do the same. It's not nearly enough to draw permanent and strict conclusions by listening to preachers and Christian radio. I recommend knowing both sides of the argument before making conclusions. You may rightfully ask, "Jim, if it's not a huge deal whether your readers end up agreeing with you, then why make such a big deal about the big bang?" There are a couple reasons why I believe it's crucial to have this debate, even if you decide to disagree with my take on cosmology and my conclusions about an ancient universe.

First, there are scientists out there who are being told by their own eyes and education that the universe is huge and very old, yet the Christian Church is telling them they must abandon their claim on an ancient universe in order to believe the God of the Bible. The Church often insists that their education is flawed and is not trust-worthy (even though it's this same education that creates airplanes and rocketships). I think this is tragic, because it truly prevents peo-ple from entering the Kingdom of God. Hugh Ross's organization *Reasons to Believe* studies the universe and publishes information about why an intelligent, loving Creator God has to be at the heart of it all. They, by the way, believe in big bang cosmology and an ancient universe. So now scientists who are searching for a transcen-dent God are allowed to believe in an ancient universe *and* the God of the Bible and are actually finding Christ as a result of Ross's ministry. Awesome!

A second reason that this debate on the age of the universe is important is that it teaches us that the primary goal is *not* to prove the other side wrong. The debate can easily be framed in such a way that we all gather around the table, have communion, break bread and drink wine together, then debate the age of the universe in brotherly love and respect.

A few years ago, I read one young-Earth apologist's opinion that a particular old-Earth Christian scientist should not even be allowed to teach Sunday school at church because he didn't believe that the universe was less than 10,000 years old. Good luck trying to find biblical support for that one! This, from a man who insists that biblical literalism is the all-important criterion for Christian service. Where does the Bible literally and clearly tell us the importance of our opinions on the age of the universe or the science God used to create it? This particular old-Earth Christian has been the subject of ridicule and called a heretic more times than I can count. All because he seeks to reconcile what God created with what God says in the Bible.

A third reason why I think this debate is important is that I believe those who believe in an ancient universe are actually right. I just simply believe that the insistence on strict biblical literalism is misguided in the debate on the origins of the universe. I believe that we can and should trust science, since the science that tells us the universe is ancient is the same science that makes most of modern life possible. If we witness a star exploding (like we did in 1987) and calculate that it's 100 million light-years away, then we know that the event must have happened 100 million years ago, since it took that long for the light from the event to reach us.

To insist that God created the universe 6,000 years ago with all these light beams and evidence of "fictitious events" already in place is to insist that God gave us evidence of a bunch of astronomical events that never actually happened. This is deception at best, since God is the one who gave us the minds that love to do science and discover truths about our universe. What possible reason could He have for creating illusions of events that didn't really happen, yet giving us scientific information that tells us that these events really did happen, as well as the ability to actually perform these mathematical equations?

Yes, I am passionate about this topic, and at its root this passion exists because I believe in the value of Christian unity. Unity does not mean forcing others with whom we disagree to agree with us. That's called coercion and bullying. Sure, there's a place for biblical correction and discipline, but this is not one of the areas that qualifies for that kind of treatment. As brothers and sisters who allegedly love one another, we ought to be able to worship side by side and accept and be challenged by one another no matter what our views on the age of the dirt under our feet.

The Big Bang and Our Old Earth

So, allow me to provide a brief synopsis of what us whacky old-earthers (or at least what I) believe, since it has a very strong impact on our discussion of quantum physics and God's ultimate realities:

I believe that the big bang is a good estimate of the method God used to create the universe.

I believe that a God who can create the universe over billions of years using the scientific processes that He Himself designed is just as amazing and sovereign as a God who can immediately speak the universe into existence.

I believe that God would not create records of fictitious events in the universe whose only effect could be to lead us astray and cause dissention. I believe that God gave us the kinds of brains and thought processes that cause us to love knowledge and learning, especially learning about the universe in which we live, and He will honor what these exploring minds discover about His universe.

I believe that quantum physics is a valid scientific language and a good expression of reality on a subatomic level. I believe that it's God's invention, and He uses quantum mechanics and other difficult-to-understand scientific disciplines to describe His incredibly complex creation.

In addition to all this, I believe in a God who is personal, loving, caring, and infinitely kind and patient, who sacrificed His own Son so that the human beings He created might have life in spite of all their disagreements and shortcomings. It is this kind of approach that I believe can unify all of my Christian brothers and sisters as we approach this immense topic of science, creationism, and the interface between the visible and invisible realms of existence that we live and function in every day.

So let's begin by agreeing to travel together as friends. None of us have a corner on truth, but we can all explore together. By combining our resources and eliminating the inefficiency and waste that come from bickering, we can make faster progress toward knowing all that we can know about this God who loves us all to distraction. And this, after all, is the goal: that the eyes of our hearts be enlightened so that we may know Him better (see Eph. 1:17-18).

Endnote

1. Young Earth creationists mainly rely on biblical genealogies to establish the age of the Earth at 6,000 to 10,000 years old.

CHAPTER 30

Prayer, Thoughts, Motives

Prayer is conversing with God.

Since God is immaterial, I can't really provide a "scientifically" accurate picture of how conversing with Him works. But I do know that He is a person, and He loves all people equally, and He desires the very best life here and now for those who want to walk through life in relationship with Him. I have conversations with Him daily.

Prayer can be accomplished verbally or merely in one's mind. God hears either way. There is a fascinating description of this in First Chronicles 28:9:

> *And you, my Son Solomon, acknowledge the God of your father, and serve Him with whole-hearted devotion and with a willing mind, for the Lord searches every heart and* **understands every motive behind the thoughts**. *If you seek Him, He will be found by you....*

There are thoughts, and then there are the motives behind the thoughts. I once believed that my thoughts were the most rudimentary expression of my mind, but here we are faced with the reality that there is a more fundamental layer of motives that influence my thoughts. The Hebrew word for *motives* here suggests that this structure is the stuff on which our thoughts, and therefore, the rest of our existence, are built upon. It includes all of our experience, our paradigms, our assumptions about ultimate reality, and it operates at a level that is often unrecognized even by our own minds.

This structure of motives is a composite of our experience and our environment, and rooms full of books have been written about how these things affect an individual's present state of existence. I want to simply point out that this underlying structure is at least one step closer to that interface between the spiritual and physical realms we inhabit. The stuff that shapes and influences my thoughts constitute the "real me," and I would do well to nurture and take care of that most precious possession if at all possible.

Nurturing Our Spiritual Life Through Prayer

Probably the best way to nurture my "inner stuff" is through prayer. People have long recognized that prayer, even outside the realm of traditional Christianity, has the power to change reality. Thoughts and the spoken word contain power to change physical reality. Somewhere along the line from immaterial thought to physical action, we pick up enough momentum, enough strength and authority, enough sheer power to make changes to the physical world we inhabit—more proof that perhaps these two realms of existence are actually one and the same.

As modern Christians, we have a tendency to boil things down into their most basic scientific constituents. This includes our viewpoint and interpretation of the command to pray and the power inherent in prayer. We tend to have a very pragmatic view of prayer, and believe it to be a simple cause and effect kind of activity. If I pray, then something might happen. I would like to suggest that it gets much deeper than that, with far more nuance than what we may believe.

God understands the motive behind the thoughts. We may think we are having great thoughts when we pray lofty prayers, but what God is mostly interested in is the structure behind our words, emotions, and thoughts and what makes that structure function as it does. That structure exists at a level that even we can't reach, for it is spirit and it is inaccessible to the natural mind: *"The sinful mind is hostile to God. It does not submit to God's law, nor can it do so. Those controlled by the sinful nature cannot please God"* (Rom. 8:7-8).

It is clear that to have any hope of getting synced with God's Spirit, we must first be in a committed relationship with Him. When we take that first step, we are recreated into creatures who can tune in to God's wavelengths. We can hear and understand His voice. Unlike the sinful mind that does not even have the ability to please God, we become His beloved children. Our entire existence begins to revolve around God and His ideas about who we are and where we are going in this life. As this paradigm is cemented in our psyches, we are changed bit by bit on the spirit level, down deep in that place where God knows us better than we know ourselves. It's a process— it's not going to happen overnight! It is this fundamental, invisible level of existence that informs the rest of our lives. It is from here that the "motives behind the thoughts" arise and become the force within that guides our thoughts and words and, therefore, our actions and the realities that we create in our everyday lives.

We can't just will ourselves to change. While it's true that the will is our primary source of strength and discipline for living, fundamental spiritual change can only happen as a result of the work that the Spirit of God does inside us, melding us as one with His Spirit so that we know His thoughts and think the same way He thinks: *"We have the mind of Christ"* (1 Cor. 2:16).

When we think like Jesus thinks, when we have the actual mind of Christ, when we are tuned into the thoughts and desires of God Almighty, then we can't help but have our prayers answered! If we are thinking God's thoughts, then we will not be asking for things that are contrary to His will. If we only ask for things that we know are according to His will for our lives, then we know we will receive the answer:

> *This is the confidence we have in approaching God: that if we ask anything according to His will, He hears us. And if we know that He hears us—whatever we ask—we know that we have what we asked of Him* (1 John 5:14-15).

Therefore, we can live a life in which we always receive the answer to our prayers, since we first determine exactly what God intends to do. Once we know that, then we simply ask Him to do it. Of course we will get the answer! He knows our motive, and we know His will. He trusts us because we have been tested and proven obedient, and He rewards us with an intimate relationship in which we are absolutely convinced that we are loved, provided for, taken care of, and are put on the track of growth and continuous upgrades. What a way to live!

This structure behind the thoughts can be likened to a physical structure like a building. It's unseen, like the foundation. A few months ago, while I was visiting Los Angeles, I saw a huge excavation where a construction company was preparing to erect a multi-story building. It was a gigantic hole in the ground, the depth equivalent to the height of a three or four-story building. They had begun pouring pilings and foundational components upon which the building would be built. Several months later, on a subsequent visit, I saw the building itself, unfinished but standing several stories above the streets below. The foundation was completely hidden, but I knew it was there. It had to be. There has to be something there to support that massive structure.

Establishing a Good Foundation

God has to start us with a good foundation. For some of us, we may have some massive structures that have been built on a poor or non-existent foundation. In some cases, God has to tear it all out and start from scratch. This can be an unpleasant experience, but it's not necessarily required. If we cooperate with Him, the whole process can actually be enjoyable, as we see old paradigms, old foundations, and sold structural weaknesses destroyed and replaced with His beautiful truths. The building of the foundation in a person can take a while. Perhaps years, depending on our level of stubbornness or immaturity. Sometimes God chooses a massive, short-term demolition. I've experienced one of those. Not a pretty sight, but it was my own fault. I sometimes think that certain people only require a nudge here or there to keep them on the path to truth. I am one of those that required a toss over a cliff, smashing in a bloody mess on the rocks below, to get my attention.

As the old foundations are replaced and the "structure behind the thoughts" is built on the solid Rock, then we begin to see like God sees. We see into the invisible realm. We gain an intuition about the struggles, motives, and attitudes of the people around us. God shows us the things that He can trust us with, and we learn to act upon those intuitive inputs with prayer, encouragement, or whatever the situation calls for. As God trusts us more and more, He gives us greater and greater responsibility. The structure or foundation upon which our motives and thoughts are built becomes the driving force, the source of wisdom, and the motivation behind our actions.

It is this foundation that is being built up and strengthened by the trials and troubles we face. James 1:2 says, *"Consider it pure joy...*

when you face trials of many kinds, because you know the testing of your faith develops perseverance." The end result is that we may be *"perfect and complete, not lacking anything"* (James 1:4). The changes in us have to happen at a fundamental level that is deeper than our thought life because in the heat of battle, we need to act instinctively. We may not have the time or ability to stop and think and strategize in certain situations so our faith, our spiritual strength and authority, our wisdom, and our insight need to be automatic and authoritative. Of course there are times when we need to stop, pray, strategize, and consult with others, but like a star athlete, the best performance comes from years of intentional focus and practice and it becomes instinctive. Once a tennis player steps onto the tennis court, it's no longer practice, it's the real thing, and instincts and intuition take over.

These fundamental changes can only be accomplished by the work of God's Spirit within us. What this means for us is that we can't change ourselves; we can only cooperate in ways that allow God to do His work. This means obedience to His words, agreement with the direction He wants to take in our lives, and intentional focus on His teachings and His will for our lives. As we cooperate with Him, He changes us from the inside out. These are changes that stick. We can go through programs or attend seminars that will teach us God's higher ways, but the real change comes from within, and it is permanent. God *understands every motive behind the thoughts.* And He is the only one who can change them.

CHAPTER 31

Logic, Truth, and the Most Real Being

I s creating photons and galaxies any more difficult than creating bread and fish? The process must be very similar, except that one is on a bit larger scale than the other. But when you are God, the physical scale of things really doesn't matter that much.

The big bang theory describes the same process as making bread from air. First there was "nothing" (at least nothing physical or material). God rearranged energy and *"stretched out the Heavens"* (Isa. 44:24), which He later organized into galaxies, stars, and the constituents from which all known matter is made.

Scientists have studied the process of the big bang for decades, and they predicted more than 40 years ago that the creation event would have had to leave an imprint in space—a measurable background radiation that could be predicted by math and observations. This math was performed under the assumptions of big bang cosmology, so if that background radiation was indeed discovered, and if it matched the values that their mathematics predicted, it would be a step forward in authenticating big bang cosmology.

Finally in the 1960s, Arno Penzias and Robert Wilson used the COBE telescope to detect this background radiation, and it agreed closely with the scientists' predicted formulas. Scientist George

Smoot said, "It was like looking at God."[1] So the universe we inhabit is really just one huge bread machine!

Some Christians do not accept the idea of an ancient universe. They believe that strict biblical literalism insists on a creation event a few thousand years ago. I admire them for their ability to stand strong for the faith, but the time has come to—at the very least—kiss and make up with those who disagree. We must not judge the relationship others have with Jesus Christ based on their opinion on the age of the universe.

Although I develop the argument for the value of intuition elsewhere in this book, logic and truth are also methods that God has given us to learn about life and our surroundings. Without applying truth and logic to our studies and discoveries, we will never be able to build a meaningful argument in any endeavor, especially in cosmology and science. Logic is the very language God uses to convince us of anything:

> Current attitudes toward reason are ultimately pathological. The culture that turns its back on reason turns its back on truth. The culture that turns its back on truth turns its back on God. And the culture that turns its back on God turns its back on life...We allow our intuitions to rule our beliefs, unchallenged. This must stop. Instead we must learn to allow reason to tutor and discipline our intuitions. If reason does not rule our beliefs, then God does not rule them and we are in rebellion against him. We need to rediscover the biblical perspective wherein obedience to God includes courageously following reason wherever it might lead...the conscious and willing subjection of our tacit intuitions to conscious rational scrutiny is vital in the quest for truth—especially in the quest for theological truth.

Crabtree uses the terms reason and logic almost interchangeably. His book is not about reason and logic per se, but he makes a strong argument for them in the beginning of the book because he correctly understands that without reason and logic, we have no way to properly understand anything. The arguments he makes in his book rely on an agreement that the reader will allow logic to rule the discussion. It can be no other way.

God Isn't Always Logical

Before we go on, however, I want to put logic and reason in their proper context. I believe Crabtree makes a good point, but he may be taking our reliance on pure logic a bit too far. From the quote above, we would conclude that he believes no understanding is possible without logic and reason. Technically, that's true because even if God chooses to communicate to us through strictly intuitive channels, we must at least have enough capacity to reason that we are able to relate that intuitive communication to our own circumstances. There can be no 100 percent intuitive communication that completely bypasses reason, else we would not be able to actually translate or understand the message. However, the initial source of communication or the transmittal of truth into our lives need not be logical or reasonable. There is plenty of biblical evidence that many of God's dealings with humankind did not follow any logical process.

The original idea and God's choice of methodology to enact it are often illogical and unreasonable, but either the execution or the result always is rooted in the natural laws that follow logic and science. It may seem illogical to us for God to whittle down Gideon's army to 300 men when he was about to go into battle against tens of thousands. But the steel in the blades that killed Gideon's opponents were as real and logical as it gets. It may not have been logical to march around Jericho for a few days in order to capture the city, but when the walls came crashing down, they were obeying the logic and reason of gravity.

We get into muddy water when we insist that God must always act in a certain way. He is the God of both reason and intuition, of logic and emotion, of mind and matter. He can and does communicate in different ways to different people at different times. Elsewhere in this book we discuss intuition in more detail. For now, let's look further into this realm of logic and reason.

It is logic and reason that enable us to translate Scriptures from ancient languages. It is logic and reason that enable us to know what the first chapter of Genesis says in our own language. Those who demand strict biblical literalism do not deny the usefulness of science and logic when studying ancient manuscripts and ancient cultures in their quest for biblical interpretive accuracy.

According to Crabtree, the ancients called God The Most Real Being ("ens realissimus"), and He should be the very center of what is real, tangible, and knowable to the people on this planet. His personality and character should be the things that we most ardently strive for. It will require both intuition and logic to understand all of Him, because He has manifested Himself to us in both of those ways—intuitively through His Spirit and logically through the revelation of His created universe and His written Scriptures.

Logic and the Origin of the Universe

The logical revelation of God—the created universe—communicates to us in a very straightforward way, interpretable by scientific discovery. It is my opinion that we should not have to rely on convoluted descriptions of why the universe looks old, but really isn't. We should not be expending such huge efforts, money, and brainpower in trying to force modern cosmology into a young-Earth interpretation of Genesis. God cannot deceive us. The universe and the Bible will ultimately agree with one another. It is God who designed us in such a way as to "do science." He created us with the mental capacities to discover scientific realities and the cultural community-centric character to be able to build upon cumulative knowledge as a species. It would be quite misleading of Him to create this universe the way it is, teach us to discover things about it, and then tell us that the things we are discovering are actually completely wrong.

In the 1980s, we witnessed a star exploding—a supernova being born. Through our calculations, we determined that this event is about 160 million light-years away. In other words, that event was so far away that it took the light from the explosion 160 million years to get here. It actually happened 160 million years ago. Now we have two choices.

A young-Earth creationist might claim either that the universe was created only a few thousand years ago with the light from that explosion already in transit to make it *appear* as if the supernova took place a long time ago when in reality it never happened at all. In my opinion, that is deceptive. That is not God's modus operandi. Or a young-Earth creationist may try to prove that the speed of light has changed tremendously during the last few millennia and therefore reconcile how the light could have traversed such a huge distance in only a few thousand years.

There are huge philosophical and scientific problems with both of these scenarios. I will not take the time to go into all that here as it would fill an entire book, but it is sufficient now to simply say these are deceptive conclusions. God designed us to discover. We have discovered truths about the speed of light and the nature of matter. This knowledge allows us to design technologically marvelous creations based on the necessity of our knowledge of things like the speed of light and the behavior of subatomic particles.

Those who insist on interpretations of the Bible that defy logic and discovery of modern science (the exact same science we trust to give us airplanes and computer chips) and who challenge the spirituality and faith of those who disagree with them are possibly accomplishing exactly the opposite of what they hope. Strict biblical literalism at any cost—especially when dealing with ancient manuscripts and ancient cultures that are not well understood today and whose stories were recorded in writing only after existing as oral tradition for centuries or perhaps millennia—can be dangerous.

I am passionate about finding harmony between the Bible and science, but we must draw the line at insisting that the Bible is a science textbook. The Bible is a history of God's activities throughout history, of His plan of redemption for the human race, and is a very effective handbook for personal behavior and growth. It is full of His wisdom, advice, and beauty. The Bible is not, however, God's only revelation to humankind. A very effective revelation from God is the created universe, which speaks volumes about His abilities and character.

Okay, I realize I need to calm down a little. I have close friends and family who are young-Earth creationists, and I love them dearly. I believe they are wrong, but they have complete freedom to believe the way they want to believe. I simply want to point out that making this a salvation issue can turn people off to the God of the Bible because people's belief about the age of the universe has nothing to do with their ability to have a personal relationship with the God who created it. When we claim that a young-Earth cosmology is the only allowed interpretation of the Bible, we are stuffing God into a very tiny box, whether we are right or wrong. We can be free to believe what we want to believe about the age of the universe, but we must leave room for other interpretations and even welcome the debate as loving brothers and sisters.

It's time to take control of what our minds are doing to us (and for us) in the arena of science, discovery, and biblical interpretation. Perhaps we should occasionally put aside the Bible completely when we study science. Why not? How often must we consult the Bible when designing a robot or starting a car or launching the space shuttle? Where in the Bible does it tell about the atomic construction of a carbon atom or the speed of light or the mechanism behind the effectiveness of penicillin? Do we need the Bible on our desks while we are building space shuttle fuel tanks, or planting a garden, or riding a bike? Neither do we need the Bible open to Genesis 1 in order to study and understand the cosmos.

Thoughts and words are exceedingly powerful, and by taking a stance that equates one particular interpretation of the Bible with the scientific reality that surrounds us, we are in danger of causing a backlash that will only be understood on the other side of eternity. Much damage can be done by dogmatically forcing one interpretation as the only valid one. Let's show more grace and flexibility than we have in the past and show God for who He really is—not a dogmatic gavel-pounding judge, but a loving Creator who wants His people to discover the true majesty of His creation.

Endnote

1. "U.S. Scientists Find a 'Holy Grail': Ripples at Edge of the Universe," *International Herald,* Associated Press (April 24, 1992).

CHAPTER 32

Prayer Changes the Past

Quantum physics has mathematically proven that time can travel backward. I know it's a bizarre thought, but it's been proven in the lab.

OK, I'll admit I'm making it sound more sure than it actually is. Truth is, it's all really just mathematical in nature. But there have been successful experiments done that seem to show certain effects preceding their causes. Other experiments have shown that certain effects seem to be capable of exceeding the speed of light, which is not supposed to be possible. As we already discussed, a large distance can separate an "entangled pair" of electrons. While some kind of influence acts upon one of the electrons, the distant, "twin" electron will exhibit identical results at the very same instant as the original electron. Because of the distance separating the electrons, the influence on the distant electron had to be transmitted faster than the speed of light so that the twin was affected at the same time. This, in effect, implies that time does not necessarily always flow in a forward direction or, perhaps more interestingly, that time is not always in control.

Only recently have we possessed the technology to measure the exceedingly short time periods involved in such calculations, but scientists have proven that an *effect* can precede its *cause*. Just another of the strange and non-intuitive characteristics of our world that have been exposed by the science of quantum physics and quantum mechanics, but makes total sense when explored from God's viewpoint.

The immaterial spiritual realm works in the same way, and I'm suspicious that perhaps the same mechanism is at work. What I'm talking about is the idea that prayer also changes the past in much the same way as our friendly little pair of electrons has demonstrated.

In the simplest of examples, prayer for healing can restore the patient to a previous state of health. Time travels backward! Prayer can restore one's financial condition—restoring the years the locust has eaten, in the parlance of the Old Testament (see Joel 2:25). Time travels backwards! Prayer can cause emotional healing to occur so that a person is in a state similar to before the emotional damage was done. But is this really the same as time travel, or are these just clever ideas and semantic manipulations?

Defining Time

First, let's talk about what time is. We tend to think about time as a thing, a noun, but it's not quite that easy. Time—or more accurately, the passage of time—is relative, as Mr. Einstein taught us, and it depends strongly on certain influences, gravity, and speed to name a couple. On a planet with huge gravity, time would travel more slowly than on earth. Also, if you were on a spaceship traveling close to the speed of light, time would travel more slowly. But even this is relative. What do I mean by that?

If you could get on a spaceship and travel near the speed of light (186,000 miles per second), your watch would continue ticking normally. You would age the same way as your body ages here on Earth. Time would seem to be passing by normally to you. However, if I were able to watch you and your activities during your journey through a powerful telescope, it would look to me like your activities were painfully slow, possibly not even noticeable to me. It might appear that you are not even moving. That's because the passage of time is relative, and your speed relative to mine is causing a big discrepancy in what looks like the passage of time. When you returned home from your journey, you would find me much older than when you left—perhaps years older—even though you may have only been gone for only a short period of time.

Now, if during your high-speed journey, you were able to watch my activities back on Earth, it would appear to you that I would be moving so rapidly that I might just appear as a blur to you. My life would be passing by very rapidly from your perspective, and I might grow old in front of your eyes. However, my watch and my years ticking by would seem normal to me. The passage of time is relative.

Cheating Time

When prayer restores a person to some previous condition, this is, in essence, cheating time. The rate at which our relationship with God, our knowledge of Him, our ability to wield the instruments and weapons of righteousness that He has prepared for us, and the growth and appropriation of the riches of our inheritance in Christ, can all move at various speeds, depending primarily on our willingness and ability to cooperate with God's dealings in our lives. In God's eyes, my life might be passing by painfully slowly, like when I'm being stupid about some simple lesson He's trying to teach me that I'm just not getting. Or time can be greatly accelerated, where I receive an abundance of revelation and upgrades in my spirit because of my obedience to God's words and my passionate pursuit of who He is in my particular life circumstances. The flow of time on the clock in my office may be relatively constant, but in God's world, the passage of time is certainly capable of changing significantly.

Think of it this way: Job lost everything he had: his house, his livestock, his riches, his health, all his children; it was all gone. Through obedience and humility, he showed himself faithful, and God restored twice as much as what he first had. This is a compression of time, because in the natural it would have taken a very long time for Job to double his riches.

Abraham and Sarah had a baby in their old age. A reversal of time! Shadrach, Meshach, and Abednego, after being proved obedient to God and impressing the king with their incredible faith, were catapulted to positions of authority and power, something that may have otherwise taken them years or decades to accomplish.

These examples portray the power that God has to transcend the limitations that time places on us physically. Most of us live as if we are absolutely subject to the inexorable flow of time. While that may be true in one sense—every day that passes brings us one day closer to our ultimate end—in a broader and more important sense it is absolutely untrue, because God has called us to live as if things on Earth were as they are in Heaven. Heaven is not constrained to the flow of time like the Earth is. In Heaven, there is freedom from the limitations that time places on us, and as children of God and co-heirs with Jesus, we too are to be free from the constraints caused by time. We have the mind of Christ (see 1 Cor. 2:16), we are presently and literally seated with Him at His throne (see Eph. 1:20), and we are not to be subject to any of the limitations that the physical creation puts on us. This is the ultimate freedom, and it is ours in Christ right now.

Does that mean that time is of no meaning to us? No, because although we need not be constrained to time like most of creation is, still it is a resource to be wisely used as we do God's work on Earth. We may not be constrained by time, but the world we live in and the people we are to be witnesses to are bound by it. Our job is to bring the freedom of Heaven to Earth and to share with others the wondrous miracle of life unconstrained, free from sin, free from guilt, and full of redemption. Included in this is the redemption of time and the restoration of lost years.

Although lost time can be restored, and we can return once again to a place in our lives that was fruitful and pure—time traveling backwards—we can also in a sense travel forward in time. When we become intimate with God and are really living in a close relationship with Him, in which we are tuned into His heart for us and His plans for our lives, God reveals to us what's coming. Normally this is not a long-term view into the future, because I think most of us couldn't be trusted with prior knowledge of the riches that will be revealed to us, but at least we receive glimpses of who God wants us to become. He wants to show you the plans He has for you, the person He is shaping you into, so that you can learn from the lessons that you are struggling through right now and see them in the bigger context of the direction God wants you to go.

Most of us, admittedly, accept the life that comes at us. We are too involved in just meeting all of our perceived responsibilities to be aggressively proactive about what's coming in the future, let alone being aggressively active in *changing* the direction we are heading. But God is urging us to be out there on the front line where nothing is certain (*"Do not lean on your own understanding"*; Prov. 3:5 NASB). We desperately need the ability to see into the future, take control of that vision of who we will become, and work hard in the present to compress time and become that person as quickly as possible. There is no rule that says you have to move at a particular limiting speed in your spiritual development. Nowhere does that concept appear in Scripture. But the Scripture is explicit in talking about God's ability to redeem time and restore years (see Joel 2:25).

The only limitation to our advancement in life is self-imposed. God is perfectly willing to move at whatever pace you desire, whether a snail's pace that just keeps you surviving until eternity arrives, or whether a life screaming with excitement with the wind in your face. It's up to you, but I really believe God prefers the latter. He wants to demonstrate to you His mastery over time and its perceived passage and teach you some new things about where you are in life, where you are going, and how long it's going to take to get there. My recommendation is to let go of the uncertainty, the fear, the trepidation; to put all your trust fully and confidently in the one person who can never make a mistake; and to sprint forward with abandon. This is the only way to live. Cheat time, but do it on God's terms!

The Dam Breaks

After I concluded this book, I realized that my analogy of a dividing wall between these two realms of existence does not quite describe what I've been seeing and thinking about. As I dwelled on the subject matter of this book and the things that God was speaking to my spirit, I realized that a much more accurate picture of God's desire for His Church—us, His collective Body on Earth—is that of a dam holding back the infinite provisions of the Kingdom. I think that we, through our inadequate and sometimes—let's face it—downright stinkin' thinkin', we dam up the flow of God's Spirit and all that He wants us to experience in this life.

A wall between two worlds implies that those two worlds are separate and distinct, and even if we succeed in breaking it down, two worlds will still exist, even though we are free to move between the two. But I believe God wants much more than that. I believe that God wants to flood our time-space continuum with a new Kingdom reality that buries once and forever everything we know, maybe even a few things we hold dear.

We must realize that as followers of the Way of Jesus, we are not subject to the constraints of this physical world. We are not subject to the financial constraints, the health and wellness restraints, the diseases and depression, the broken relationships, the uncontrolled emotions, the lack of success, the lack of direction, the lack of vision, or the lack of resources that others struggle with. At least we shouldn't be.

Yet many Christians are seemingly trapped in a lifestyle that feels nothing like victory, where every day is a struggle, where the power of God is more a good idea than a strong and vigorous reality.

All of us encounter times like these, but this should not be our lifestyle. We ought to be living primarily in victory, with a few battles now and then to keep us in a mode of dependence upon God. The problem is, we're dry. The valley is dry. The river is barely a trickle. The dam has been well-built, and what little water gets through is nowhere near enough to guzzle.

The dam must break.

We must train our vision to rise above the humdrum of everyday life, above the Hotel Mattresses part of our existence. We must invite the Kingdom into our lives, into our hearts, minds, and souls. We must earnestly seek what that means for us specifically in the middle of the everyday tasks and relationships of life. It won't come easily, not because we have to faithfully follow some kind of tough-minded formula and strict asceticism. It all comes through the renewing of our minds (see Rom. 12:1-2), an aligning of our thought processes with those of the Spirit of God. Easy to talk about, not so easy at times to implement.

God assures us that if we seek Him, He will be found by us (see Jer. 29:12-14). Be sincere in your pursuit. Be willing to let Him strip away all that junk that you don't want in your life anyway. Sure, it might be uncomfortable. But so is a tough workout at the gym. We all know what a good workout can do, especially if practiced faithfully. Work out your faith, your knowledge of God, your relationship with Him. It can only lead to a depth of life in which His goodness will flood everything about you.

The dam will break. Then the old physical realm will simply disappear, supplanted by the glorious life that is inherent in God's Kingdom.

In other words, *"Seek first His kingdom and His righteousness,"* and everything else you need and desire will be freely given.

I want to sincerely thank you from the bottom of my heart for sticking with me this long. If you've actually survived this journey, I trust that it has at the very least helped you to think about some things that perhaps had not before entered into your sphere of active thought.

We've talked about quantum physics, science, theology, God, people, relationships, love, intentionality and a whole lot more. But it mostly has to do with learning to see from God's point of view. His is a point of view that is unhindered by the physical limitations of our physical eyes and the constraints of our limited thoughts and dreams. His point of view sees majesty in you no matter what you're going through. He sees beauty in the midst of ashes and victory in the jaws of defeat. He sees perfectly clean, sinless people when He looks at His children because they have been placed inside the perfection of Jesus. He sees incredible potential for you that far surpasses what you can even imagine or dream. He sees a huge pile of provision just waiting to be lavished upon you so that you may most effectively do the things He has prepared for you, and these things are consistent with your deepest dreams and desires.

In His world, science, quantum physics, and prayer are inseparable because one begets the other. The authority and reality of the unseen realm is the very foundation upon which the entire physical universe is built. And God wants you to see it as clearly as He does.

He's ready to reveal it to you, perhaps in small steps, perhaps in large doses, depending on your particular journey with Him. But He will show you. Just ask. Obey Him. Love Him. Give Him your life, mind, and spirit; and watch what He can do with a person who is fully submitted to Him and His methods and dreams for you.

Thanks for coming along on this whacky and wonderful journey. And may the God of prayer, quantum physics, and hotel mattresses richly bless you.

About Jim Berge

Jim Berge is a self-professed armchair physicist, a lover of God, student of the ultimate origins of the universe, and by trade a robotics engineer and consultant. He is a frequent speaker and author on the topic of robotics, technology, and manufacturing and owns his own consulting and engineering business, assisting corporations who own and use robotic technology.

Berge has been a follower of Jesus virtually his entire life, never remembering a time when he did not know and trust Jesus as his Savior and Master. An accomplished musician, active on his church's worship team, and a voracious reader, he is constantly pursuing a deeper relationship with the Ultimate Scientist—the God who created the cosmos, yet loves His children intimately.

Jim lives in Shreveport, Louisiana, with his amazing wife, Kayla, and his son, Bax. He is surrounded by a huge godly family and loves music, the outdoors, travel, photography, and of course writing.

In the right hands, This Book will Change Lives!

Most of the people who need this message will not be looking for this book. To change their lives, you need to put a copy of this book in their hands.

> *But others (seeds) fell into good ground, and brought forth fruit, some a hundred-fold, some sixty-fold, some thirty-fold* (Matthew 13:8).

Our ministry is constantly seeking methods to find the good ground, the people who need this anointed message to change their lives. Will you help us reach these people?

> *Remember this—a farmer who plants only a few seeds will get a small crop. But the one who plants generously will get a generous crop* (2 Corinthians 9:6).

EXTEND THIS MINISTRY BY SOWING
3 BOOKS, 5 BOOKS, 10 BOOKS, OR MORE TODAY,
AND BECOME A LIFE CHANGER!

Thank you,

Don Nori Sr., Founder
Destiny Image
Since 1982